A History of
The Actors'
Fund of America

A History of
The Actors'
Fund of America

by
LOUIS M. SIMON

with Special Contributions by
RUTH GORDON
NEDDA HARRIGAN LOGAN   CORNELIA OTIS SKINNER
JEAN LOGGIE

Theatre Arts Books

NEW YORK

Library of Congress Catalog Card Number: 72-87118
ISBN 0-87830-057-0

Designed by Bernard Schleifer

Published by Theatre Arts Books
333 Sixth Avenue, New York, New York 10014
Printed in the United States of America

The concept of a book on the Actors' Fund originated with
the late Milton I. Shubert. A committee carried on his work:
Earl Benham, Chairman
Jacob I. Goodstein, Max Gordon, Warren P. Munsell

PICTURE CREDITS: The following illustrations were obtained from
the following persons and organizations, to whom the Publisher
and Author are grateful: Photographer David A. Loggie: 1, 2,
3, 4, 5, 16, 23, 24, 37, 39, 41, 42, 43, 62, 63, 64, 65, 66, 69, 70, 71;
Theatre Collection, New York Public Library: 6, 9, 10, 12, 13,
15, 22, 45; The New York Historical Society: 7, 14, 18; The
Museum of the City of New York: 8, 19, 20, 34, 36, 38.

*This book has been made possible financially
through a bequest in memory of*

SAM S. SHUBERT

LEE SHUBERT

and

MILTON I. SHUBERT

CONTENTS

LIST OF ILLUSTRATIONS

CURRENT OFFICERS AND TRUSTEES
ACTORS' FUND OF AMERICA
1972–1973

LOUIS A. LOTITO
President

ALFRED de LIAGRE, Jr.
First Vice-President

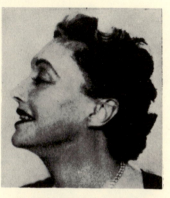

KATHARINE CORNELL
Second Vice-President

SAMUEL H. SCHWARTZ
Treasurer

WARREN P. MUNSELL
Secretary and General Manager

William P. Adams

John Alexander

Mrs. Martin Beck

Earl Benham

Alexander H. Cohen

Maurice Evans

Lillian Gish

Jacob I. Goodstein

Max Gordon

Alan Hewitt

Lawrence Shubert
Lawrence, Jr.

Nedda Harrigan Logan

Louis R. Lurie

Frederick O'Neal

Harold Prince

Richard Rodgers

Cornelia Otis Skinner

Beatrice Straight

HONORARY MEMBERS

W. S. ANDREWS
BROOKS ATKINSON
JAMES GORDON BENNETT
MME. SARAH BERNHARDT
JACOB A. CANTOR
GROVER CLEVELAND
WALTER DAMROSCH
A. B. DeFREECE
CHAUNCEY M. DEPEW
A. J. DITTENHOEFER
DANIEL DOUGHERTY
THOS. E. GILROY
WILLIAM R. GRACE
HUGH J. GRANT
ABRAHAM S. HEWITT
REV. G. H. HOUGHTON, D.D.
ROBERT G. INGERSOLL
OTTO H. KAHN
HONORABLE JOHN V. LINDSAY
ROBERT NOONEY
HONORABLE WILLIAM O'DWYER
RIGHT REV. JAMES B. O'REILLY
IGNACE J. PADEREWSKI
PROF. WILLIAM LYON PHELPS
HORACE PORTER
REV. RANDOLPH RAY, D.D.
C. C. RICE, M.D.
THEODORE E. ROESSLE
H. H. ROGERS
ADOLPH SANGER
MME. MARCELLA SEMBRICH
WILLIAM T. SHERMAN
DANIEL E. SICKLES
ARTHUR G. SMITH
WILLIAM H. TAFT
ANTONIO E. TERRY
HONORABLE ROBERT F. WAGNER
STANFORD WHITE
WILLIAM WINTER

INTRODUCTION

WHEN I WAS A cub reporter on the *Boston Evening Transcript* many years ago I was once assigned to cover an Actors' Fund matinee. Dan Frohman, president of the Fund, was the speaker. I can still remember him on the stage—his long neck and high starched collar, his pointed beard—and I can still see him reading his speech from loose sheets of paper. He concluded with a line from *Hamlet:* "See the players well-bestowed." As an apprentice writer I envied him the pertinence and erudition of that final remark. That was my introduction to The Actors' Fund.

Now I am much more familiar with it; and like everyone else on Broadway I have consistently admired it. Although the Fund is by nature a rather shy institution, this book gives it a winning personality and it also provokes some random ideas. Why has The Actors' Fund worked so well for ninety years? Because it is all theatre. Because it has style. Because it has inherited the natural generosity of theatre people. Among its officers and trustees there have been many temperamental actors who have been entranced with showy ideas. At one time some of them wanted The Actors' Fund to join what later became Actors' Equity. That must have seemed like a plausible idea in the context of 1910. But it was not a public accountant but a jovial actor, Tom Wise, who pointed out the fallacy of trying to combine an organization dedicated to the sick and needy with a labor union dedicated to the interests of working actors in good health. The Actors' Fund and Actors' Equity have long had a close relationship and Actors' Equity has contributed generously to The Actors' Fund. But the decision in 1910 not to amalgamate was a crucial one, and it was an actor who understood the conflicts at stake.

Has it ever occurred to you that the theatre is never better than when it is not trying to make a profit? That is an immoral idea and I like it. When a production is completely spontaneous, when the actors, directors and technicians are working free, the performance is likely to be completely captivating. The emotion it generates is direct, intimate and ardent. That has been the case with The Actors' Fund all the years I have known it.

It originated with a feeling of loyalty to the theatre. Harrison Grey Fiske, then the young editor of the *New York Dramatic Mirror*, was annoyed because the theatre was forever giving benefits for many good causes but never for itself. There was no self-interest in Mr. Fiske's idea; he got nothing out of the proposal; he was not even an officer or trustee of the original board. In fact, and this is characteristically irrational, there was no board or organization when the Fund began in 1882. There was only the enthusiasm of A. M. Palmer, a theatre manager when he was not being a politician, and many of his associates. By holding a series of benefits he and his colleagues raised $34,596.30 for needy actors; and James Gordon Bennett, publisher of the *New York Herald*, gave $10,000 more. With that money deposited in a bank before the Fund even had an elected treasurer, Mr. Palmer and others who were interested got a charter and elected officers. Among the incorporators were Edwin Booth, Joseph Jefferson, Lawrence Barrett, Lester Wallack, A. M. Palmer, Edward Harrigan and P. T. Barnum, a showman better known outside the theatre. It was a good beginning. Good will was the principal asset.

In two respects the Fund reflects the spirit of the theatre. In the first place, the early festivals organized to raise money were fun. The fair put on in the old Madison Square Garden

in 1892 was designed and staged by Stanford White and con-
sisted of all sorts of gay and bizarre plazas and pavilions. It
also included booths presided over by costumed clowns and
comedians. The most colorful actors of the day took part in a
series of performances. All that must have given everyone, including the actors, a royal good time. These early fairs were
patronized by some of New York's haughtiest society folk. In
1910 President Taft came from Washington to attend the fair.
Actors' Fund benefits and festivals were never stodgy.

In the second place, the Fund has always drawn on the in-
stinctive generosity of show people. To read this book is to
be impressed by the amount of time and energy theatre people
have lavished on the Fund. A. M. Palmer, a founding trustee
and president from 1885 to 1897, was a dynamo; he endowed
the early days of the Fund with energy. Dan Frohman gave
the Fund a good part of his life. He was president from 1904
until he died in 1941. If he had been less bountiful by nature
he could have spent all his time working in his own theatre, the
Lyceum, and with his famous acting company. Walter Vincent,
a self-effacing man, was president from 1941 to 1959, and gave
not only money but counsel and ideas; and Vinton Freedley,
another large benefactor and a conscientious business man,
served from 1959 until he died ten years later. Louis Lotito,
the current president, has been active in the Fund for more than
twenty years. Warren P. Munsell, currently secretary and general manager, began his association with the Fund in 1937.
Being a trustee is not for figureheads. It involves making touchy
decisions that intimately affect human beings. Many of the
most illustrious people in the theatre have been trustees.

Thanks to large gifts and legacies, which have been well
administered by knowledgeable people, the resources of the
Fund are now substantial, and money-raising is not the anxious,
ever-recurring crisis that it was in the first twenty-five or
thirty-five years. Now Actors' Fund benefits are not huge fairs.
They consist of a week of passing the hat during intermissions,
and in special Sunday performances of current plays. The pub-

lic does not have to be seduced so artfully as in the days before the Fund had a backing of investments.

The Fund is not only a charitable organization but the conscience of the theatre. It is scrupulous and merciful. It preserves the privacy of the sick and needy. Broadway is a gossipy place. But there is no gossip about the Fund. Except in the case of individuals whose troubles were known to me personally, I have never heard anyone discuss applicants for assistance or the plight of those who are receiving assistance. The Home in Englewood has all the comforts and freedoms of a private residence. In short, the Fund is administered with warmth and respect, and its charity is neither smug nor patronizing.

The Actors' Fund is no monolith. It is all theatre. Theatre people founded it and administer it now. I have enjoyed reading this book because it retains the fever, excitement and the sweeping gesture of the theatre.

Brooks Atkinson

I

Narrative History

BACKGROUND AND EVENTS
LEADING TO INCORPORATION

In 1892 The Actors' Fund had completed the tenth year of its existence. The annual meeting for that year was held on June 7, 1892, at the Madison Square Theatre. Following it there was an elaborate program of "commemorative exercises" during which A. M. Palmer, as President of the Fund, gave an account of the founding of the Fund. In his address, Palmer briefly mentioned the American Dramatic Fund Association as having "stood for many years as the only charitable fund of the dramatic profession in America." He said nothing about three other organizations which existed at the time.

Let us examine the nature and status of the groups which occupied the field when The Actors' Fund entered the scene. This is important, for in setting up an actors' fund, the founders apparently wanted to make certain that they would not repeat the mistakes of other organizations which may have been failing to fulfill their ostensible missions. Fortunately, among the various bits of theatrical memorabilia which have accumulated at The Actors' Fund over a ninety-year period, there are a few relics which provide clues as to the nature of these other associations—now all but forgotten.

In the somewhat dusty files of The Actors' Fund's offices there is a handwritten document bearing the date February 27, 1848. The ink and paper are brown with age but the meticulous penmanship with which it was written makes the manuscript easily legible. Its title is: "Original Draft of Rules and Regulations Submitted to the Members of the Profession as Ground Work of the American Dramatic Fund."

On the wall in one of the offices there is an elaborately engrossed certificate, handsomely framed in carved oak. It is headed, "Shakespeare Lodge, Actors' Order of Friendship, #1." This certificate, dated April 5, 1888, grants a charter to a group of distinguished "brethren"—among them Louis Aldrich, John Drew, and Otis Skinner—to operate in New York as the "Edwin Forrest Lodge, Actors' Order of Friendship, #2." The Actors' Order of Friendship, the parent organization (together with its "Shakespeare Lodge, #1"), had been chartered in Philadelphia by the Superior Court of that city as far back as 1849; just one year, in fact, after the founding of the American Dramatic Fund in New York.

A third relic possessed by The Actors' Fund is a ceremonial gavel, executed in silver and mounted with three gold plates. One, at the center of the mallet-head, states, "Presented by the Baltimore Lodge, #14, TMA, to the Actors' Fund Fair, May 2, 1892." On either end of the mallet-head of the gavel are two other filigreed gold plates, each bearing the insigne of the Baltimore Lodge, #14. Research discloses that TMA stands for Theatrical Mutual Association; that it was founded in 1861 as the Theatrical Workmen's Council and that it became affiliated with the Knights of Labor (later the American Federation of Labor); also that in 1886 the labor union functions of TMA (which the Workmen's Council had become by that date) would henceforth be separate and would operate under the name of "Theatrical Protective Union, Local #1" (now officially Local #1, I.T.A.S.E.), while TMA would continue independently as a welfare group, administering to the needs of stage hands who are ill or financially distressed. Of the three organizations to which these relics once belonged, the only one existing today is the Theatrical Mutual Association.

Among these three, the American Dramatic Fund was the

The first page of a document preserved in the files of the Actors' Fund of America. It is "The Original Draft of the Rules and Regulations Submitted to the Profession as the Ground Work of the A. D. F. A." (American Dramatic Fund Association) The document is dated February 27, 1848.

A silver ceremonial gavel (above) presented to The Fund by an antecedent of the Stage Hands Union on the occasion of the Actors' Fund Fair in May, 1892.

A sterling silver bouillon spoon bearing the likenesses of five famous actresses on the obverse side of the handle; five male stars are on the reverse. The bowl is embossed with a view of the Park Theatre. A number of these spoons were struck as souvenirs to be sold at the 1892 Fair.

one most closely associated with the early days of The Actors' Fund.

The hand-written "Rules and Regulations" of the American Dramatic Fund were adopted, with minor amendments, at a meeting held in New York shortly after they were drafted. According to the Dramatic Fund's own documents, it was on March 3, 1848, that the American Dramatic Fund Association was "established" by the adoption of the "Rules and Regulations." It became a legal entity when its incorporation was validated by the New York State Legislature in April of 1848.

The Association's stated purpose was: "To raise by subscription from the members thereof, by voluntary donations and bequests from members and others—by Public Donors and Theatrical Benefits—a stock or fund for making a provision, by way of annuity, for aged and decrepit Members, and such provision for the Nominees' Widows and Orphaned Children of Members and also for Funeral Expenses." In the manuscript, the words "aged and decrepit" are lined through and the word "subscribing" substituted. Eligible to be members were "all persons who practiced the art of Acting, Singing or Dancing as a means of subsistence in the United States of America or elsewhere, and who have practiced, for a term of not less than three years, in one or more regularly established theatres, and also the Prompter, Leaders of Orchestra, Scene Painters and Master Carpenters. . . ." The document continues with complex provisions as to internal government, classes of membership, eligibility for "benefits," withdrawals and expulsions, etc. However, reduced to its fundamentals, the Association was simply a combined fraternal organization and life insurance society—typical of many such institutions of that day and comparable to the "Elks," the "Woodmen of the World," and certain farmer counterparts known as "Granges."

But, even as The Actors' Fund seemingly had a direct predecessor in the form of the American Dramatic Fund Association, so that organization was preceded by a still earlier one called the General Theatrical Fund. This earlier organiza-

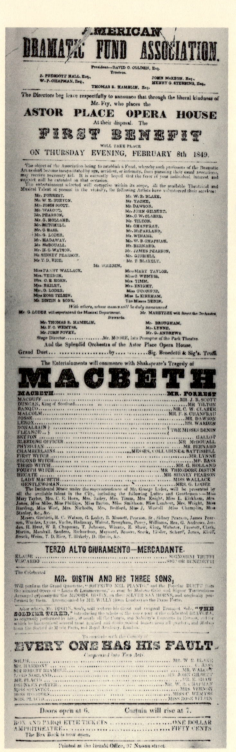

Playbill of the first performance to benefit the American Dramatic Fund Association; February 8, 1849. The major item
on the program, "Macbeth," starred
Edwin Forrest.

As a loyal Philadelphian Edwin Forrest
resisted the dissolution of a Philadelphia
organization so that it could be merged
with the A.D.F.A. Nevertheless he eventually lent support to the newly formed
American Dramatic Fund Association.

tion was started in Philadelphia in 1829; nineteen years before the Dramatic Fund, twenty years before the Actors' Order of Friendship and fifty-three years before The Actors' Fund. Original correspondence relating to the two "funds" is preserved in the American Dramatic Fund's file of manuscripts at the New York Public Library. Particularly pertinent are letters from one Quintin Campbell of Philadelphia to F. C. Wemyss, an officer of the Dramatic Fund in New York. These letters reveal that Mr. Campbell, a trustee of the General Theatrical Fund, was getting on in years, that the General Theatrical Fund was faltering, and that Campbell was anxious to wind up its affairs by assigning its assets to the newly established Dramatic Fund. A typical letter on the subject, dated April 21, 1849, concludes as follows:

> I wrote Mr. Forrest a letter on the 7th of this month but have no reply. I should wish him to see this presuming he would make no objections.

But the matter was not to be resolved as quickly or as simply as the Messrs. Campbell and Wemyss wanted. Further correspondence from Mr. Campbell discloses that Edwin Forrest did object, and very strongly, to transferring the Philadelphia organization's funds to New York. He contended that all the money should be divided among the original members. Campbell then countered that this could not be done inasmuch as all the members had not complied with every rule of the organization. Nevertheless, the wishes of Edwin Forrest, particularly since he had been one of the largest contributors to the General Theatrical Fund, could not be safely ignored. Campbell made it clear that under no circumstances would he face up to the formidable Forrest all by himself and that he would, therefore, be obliged to consult other trustees. Communications among them were cumbersome and slow. Then lawyers entered the picture, to complicate matters still further. But as time went on and some of the obstacles were overcome, the stickiest problem continued to be how to get around Edwin Forrest's objections; this, despite the fact that he held no official position, either in the General Fund or the Dramatic Fund. But he let no one forget that he was the most important theatrical figure in the country. And his overweening vanity demanded deference to his every whim.

At this juncture of theatrical development in America, Philadelphia and the cities to the south of it were rapidly losing out to New York as centers of theatrical production. The heavy immigrations, which were causing New York to mushroom faster than any other city, during the late 1840's and early 1850's, were predominantly Irish and German. Both of these groups brought with them their great love of theatre and music. As their native cultures took root in the new land, Puritan prejudices against theatre were diluted far more quickly in New York than elsewhere. So, by 1855 New York was indisputably the theatre capital of the country. However, Forrest was an intensely proud American and a rather provincial Philadelphian. He obviously felt that to give in to the Campbell-Wemyss proposition would in some way slight the city of his birth and might be construed as symbolizing a deterioration of native American influences which he had so painstakingly been nurturing within the theatre. Forrest even went so far as to enlist the weight of Mr. Swift, the ex-mayor of Philadelphia, to try to prevent transference of the funds to New York. In this he failed. Nevertheless, it was not until 1856 (some seven years later) that the transfer was finally effected. Campbell was then eighty-one years old and the remaining assets of the General Theatrical Fund had dwindled to a mere $700.

Having finally taken over the General Theatrical Fund, the American Dramatic Fund functioned successfully, albeit subject to its self-imposed limitations, for more than thirty years. But by 1880 its weaknesses had become readily apparent. The troubles that beset the American Dramatic Fund, and eventually caused its gradual disintegration, were those that invariably have plagued so many groups comprised of people professionally engaged in the field of entertainment; namely, the instability of theatre as "a business." (Yet, until very recent times this has been the category in which all theatre had always been placed in the United States.) The American Dramatic Fund, as an "insurance" company, depended on the regularity with which its ordinary members paid their quarterly "subscriptions." Although it could, and did, get some revenue from "benefits," donations from "honorary members" and also "bequests," major income derived from what would now be called "insurance premiums." Yet the average theatre person (who even today is considered a poor "insurance risk") was the very one most likely to need assistance. Nevertheless, he was exactly the one most often "in default," and thus ineligible to receive any benefit from the Dramatic Fund.

By the winter of 1881-82 the Shakespeare Lodge of the Actors' Order of Friendship, having prospered in Philadelphia for thirty-two years, decided to look into things in New York. The president of this Philadelphia counterpart to the Dramatic Fund, was a prominent actor by the name of Frank Findley Mackay, who happened to be playing in New York. Mr. Mackay was asked to seek out and report back to the Philadelphia "Lodge" the names of all "sick and distressed brethren in New York." Whether Mr. Mackay's investigations were actively resented, or whether they proved to be a healthy stimulus, can only be conjectured. In any event, as early as 1880, the *New York Dramatic Mirror* had created a considerable stir by loudly objecting to the use of theatrical performances as benefits for every imaginable "cause" looking for easy ways to raise money while, at the same time, the profession was doing little or nothing to relieve the distress of those within its own ranks.

The situation was brought to a head when, in February of 1880, the *New York Herald* challenged the City of New York to raise $100,000 for the relief of the starving people of Ireland. Much to the distress of the *Mirror*, which considered itself the fountainhead of wisdom in all matters theatrical, the *Herald* had engaged the goodwill of Dion Boucicault and various other prominent theatrical personalities to help in raising this $100,000 sum. The *Mirror* did not object to using playhouses as locations where audiences could contribute to the sum being collected by the *Herald*. In fact, the *Mirror* advocated the installation of "contribution boxes" in all the theatres so that the public could voluntarily contribute whatever they wished to the Irish relief program. The feature of the *Herald*'s plan to which the trade paper took violent exception was the plan that on St. Patrick's Day (March 17, 1880), all New York theatres would give "benefit" performances for the Irish charity; the actors, and presumably everyone else involved in them, not being paid for these performances. If the entire proceeds were turned over to the *New York Herald*, the theatrical community would be contributing a vastly disproportionate share to the cause, argued the *Mirror*. In its editorial dated February 14, 1880, it said:

> We would not do anything to check the torrent of benevolence which is pouring through the *Herald*'s channels on the barren fields of Ireland; but we should like to check the general inclination to demand help from the theatres when *anybody* needs relief. The theatres have their own good work to do and they have no chance to do it properly because of the incessant requirements of these outside charities. Since the newspapers have taken up the task of supplying Ireland with funds, let them carry it out and let all of us help them to the fullest extent of our means, reserving the theatrical channel for another occasion.

The *Mirror* then became very specific about what it had in mind in the way of something it called a "Sinking Fund" for the theatre.

> One of the good works which has been too long neglected in the theatres is the establishment of a Sinking Fund, to be man-

aged by an executive here in New York for the prompt relief of actors in distress and for the prompt remedy of any wrongs from which professionals may suffer. We do not need for this purpose any great benevolent association like that of the Elks —which does its own noble work in its own way—nor like the old Dramatic Fund. All that is necessary is for the managers throughout the country to agree to raise a Sinking Fund by giving one benefit a year at each theatre, and to vote some such practical and responsible New York manager as Lester Wallack, A. M. Palmer or J. H. Haverly into office for a year as custodian or treasurer of the fund, with a strong committee of leading managers of the country to meet here every summer to supervise and audit the accounts. By this simple plan, without any great trouble to anybody and without any individual expense, a fund would be raised and managed that would do more to relieve, elevate and strengthen the profession than any other scheme which has ever been devised. Once in practical operation it would be self-sustaining. Within five years every lease of theatre, every contract for the lighting or the printing for a theatre, every agreement with every member of a theatrical company would contain a clause donating one day's rent or charge or salary to the Sinking Fund so that all the proceeds from the benefits would be clear profit. One of our ablest managers is willing to guarantee the sum of $25,000 from New York City alone to start the fund, if the other managers will join him heartily in the work, and if managers throughout the country will send in their adhesions to the proposal to give one yearly benefit for this purpose. Who speaks first? Who will start the roll call? Who will sign an agreement to give one benefit a year to a theatrical Sinking Fund and take part in the appointment of a responsible New York manager as treasurer?

The *Mirror* editorial then went on to berate the lack of system whereby people of the theatre who had met misfortune were helped. It cited a number of examples of individual benefits that were given in particular cases. Huge sums of money were raised at these benefit performances and the *Mirror* gave the opinion that much of this money was wasted. They cited one benefit which had raised $17,500 for a single person. Referring again to the idea of a single fund, the editorial concluded:

> We ask for it no money contributions, no monthly dues, no initiation fees,* nothing but the proceeds of an annual benefit to be given at every theatre in the United States. . . . The relief of Ireland is a personal charity which ought to appeal to every heart without delay; but this theatrical Sinking Fund is a professional charity which ought to get precedence of any other organized charity benefits at the theatre. We should be glad to have the *Herald*'s views upon this matter and we rely upon its support as sincerely as it may rely upon our own for the Irish Relief Fund.

The benefit performance which had raised the incredible sum of $17,500 "for a single person" was, in truth, a whole series of benefits. They had come about in this way.

On March 18, 1879, a touring company, headed by Maurice Barrymore, played a one-night stand in Marshall, Texas. This small town is near the Louisiana–Texas border—not too far from Shreveport. It seems that after the performance in Marshall, Barrymore, an actress named Cummins and an actor named Benjamin C. Porter were waiting for the 2:00 A.M. train which would take the company to its next stand. Typically, this threesome thought a light snack and some coffee would help pass the time until the train arrived. They were told that the one place in town which would be open late at night was a lunchroom. It was connected with a saloon. The three members of the company found the place and were seated on high stools at a counter enjoying their refreshment when a drunken ruffian lurched out of the door from the adjacent saloon. He made some slurring remarks about Miss Cummins. At first Barrymore and Porter merely tried to silence the ruffian's tongue. Their attempt at verbal persuasion did not

* (the reference to monthly dues and initiation fees was an obvious slap at the Dramatic Fund's method of maintaining itself)

succeed. Thereupon, the incident swiftly deteriorated into a physical quarrel.

Maurice Barrymore had achieved considerable eminence during his college days in England as an amateur boxer. Therefore, he did not hesitate to challenge the drunkard to a fist fight. The actor was well enough versed in the ways of small towns in the American West to be suspicious of gun play. True to the English tradition of fair play, he first demanded to know if his opponent were armed. The man, later identified as one Jim Currie, swore that he was not. Upon this assurance Barrymore started to whip off his jacket and was in the midst of doing so when Currie swiftly drew two pistols from beneath his jacket and fired. One bullet hit Barrymore in the arm; the other found no target. Barrymore tried to pick up one of the lunch-counter stools as a weapon with which to assail Currie. But the stools were securely fastened to the floor. At this point, realizing that he had no way of defending himself against an armed maniac, he motioned to Porter and Miss Cummins that all three had better leave as fast as they could. When they started for the door, the drunken Currie fired again. This time he felled Porter, wounding him fatally.

Porter's body was sent to New York, the tour was cancelled, and Barrymore returned to Philadelphia. In Philadelphia the newspapers descended on Barrymore to get a detailed account of the murder. Barrymore's interview not only received widespread publication but instigated a tremendous furore in which the theatrical communities of both New York and Philadelphia became heavily involved. Some elements in New York began demanding that no more companies be booked in Texas. Some opinion in Texas responded by casting aspersions on the theatrical profession in general. The battle of words mounted. The whole thing reached almost the same dramatic proportion as had the Forrest-Macready feud of a previous generation.

Funeral services for Porter were held at the Little Church Around the Corner on Wednesday, March 26, 1879. Although

he had not been a particularly well-known actor, the name of
Porter now became the focal point of a *cause célèbre;* the up-
shot being that in Texas, as well as in New York, benefit
performances were wildly encouraged to preserve Porter's
widow and orphaned children from want. The total of these
benefits added up to the $17,500 which was turned over to
Mrs. Porter. Her grief appears to have been rapidly assuaged
by such a tidy sum. The record reveals that in the course of
a very few months, after she became possessed of this substantial estate, the widow Porter found herself another husband.
The *Mirror* cited this particular case as one which pointed up
the necessity of a general actors' fund so that a woman like
Mrs. Porter could have been given whatever was necessary to
support her and her children over such period of time as it
would actually be needed, but not beyond.

What sort of picture did New York present as the hub
of the entertainment world in America in the year 1880 when
the *Mirror* began its campaign to create a charity system by
which the theatre could properly "take care of its own"? The
Union Square area, where Broadway is intercepted by 14th
Street and for three blocks north of 14th Street—bounded by
Fourth Avenue on the east and Broadway on the west—had
held its preeminence as the city's theatrical center for more
than a generation. But now the area began to yield its dominant
position. New York was restlessly pushing its complex of retail
shops, hotels and theatres northward on Broadway and west-
ward to Fifth and Sixth Avenues. Eleven years earlier Booth's
new theatre, the most lavish and technically advanced yet to be
conceived, had opened on the southwest corner of Broadway
and 23rd Street. Wallack's new theatre, replacing the old Wallack's at 13th Street and Broadway, was being erected on the
corner of 30th Street and Broadway, opposite to Daly's. These
two theatres were becoming celebrated as *the* prestige houses
of New York, where full evening dress, or at least that new-
fangled tailless dress jacket for men, the tuxedo, were *de rigueur*
for a gentleman occupying a seat or a "stall" on the orchestra

floor. True, the Union Square, under A. M. Palmer's direction, was still popular in its old locale. But it would not be very long before Palmer leased the Madison Square, ten blocks to the north. The Madison Square, although a small house, was remarkable for its double stage, elevated and lowered by hydraulic pressure, which made possible "scene changes in less than one minute"! The *New York Mirror* still occupied offices in its own building opposite the Union Square Theatre and immediately adjacent to the Union Square Hotel. Nearby stood Steinway Hall. Not far away was that bastion of the "old aristocracy," the Academy of Music, exclusively devoted to Grand Opera. Being a box-holder at the Academy of Music, where there were only eighteen boxes, was, above everything else, a mark of social leadership. Vanderbilts, Morgans, Rockefellers, Goulds or Whitneys—the "new" post Civil War capitalist oligarchy—could not buy their way in, even though as much as $30,000 had been offered by one of them for an Academy box. Because they were proscribed by the then reigning aristocracy, the *nouveau riche* embarked upon building their own opera house, the Metropolitan. It opened in 1883, where its hideous yellow brick structure occupied the entire block on Broadway from 39th to 40th Streets. At the new "Met" there were three tiers of boxes for a total of 108—a number subsequently reduced to 72—arranged in two tiers, the legendary "Diamond Horseshoe" and the less exclusive "Grand Tier."

Ten blocks above Union Square the stretch of Broadway from 24th Street to 42nd Street was rapidly becoming known as "the Rialto." Up and down its length new theatres occupied the more prominent locations. At 33rd Street was the Standard. This theatre was the American home of Gilbert & Sullivan's operettas which were beginning their indestructable careers. And there was the Casino, at 40th, where the fabulously beautiful Lillian Russell reigned like a queen in operettas by Strauss, Offenbach and Lecocque and where the chorus girls were the cynosures of the wealthy young blades.

In 1882, when The Actors' Fund began, Union Square was beginning to wane as the theatrical hub of New York. But the Union Square Theatre still thrived—as did the nearby Academy of Music, Pastor's, costume companies, piano companies, "The New York Mirror" and several prominent hotels and banks.

Wallack's Theatre, Broadway and 13th Street, the second theatre to be operated in New York by Lester's father James. (The first Wallack's was a rebuilt theatre at Broadway and Broome Street). This theatre was opened in 1861. When James Wallack died, in 1864, Lester continued to manage it and to act there.

Interior of Wallack's "new" theatre, built by Lester at Broadway and 30th Street. The theatre had barely opened in 1882 when, on July 15th, the first official meeting of the Actors' Fund (after incorporation) was held here.

On November 8, 1880, one of the most important premieres ever to be offered on the New York scene was given, when Sarah Bernhardt, whose arrival in America had been trumpeted in advance for more than a year, made her American debut at the Booth Theatre. The play was *Adrienne Lecouvreur*. The house was packed with all of New York's smartest and richest. They had paid as much as forty dollars for a ticket. While it is true that many came out of curiosity to see this widely publicized and "scandalous" personality, they remained to give her fitting adulation for the exquisite artistry which they witnessed. Her triumph was crowned with twenty-seven curtain calls.

Although Edwin Booth had done much to raise the standards of acting in the American theatre and Daniel Frohman, with his newly formed but excellent stock company at the Lyceum Theatre, was doing much to introduce native American playwrights like Bronson Howard, Henry deMille and David Belasco and their modern plays dealing with the contemporary American scene, it can still be said that the arrival of Sarah Bernhardt revived a type of theatrical press agentry that had been going out of style since P. T. Barnum had reached his peak some years earlier. Thus, the appearance of Sarah Bernhardt in America did much to revive the hostility between church and theatre which, for twenty years, had been slowly diminishing. Bernhardt was widely regarded as a "fallen woman" because of her open acknowledgment of and devotion to her illegitimate son and for her well–publicized flaunting of conventional decorum in every possible way—dress, love affairs, the parts she played, and her much touted concern for money. She was castigated throughout the country by preachers in sermons and in church publications. One of her managers, Henry Abbey, was so delighted with the "free" publicity being extended by the churchmen that he sent "$200 for the poor of your parish" to the Episcopal Bishop of Chicago, explaining that he had been able to cut his advertising budget by that amount because of the advertising the bishop had given Mme. Bernhardt. So, perhaps the time had become really ripe for the

Harrison Grey Fiske, the youthful and energetic editor and owner of the "New York Mirror." His weekly initiated propaganda for the creation of an actors' fund and was persistent in its agitation for more than two years.

New York Mirror to intensify its campaign for a theatrical charity which might also bring an aura of respectability to a profession so constantly sniped at by the moralists of the day.

Harrison Grey Fiske had only recently become editor of the *Mirror*. He was the son of a wealthy hotel owner whose views on educating his son were unconventional, to say the least. The father allowed the boy complete freedom to indulge whatever intellectual pursuits he fancied while, at the same time imposing a rigorous and tightly disciplined regime of physical activity. When the lad was still in his teens, a childhood fascination with a toy theatre which had been followed by ever-expanding interests in the drama, led to his appointment as dramatic critic on the *Jersey City Argus*. Harry was under the impression that he had been given the job solely on merit. He was bitterly disillusioned to learn that the *Argus'* indebtedness to his father had more than a little to do with his assignment. A year later his entrance to New York University was delayed because a bout with malaria had left him physically weakened. The family doctor had prescribed an extensive trip abroad to rebuild his strength. On his return, he matriculated at the university. Along with all freshmen, he had to sign a pledge that he would not frequent theatres or other "unholy places." The young theatre buff nevertheless contributed an article to the newly formed *Mirror*. It was so well liked that he was assigned to do interviews with theatre personalities. The university authorities chose to ignore such undeniable evidence of blatant disregard for the pledge, for he experienced no difficulty in returning for his sophomore year. It was during his second year at college that the budding journalist was offered an opportunity to buy one-third of the *Mirror*'s stock and become editor of the paper as well. Harry's father promptly put up the money, the boy quit school, and in 1879, at the preposterous age of seventeen he occupied the editor's chair of a weekly that would rapidly become the country's most influential theatrical trade paper. Then, within two years, the balance of the *Mirror*'s stock was put up for sale at a price of $12,000. Harry Fiske had only $2,000 available and, unfortunately, his father was away on an extended trip. Not even a series of urgent telegrams was able to find him. When it seemed that all opportunity to acquire full control of the paper was lost, Edwin Booth, quietly and without solicitation, offered a loan of $10,000. Fiske's first act as sole proprietor of the *New York Dramatic Mirror* was to launch a campaign for an American equivalent of England's Actors' Benevolent Fund.

Toward the end of 1881, the *New York Dramatic Mirror* renewed with greater intensity than ever its drive for an actors' fund. The front page of its December 24 issue was devoted

In the circle, at the upper right of this front page of "The Mirror" issued the day before Christmas, 1881, is a sample of Fiske's propaganda for an actors' fund.

exclusively to a cartoon which summarized two causes which had been the subject of numerous editorials for the better part of two years. One cause was the establishment of a copyright for a dramatic work—the other the proper relief for impoverished and also aged actors. On January 28, 1882, there appeared an editorial captioned "Who Will Start the Actors' Fund?" After citing two tragic cases of neglect the editorial continues: "Every day, even in these prosperous times of the profession, need for the Actors' Fund arises. And yet, the weeks slip by and the work of creating a Fund is neglected. Everybody admits that such a Fund would be the best possible benefit to the profession. We have induced all the leading actors to agree to play for us and yet nobody will take the initiative. Never before did so easy an opportunity for immortality go begging." The *Mirror* then went on with its outline of simple mechanics detailing how such a fund could operate. "After the first $1,000.00 is in the bank, the treasurer appointed, the first case of distress relieved, all the rest will come of itself. Managers, stars and companies everywhere will eagerly volunteer to give one benefit a year for the fund. In two years, supposing that each benefit nets only $500.00, there will be at least $100,000.00 out at interest to help the poor, the sick and the afflicted." They offered to organize the fund themselves if no one directly within the profession would do it. But they pointed out the pitfalls of having a newspaper organize such an undertaking. On February 4, 1882, things finally began to take shape. The *Mirror* waxed enthusiastic. In a prominent spot on the editorial page they published a letter from Fanny Davenport, corroborating their previously unsupported statements concerning the willingness of stars to give benefit performances. That letter was written from the Southern Hotel in St. Louis; it was dated January 28, 1882, and was addressed to the Editor, *New York Mirror*. The letter goes on to say: "It has long been my ambition to further the praiseworthy idea of founding an actors' fund and the way suggested by the *Mirror* is so easy that it will enable me to begin the good work." In her letter Fanny

Fanny Davenport, a reigning favorite with the public and a good friend of Harrison Grey Fiske, was the first star to volunteer a benefit performance to forward Fiske's idea.

Davenport admitted that she had thought it would require a great deal of capital to start something like an actors' fund, but having read the *Mirror* editorial, she says she decided that the idea of giving a benefit would certainly start the ball rolling. Her letter advises: "Fix on a date to give the first benefit possible. I suggest the afternoon of May 10. Ask every artist of note to send their names to me in care of the *Mirror* and have every manager contribute not less than $100 in every city on that day." The *Mirror* then recommended that Mr. A. M. Palmer really start the ball rolling for the managers.

The *Mirror* was very realistic in the way it handled the actual campaign for beginning a fund. It published a story about a young actor who was determined to go among the members of his company to see whether he could not immediately, and personally, do something for such an actors' fund.

The story relates that in an hour he returned to his room, his enthusiasm completely dampened. He informed the *Mirror:* "Older actors have said, 'oh, the best fund for an actor is money in the bank,' or 'we have a dramatic fund already, my boy.' " And they altogether pooh-poohed his project. The *Mirror* then reports that actors always have felt this way and draws the obvious conclusion that if they had money in the bank there would be no need for a fund. Commenting on the young actor's quotation about the fund that already existed, the newspaper declares: "True, also, that there is a Dramatic Fund, which probably does good by stealth and blushes to find itself fame (*sic*) so little do we hear about it. But the Dramatic Fund only helps its own members, like the Elks, Odd Fellows and the Masons and other admirable institutions." Then the *Mirror* thunders: "WE DO NOT INTEND THAT THE ACTORS' FUND SHALL SUPERSEDE ANY OF THESE SOCIETIES BUT THAT IT SHALL SUPPLE-MENT THEM." In that same issue of February 4, another actor wrote in to say, "How shall we know which of those in the profession are really deserving. . . . May not the loafer or idle actor say, 'Help me, I faint'?" The *Mirror* suggests that agents be appointed to ascertain the truth in each case. It winds up by saying: "We want a matinee given on a single day with every theatre in the country and every star called on to give benefit performances on that day in whatever city they play." Later on Fanny Davenport continued her warm and very public espousal of the "cause." She wrote to the *Mirror:* "The Misses Morris, Eytinge, Ward and Jewett will help. Others will follow." But she wanted to make sure that everything was very economically arranged. Then about the eleventh, it became possible to report that there was another performer who committed himself publicly to play a benefit for the fund. Enthusiasm became almost ecstatic! The reason for all this was that J. K. Emmett had promised a benefit when he played New Orleans. At that point the *Mirror* specifically and emphatically proposed A. M. Palmer to be appointed honorary treasurer

GRAND OPERA HOUSE!
COMMENCING
MONDAY, MARCH 28
Matinees Wednesday and Saturday.

Fritz-Emmet

STROBRIDGE & CO LITH CIN O.

J. K. EMMET.

J. K. Emmett gave immedi-
ate response to "The Mir-
ror's" appeal to stars for
benefit performances.

with the power to distribute relief, loans or donations to the
distressed. "All monies may be forwarded directly to Mr.
Palmer and will be duly acknowledged by him in the *Mirror*."
The weekly trade paper now took the bull completely by the
horns and went so far as to propose a board of trustees to
supervise proper investment of the fund and to certify Palmer's
accounts quarterly. It put forth that Manager Wallack and

Manager Abbey be named as trustees for the profession, the Reverend Dr. Houghton of the Little Church Around the Corner to represent the clergy, the Hon. Leon Abbott the legal profession, and Mayor Wickett the general public. The *Mirror* noted that it would be "impractical" to hold a meeting to vote on these nominations, and therefore opened its columns to suggestions or objections and said it would consider "that silence will mean assent." The paper thus having asserted itself, went on boldly to declare: "if there are no objections to these names they will stand as trustees. The strength and simplicity of this organization will appeal to every professional. Not less simple will be the method of distribution. Who is ill and in want can simply notify the nearest manager and a draft on Treasurer Palmer for the money with the clear statement of the case will be honored. Of course, the names and circumstances of recipients will be kept private, except from the board of trustees, and the treasurer will be *ex officio* a member." After deciding matters thus—at least to its own satisfaction— a renewed appeal for benefits was made so that at least $10,000 might be on hand for the commencement of the new season. Surprisingly, very little objection was immediately expressed to the arbitrary method in which the *Mirror* engaged to implement a "cause" it was so vigorously thrusting on a rather supine profession. Any other paper but the *Mirror* might have been quite satisfied with the progress it had made during the first six weeks of the year 1882, what with the promises it already had from J. K. Emmett and Miss Fanny Davenport that they would play benefits for the fund. But the *Mirror* was not to be satisfied so easily. On February 18, 1882, it stepped up its barrage by publishing an editorial entitled "A Greek Unburied." The case concerned one Eliza Newton, "formerly well-known actress of the Olympic Theatre" who lay unburied in a vault because sufficient funds for a decent funeral could not be collected. The editorial went on to say: "All week the daily papers published appeals to the profession, made comments on their indifference, and expressed astonishment that an actress, once a favorite, should be so neglected." At last, however, enough money was subscribed to give the poor woman a respectable burial and the funeral took place according to the *Mirror*, "last Monday, at the Little Church Around the Corner." The *Mirror* then says: "Now, in the face of a fact like this, what becomes of the statement put forward by some old professionals that we don't need an Actors' Fund?" And it took particular pains to dig at a Mr. Duff, who was Eliza Newton's former manager. A week later, on February 25, another editorial was published which said: "Another case for the Fund." "Last week poor Eliza Newton lay at the morgue, unburied. This week the family of William N. Norton, an old manager, in such distress and destitution, suffering from cold and hunger, a few remaining friends are forced to make an appeal to the profession through the press and request that a benefit performance be organized for their relief. If an Actors' Fund were in practical operation it would not be worried and disgraced by such appeals." The *Mirror* then reiterated its list of proposed trustees ("no objections having been received") and said that the next step will be to publish their formal acceptance. The paper also expansively related how it had been asked to assist at the inauguration of a similar fund in England.

On March 4 the *Mirror* finally had reason for true celebration. It did so by publishing an editorial entitled: "Progress of the Actors' Fund." The editorial announced: "We have good news, and plenty of it. In the first place, all managers in New York City held a meeting on Tuesday under the call of Manager Palmer and agreed to give benefits for the Fund. Mr. Palmer has accepted as honorary treasurer, a leading physician has volunteered his services to the Fund, and the Rev. Houghton and Mr. Abbott have accepted. The benefit to be tendered by Miss Davenport will not be interfered with by the managers' group. Now we have to hear from Wallack and ex-Mayor Wickett." Then in a column called "The Usher" appeared a report: "On Tuesday there was a meeting of theatrical managers in the Morton House parlor, #159. Mr. Wallack presided. The meeting was called by means of a circular letter bearing the signatures of most New York and Brooklyn managers."

Things moved very swiftly following the managers' meeting in the Morton House on March 2, 1882. At that meeting it was decided to fix the ensuing April 3 as the date on which all theatres in Brooklyn and New York (Manhattan) would give matinees to benefit the projected fund. But some theatres, and stars, were so eager to move things along that they jumped the gun. Haverly's 14th Street Theatre announced that M. B. Curtis, starring in a piece called *Sam'l of Posen* would donate the proceeds of its March 13 performance to the fund.

The *New York Clipper* was a rival trade paper to the *Mirror*. It concerned itself, however, more with the sports world; particularly boxing, horse racing, yachting and the new sports craze, baseball, than it did with the theatre. Its pages reflected a cynical attitude toward the stir the *Mirror* was making in theatrical circles with propaganda for an actors' fund. On March 18 the *Clipper* briefly noted that the benefit at Haverly's had "yielded $366.00" and then snidely commented: "J. K. Emmett was to have given a benefit for the same purpose in New Orleans during his engagement which closed March 11th but our correspondent makes no mention of such a performance having taken place." To which the sports journal added this negative comment: "The fund is to be tried as an experiment for one year, and if it shall prove successful, benefits will hereafter be given once a year. We have little faith in it. Professional jealousies have wrecked many similar organizations. And it will be very difficult to arrange a plan of distribution in a manner satisfactory to professionals. It may be somewhat easy to raise a fund but it will be exceedingly hard work to get much money out of the hands of its custodians owing to the profusion of red tape that will probably be used in tying it up." On April 1, however, the *Clipper* felt obliged to print some tiny though positive items such as: "J. K. Emmett sent from Chicago, March 21st, $1,000.00 for this fund" or ". . . John T. Raymond had previously contributed $100.00" and "from other sources $400.00 has been received." By contrast, the *Mirror*, in its issue which appeared on the same day as the *Clipper*, devoted two full columns to the first fund benefit performance ever to have taken place.

The piece *Sam'l of Posen* has certainly not survived as a play to be remembered in the annals of the American stage. Nevertheless, apart from whatever distinction may be claimed for it as the forerunner of thousands of Actors' Fund "benefits" it does deserve attention for having been a different type of genre play than any of its contemporary dramatic pieces. In commenting on *Sam'l of Posen* as a play, the *Mirror* stated: "New figures on the stage are exceedingly rare. . . . The advent of this Hebrew with his refreshing impudence and peculiarities of expression was a genuine event that opened up hitherto undiscovered possibilities and a new field of characters. . . . That Mr. Curtis should have acquired a national reputation and a handosme fortune at an age when most actors are studying how to achieve either, is a result which speaks for the comedian louder than any words." The *Mirror* lists all the notables in the audience, tells about Thomas Whiffen auctioning off the boxes; who bought each and for how much. Then it continues: "Mr. Curtis played before an assemblage such as probably never before gathered inside the doors of a theatre in this city—a company of actors and actresses who are accustomed to sit in front of the footlights only as privileged guests, not as paying patrons." Here a tradition was initiated. Actors' Fund "benefits," down to this day are noted for a glamour and excitement in the audience that sometimes surpasses that which emanates from the stage. It is refreshing, that for all of its bias toward the project it was fostering with such dedication, the *Mirror* was honest enough to report that the auditorium for the benefit performance of *Sam'l* was by

M. B. Curtis had been sensationally successful in creating the first in a long line of Jewish comic stage characters. His "Sam'l of Posen" was the ancestor of "Potash and Perlmutter" and many others. Curtis jumped the gun by giving a benefit several weeks before the planned Actors' Fund Day performances scheduled for April 3, 1882. So to him goes the credit for giving the first Actors' Fund Benefit.

no means full. Then the paper charitably excuses this condition because of "the hasty preparation and limited time for advertising."

On the same page as the account of the *Sam'l of Posen* benefit there is published a telegram from Edwin Booth, addressed: "Harrison Grey Fiske, Editor, *New York Mirror*." It is datelined Akron, Ohio, March 9, 1882, and reads: "I accept the trusteeship, and you may use my name in any way to benefit the actors' fund." The balance of the page is filled out

with numerous communications from stars and managers outside of New York offering to play benefits for the fund and
by printing, in full, a resolution adopted by the managers of
eighteen New York theatres who met in the Union Square
Theatre on the same Monday (March 13) that *Sam'l of Posen*
was playing its benefit performance. This resolution officially
adopted the designation "Actors' Fund" and outlined those
principles which were later embodied in the formal articles of
incorporation, as submitted to the New York State Legislature
and subsequently passed into law. With understandable pride,
the editorial page for March 18 winds up with a selection of
laudatory comments which appeared in other contemporary
newspapers, including all of New York's major dailies.

It is of the utmost significance that the theatrical managers
of New York undertook to work in concerted fashion to
establish April 3, 1882, as "Actors' Fund Day." Managers were
then, as they are today, a highly competitive breed. Never before, and only rarely since that memorable day, has the same
degree of unanimity been displayed among them. Yet they
were then, as they continue to be today, the practical backbone
of the Actors' Fund. A. M. Palmer was quite obviously a man
who believed that "money talks." He was, also, very evidently
a man of enormous pride—some saw it merely as over-inflated
ego. Many of his contemporaries regarded him as a "showman,"
an impressario who exploited the creative talents of others. At
this time—the last quarter of the nineteenth century—the actor-
manager was in his hey-day. Consequently, those who held
positions of the greatest prestige were such men and women
as Wallack, Booth, Daly, Harrigan, Charlotte Cushman and
Fanny Davenport—performers who, with the notable exception
of Edwin Booth, also possessed business ability which they combined with their recognized artistry and enormous popularity.
P. T. Barnum, Haverly, H. C. Miner, Henry Abbey and their
ilk either owned theatres or were shrewd in their knowledge of
the public's taste and would exercise their expertise in ingenious
booking operations and clever publicity. However, they gen-

erally pandered to the lowest common denominator of taste, exploiting run-of-the-mill melodramas, minstrel shows, extravaganzas or such highly charged personalities as Bernhardt or the midget "General Tom Thumb." Charles Frohman, Daniel Frohman, George Tyler, Harrison Grey Fiske and Henry B. Harris had not yet emerged as producers who, though fundamentally business men, nevertheless were imbued with at least some feeling for the artistry of an actor and integrity of a playwright. A. M. Palmer was the true forerunner of this type of producer. Harrison Grey Fiske, as editor of the *Mirror*, knew what he was doing in literally foisting the management of The Actors' Fund onto Palmer even in its pre-natal period. Palmer, flattered by the attention he was getting from the *Mirror*, readily accepted the position which was by all odds most vulnerable—that of pro tem treasurer. Boldly, he forecast that the net profits from the projected Actors' Fund Day benefit performances on April 3 would exceed $30,000. The *Mirror*, itself, for all its enthusiasm, was far more conservative in its estimate of the financial result. On March 25, 1882, commenting on Palmer's expectation of $30,000, the *Mirror* had this to say: "We do not hope for so much, and shall be satisfied with $10,000.00. Our calculations are practical. Sixteen theatres will give benefits and a $600.00 matinee at each house will be a large average. But $10,000.00 will be enough from New York for the present. Now, let us see what Boston will do, what Philadelphia will do, what Chicago will do, what Baltimore, St. Louis, Cincinnati and San Francisco will do. If each of these cities sends on $10,000.00, that will make a total of $80,000.00 for the fund, and with individual efforts and benefits this may be increased to $100,000.00 before next Christmas. That is the sum we wish and intend to reach. Then the fund can live upon the interest of its money without touching the principal, which will be safely invested forever."

The $30,000.00 net income forecast by Palmer turned out to be a fairly accurate estimate. Between the special matinees

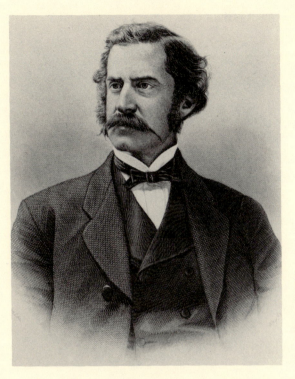

James Gordon Bennett, publisher of "The New York Herald," astonished the theatrical world with a munificent gift of $10,000 towards establishing "The Actors' Fund." "The Herald" was also generous in the publicity it gave to "The Fund" throughout his lifetime.

and individual gifts, by April 18, the acting treasurer had received $34,596.30. The matinees of the previous Monday accounted for $17,659.00 of the total. The great bulk of the tickets had been sold through the police force—over $12,000.00 worth. The most astonishing individual gift came from James Gordon Bennett—$10,000.00. He had been cabled to in Paris as follows:

New York, March 31 (1882)

BENNETT, PARIS

A fund for the relief of actors is being raised. Astor has given $2,500 and others are contributing liberally. Will you aid us?

LESTER WALLACK
A. M. PALMER

At 10:00 A.M. Monday morning Bennett's paper, the *Herald*, received this reply:

> Paris, April 2 (1882)
>
> HOWLAND, *Herald* Office, N.Y.
>
> Tell Lester Wallack I have received his telegram and that I will subscribe $10,000 to the Actors' Fund.
>
> **JAMES GORDON BENNETT**

The *Mirror* posted this exchange of telegrams in its window on Union Square, together with a list of the performances to be played as benefits on that Monday. This display of great generosity and concern by a leading citizen of New York most certainly had a beneficial effect, for the *Mirror* reported: "The densest crowds gathered at the Union Square (theatre) and Wallacks. Long before the time for beginning, these two theatres were packed to suffocation, while the overflow sought accommodation elsewhere."

Other noteworthy individual gifts were:

J. K. Emmett	$1,000	(this besides $230 from an out-of-town benefit performance)
Edwin Booth	1,000	
Municipal Gas Co.	300	
Agnes Ethel	250	
W. F. Cody (Buffalo Bill)	100	
James O'Neill	50	
R. H. Macy & Co.	25	

Sara Jewett and Maude Harrison, in their "door to door" campaign in the Wall Street area, came up with $1,500.

Palmer was interviewed by the *Mirror* on the outcome of the benefit performances, particularly with respect to the expenses and whether they would substantially reduce the glowing figure reported as gross income. The interview ran this way:

"What was the expense of the matinees, Mr. Palmer?"

"It was merely nominal. A carriage bill for Misses Jewett and Harrison's trip among the brokers of Wall Street was $8.00; a cablegram to Mr. Bennett was $14.00, and the *Herald* advertising about $250.00. All the other papers advertised the matinees without charge. The *Herald*'s invariable rule prevented a gratuitous insertion there. The expenses defrayed from the gross receipts of sixteen theatres, therefore, will be less than $300.00."

Palmer was asked where the money was being kept. He answered: "At the Bank of the Metropolis . . . where any one who may wish to satisfy himself as to the security of the money may obtain all the necessary information." He then volunteered: "Probably the Trustees, when appointed, will decide to invest the money in bonds that will make a good return." Asked if he were "now ready to begin dispensing relief from the Fund?", Palmer replied in a most emphatic manner: "No. I shall not touch one penny of the money until the managers assemble and some tangible plan is arranged. You are, of course, aware that the plan submitted is only experimental. Later on, at the convention of managers and actors from all over the country, the whole matter will be exhaustively discussed, the trustees elected regularly and other particulars adjusted. The treasurer and president of the Fund will be members of the board. I am treasurer only provisionally, and I shall insist, as Mr. Wallack will also do, probably, that my name shall either be ratified or some other treasurer appointed at the professional convention. And right here I would have you say officially that I do not want to be, and have not pretended to be, master of this Fund. On the contrary, I am its servant, ready to take off my coat and work like a Trojan for its best interests. Hereafter, I shall give one benefit every year, and if there was no other benefit given throughout the whole country, yet I would continue to do this. When I put my hand to the plow, I do not look back. I desire no notoriety, no advertisement, either personal or for my theatre. I want to see all petty jealousies sunk, and every man and woman in the profession assisting this splendid charity. You may say that is all I want to gain from my participation in this matter."

That Palmer should have gone to such lengths to make clear that he was not seeking any personal gain from the prominence thrust on him by his activities for the Fund, and that he was at such pains to make it very clear that the managers and actors as a group would set the Fund's policies and work out its mechanics of operation, throws considerable light on the man's personality as well as the rather delicate situation in which he found himself. Trained as a lawyer, and successful as a theatre manager, his statement implies a certain contempt for the highly unconventional manner whereby the *Mirror* had forced the actual creation of some sort of fund without waiting for duly called meetings in which a legally sound corporate body could be properly devised which would then proceed to appoint and/or elect officials and would carefully define both their responsibilities and the scope of their authority. Yet, he was sufficiently realistic, as well as opportunistic, to take advantage of the situation in which the trade paper placed him and to indicate that he was quite ready to exercise his leadership ability—provided, of course, that he could be reasonably certain that the profession would back up his leadership. Thus it was that he made it clear that no meeting of managers would take place until Wallack could be present. Obviously he did not want it to appear that he was setting himself up as a rival of that luminary. Yet, he must also have been aware that Wallack would serve more as a figurehead president than one who would or could devote the time necessary to the laborious work of ironing out a myriad of detail which would have to be accomplished before the fund could become a legally functioning entity.

In the ensuing weeks it became readily apparent that the wave of enthusiasm for the fund was sweeping ahead. Fanny

Davenport announced May 10 as the date for her benefit performance at the Grand Opera House; Mary Anderson had to decline joining in the Davenport benefit but she sent a contribution of $500; Henry Irving endorsed the project from London and gladly accepted the *Mirror*'s suggestion that he be "Honorary Trustee for England"; Nat Goodwin fulfilled his promise to do a benefit in San Francisco—to the tune of $1,600 net and the possibility that an additional $200 might be forthcoming; Pittsburgh added still another $200—which represented the theatre's share of the Emmett performance at the Opera House in that city. DeWolfe Hopper was unable to organize a benefit of the touring show he was in because it wasn't doing good business, but he offered his services in the Davenport benefit, if he could be fitted into it or, as he said in his letter to the *Mirror*, "Indeed in anything you can use me, I shall hold myself in readiness to do your bidding."

But there were also some undercurrents of dissatisfaction. Despite Fanny Davenport's pushing ahead with plans to play a benefit on May 10 in New York, she had this to say in a letter to the *Mirror* from Pittsburgh, dated April 24, 1882: "My opinion of the last agitation of the Fund business is this: All the profession should have a vote as to what should be done. They were the cause of the effect, and a committee of three might be chosen by their votes to decide all important questions. At any rate, something should be done, and at once." Mary Anderson echoed Miss Davenport's sentiment. Then, too, word had gotten about (albeit erroneously) that stage hands would not be eligible for relief from The Actors' Fund. In the April 15 issue of the *Mirror* Palmer corrected an item which had appeared in the *World* concerning the Theatrical Mechanical Association and its own fund raising event. Said Palmer: "The Fund recently raised was for the benefit of all persons connected with the theatrical business and no appeals from worthy persons so connected would be disregarded."

On Tuesday, April 13, 1882, in the Union Square Theatre,

only ten days after the so-called "Actors' Fund Day," there was a meeting of the New York and Brooklyn managers at which plans for the permanent organization of the Fund under the laws of the state were discussed. A committee consisting of A. M. Palmer, W. E. Sinn, Edward Harrigan, Daniel Frohman and John F. Poole was appointed which, among other things, was to try to bring about a consolidation of the new entity with the "old" Dramatic Fund.

Referring to these actions the *Mirror* commented: "This will dispose of an objection that some of the over-zealous fault-finders have had to the Fund. We mean those who wanted a charter before anything else was obtained."

But at a meeting on May 11, the appointed committee reported dolefully that the directors on the Dramatic Fund objected to any consolidation. The meeting then went on record to propose that no time be lost in submitting an application for a charter to the legislature of the state.

By June 8, 1882, the Act of Incorporation, drafted by Hon. A. J. Dittenhoefer, had been passed into law by the New York State Legislature. On Saturday, July 15, the first meeting officially held under the charter took place at Wallack's Theatre at 12 noon. Mr. William Henderson presided. Permanent officers were elected to serve during what remained of the year 1882-83.

President, Lester Wallack; Vice-President, A. M. Palmer; Secretary, Daniel Frohman; Treasurer, Theodore Moss. (On the fifth of June, Palmer had turned over to Theodore Moss a check for $38,268.16 since he had been named acting treasurer in Palmer's stead. Palmer's official accounting showed that he had disbursed $867.64 for emergency relief and $200 to the *New York Herald* for advertising. Interestingly enough, this would appear to indicate that he got the *Herald*'s advertising bill reduced by $50 and the other small expenses of the initial fund raising otherwise absorbed.) Initial trustees were, according to the Act of Incorporation, the first seventeen incorporators named in the bill. They were:

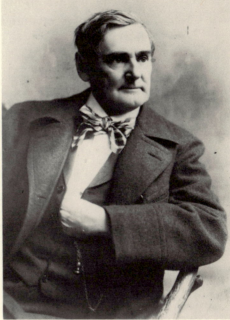

Two giants of the entertainment world in 1882 were P. T. Barnum (left) and Joseph Jefferson (right). Both were among the original incorporators of The Actors' Fund and served on its first board of trustees.

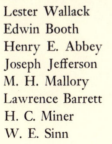

Lester Wallack	A. M. Palmer
Edwin Booth	Edward Harrigan
Henry E. Abbey	William Henderson
Joseph Jefferson	John F. Poole
M. H. Mallory	P. T. Barnum
Lawrence Barrett	W. T. Florence
H. C. Miner	Frank Chanfrau
W. E. Sinn	Bartley Campbell
	Samuel Colville

This meeting, on July 15, 1882, was marked in the records of the association as its first annual meeting, and from this all subsequent annual meetings are numerically reckoned.

On the eighteenth of July, the trustees appointed a temporary executive committee—H. C. Miner, Edward Harrigan, John F. Poole, M. H. Mallory and William Henderson.

The second meeting of the association was held at Wallack's Theatre Monday, September 14, 1882, at 10:00 A.M. A. M. Palmer presided. At this meeting the by-laws of the association were adopted; the temporary executive committee was made permanent and, because Frank Chanfrau, Bartley Campbell and Samuel Colville had declined to serve as trustees, William Birch, Joseph K. Emmett and J. H. Haverly were named in their places.

The foregoing actions completed the legal organization of The Actors' Fund of America.

FROM INCORPORATION TO
THE PRESENT DAY

THE PRIMARY PURPOSE of the Fund today is, as it was at its inception, the gathering and conserving of money—in order to be able to relieve the financial distress of those in the profession who are destitute. Inasmuch as assistance to a needy individual has most always been a matter held in strict confidence between the person aided and the Fund's executive committee, perhaps the essential story of the Fund could be told merely by relating, in chronological order, a summary of its annual statements. The official annual reports, which have been issued each year since 1883 contain meticulously prepared financial statements. The figures set forth total income, cost of administration, disbursements for relief, cumulative growth of capital assets and statistics showing number of cases assisted in a given year and the average of weekly case-loads of persons hospitalized; receiving medical or dental care at home; supplied with shoes; living at The Actors' Fund Home; buried—and so on. These reports are careful to print the names of life members, both present and past, and of persons who have made donations or bequests of substantial amounts.

These annual accountings, however, tell the reader very little about the "personality" of The Actors' Fund. Nevertheless, over the years, the Fund has developed a definite image— if not in the eyes of the public at large—at least it has in the eyes of the profession. Most recently it was dubbed "An Un-

stuffy Santa Claus" in *Variety*, the leading trade paper of today's entertainment world. But, it would be wrong to imply
that the image it has presented to those within the field has
been constant. It is only natural that the Fund's image should
conform generally to one evoked by any voluntary, non-sectarian, charitable institution of a particular era. It must be
remembered, however, that the images of all charitable en-
deavours are conditioned by ever-changing sociological attitudes
and the actions that these attitudes provoke.

From 1882, and even long before that—until 1932 in fact
—it was accepted practice in the United States for voluntary
(i.e. non-governmental) organizations to assume the major responsibility in providing for the well-being of those in need;
those who were physically or mentally ill; the financially
destitute; those who were bereft of family in infancy, old age
or death. Most of these charities were of a religious character
—a few were non-sectarian. But all were pre-eminent over the
scattering of governmental institutions which operated mostly
at a local level—like a county "poorhouse" or a municipal
"Potter's Field" or state supported "insane asylum."

Even within the category of voluntary, non-sectarian charities, such as existed in the last quarter of the nineteenth
century, The Actors' Fund had a certain unique identity. As
has already been demonstrated, in its earliest manifestation, the
Fund was essentially the creature of the *New York Dramatic
Mirror*. It was Harrison Grey Fiske, who as editor of the
Mirror, first gave public expression to the concept that membership within an organization, with its concomitant of dues pay-
ments, should not be a prerequisite to a needy actor's eligibility
for charitable assistance. And he thundered away at what he
believed were the false standards of the American Dramatic
Fund. He was convinced that the financial requirements of the
Fund could be amply met, solely from the proceeds of "benefit
performances" and therefore he devoted column after column
of his weekly in his efforts to get both actors and managers
to deny this popular form of fund-raising to charities in gen-

eral, but instead to confine them all to filling the coffers of an actors' fund. Although Fiske was neither officer nor trustee of the Fund for the first three years of the Fund's corporate infancy, there can be little doubt that his was the most powerful influence within the councils of the Fund, just as he was its most loyal and eloquent spokesman to the profession at large.

In 1885 Albert M. Palmer became president of the Fund. He was to continue in this office for the next twelve years. During his tenure, the character of the Fund was truly established and certain enduring policies were firmly fixed. In the same year that Palmer became president, Harrison Grey Fiske was voted in as secretary—a position the latter held until 1889. Undoubtedly they worked as an harmonious team in the best interests of the Fund. But, of the two, Palmer was undeniably the more practical. And his legal training and political connections, plus his managerial expertise, were all to redound to the benefit of the Fund in those early years—particularly in those few years immediately following its creation, when it could no longer bathe in the glow—and even the after-glow—of the extended publicity which had attended its birth. But Palmer was not a man of limited vision—for all his practicality. He saw the Fund as a constructive force in furthering theatre as a cultural element in the life of the community and not merely as purveyor of light commercial entertainment, which, then as now, was the way most of its professional practitioners viewed the theatre. Rather than limit the Fund to the purposes which were the primary ones expressed in its charter, Palmer constantly sought to expand them. Furthermore, he saw the Fund as a catalyst in a process of integrating theatre with the social, political and economic aspects of community life. He tried— and sometimes succeeded—in overcoming much of the provinciality that invested so much of theatrical thinking and practice.

Towards this end, one of the first things he pushed for was the creation of "honorary memberships." This made it possible to have such distinguished men as Grover Cleveland (serving his first term as President of the United States), John Jacob Astor and James Gordon Bennett become publicly identified with The Actors' Fund, and, by extension, to endorse theatre itself as a wholesome element in community life. As honorary members their identity with theatre went far beyond that of merely being spectators at a play. Thus, Palmer used his theatre-as-culture concept to encourage participation in the Fund by "outsiders," while, at the same time, he was adding to the prestige of the Fund within the hierarchy of the theatre's professional fraternity.

It is well to remember that within the United States the status of the theatre and its people had been steadily deteriorating in the years following Lincoln's assassination. A full new generation had not yet had time to emerge since that fateful April day in 1865. By contrast, during the same period—roughly 1865-1885—in England actors were becoming more and more "socially" elevated, a trend which was to reach its culmination when Henry Irving was knighted by Queen Victoria in 1895 at a ceremony in Windsor Castle. Until Palmer took an interest in upgrading the social position of theatre folk—and had discovered that the Fund was a very practical instrument towards accomplishing it—Edwin Forrest had been a rather lonely, and not too successful, pioneer in this area. Moreover, the scandal which attended Forrest's divorce proceedings did much to hamper the effectiveness of his efforts in this direction.

In the two years preceding the formal organization of the Fund, and when the *Mirror* was campaigning so ardently for its creation, instances of theatrical personages dying in circumstances of loneliness and poverty were extravagantly dramatized by the newspapers in general and the trade papers in particular.

For the press, such incidents have always appeared to have the primary ingredients essential to sensational "human interest" stories. They still do! But in the period of the early days of The Actors' Fund, these stories also carried an implication that the theatrical fraternity had a specific responsibility with respect to such tragic occurrences. Undoubtedly it was true that many young people, in determining on a theatrical career, had to run away from home to pursue it. Family ties were broken that seldom were mended. Stage names were used to hide family identity—to insure permanency of the break with family and childhood friends. It was therefore to be expected that when a relatively unknown actor died, the chance of some member of his family, or a family friend, coming forward to identify—much less claim—the body, was considerably less than in the case of members of professions considered "more respectable." Thus, it was only natural for The Actors' Fund, very early on, to try to alleviate a situation which tended to bring disrepute to the profession as a whole. Indeed, the first capital expenditure made by the Fund was for the acquisition of a burial ground. In 1886 a plot was purchased within the Cemetery of the Evergreens in Brooklyn. The plot comprised twenty burial lots for which $3,600 was paid. In 1887 a special drive was conducted to secure funds for the erection of a central monument in the Evergreen plot. The trustees concluded that they would have no right to dip into monies that had been collected "for relief" to pay for something like a monument, so the special drive was decided on. It resulted in $6,477.60 being taken in; substantially more than the monument was to cost. The surplus was added to the general relief fund. On June 6, 1887, the monument was dedicated with elaborate ceremony. The principal speaker for the occasion was Edwin Booth. William Winter, the eminent critic, wrote a special poem for the event and delivered it personally. A huge crowd was attracted to the cemetery and newspaper coverage was profuse.

By the time Palmer assumed the presidency of the Fund it was clear, at least to him, that the Fund was not going to be adequately sustained solely by income derived from membership dues, individual donations, and proceeds from benefit performances. For three years strenuous efforts had been made

The "cover" story of "Harper's Weekly" for June 18, 1887, was the dedication of the monument erected at the center of The Actors' Fund plot in the Cemetery of the Evergreens, Brooklyn. Edwin Booth was the chief speaker and it was claimed that attendance exceeded 10,000.

to recruit new members. It was continually stressed that the annual dues, only two dollars, were extremely modest. Yet, in the fiscal year ending in June, 1885, only a few more than five hundred—out of a potential of some twelve to fifteen thousand professionals working in the field—had seen fit to become members of the Fund. And benefit performances had proven to be a very fluctuating proposition. So the question of how the Fund was to maintain a steady income, sufficient to meet ever-increasing demands, became paramount in the minds of the officers and trustees. Yet they resolutely dismissed suggestions that assistance be given only to members, with a concomitant upward revision of the dues structure which would presumably generate sufficient income to meet demands limited to taking care of members only. The American Dramatic Fund had fallen into this pitfall and they had no intention of having The Actors' Fund follow suit. Fortunately, at the annual meeting of June 8, 1886, President Palmer was able to report a source of continuing revenue. And it was a substantial one.

For a considerable time there had existed in New York an organization called the Society for the Reformation of Juvenile Delinquents. This society was supported by money from the New York City Treasury, which, in turn was enriched by license fees paid into it for the privilege of operating theatres. Each playhouse in Manhattan and Brooklyn paid a licensing fee of $500. It is unclear whether the state law which authorized the collection of such fees applied to theatres in other cities. The question, however, is academic because Manhattan and Brooklyn were the only places where there were enough theatres to bring in any sizeable amount of money. Unsuccessful attempts by theatre owners to have the law abolished had been made repeatedly. The law was particularly obnoxious to A. M. Palmer because the philosophy on which it was based ran directly counter to his concept of theatre's rightful place as a cultural element, and because he thought the law discriminatory and the fee collected exorbitant. But what angered him most was the disposition of the fee to a single charity which he claimed had a very unsavory reputation. The so-called "reformation" society, to which the entire proceeds of the theatre license fees were turned over, had persuaded the state legislature and the New York and Brooklyn Boards of Aldermen that theatre was a major cause of juvenile delinquency and that it therefore was justified in receiving these funds to aid in its effort to combat what it called the evil effects of theatre on juvenile morality. Palmer was fired by an ardent belief that, quite to the contrary, theatre could have a very beneficial effect on juvenile minds. By utilizing his very considerable political connections, he was able to get 50 percent of the theatre licensing revenues allocated directly to The Actors' Fund. In 1886 the coffers of the Fund were thus enhanced from this source to the tune of $6,350. This sum was more than $1,000 greater than the Fund had earned from all the benefit performances which had been given in the preceding year. In a sense it was a triple triumph for the theatre and the Fund. By getting both the state legislature and the city fathers of Brooklyn and New York to agree at least to a division of the money, the Society for the Reformation of Juvenile Delinquents' argument that theatre was inherently immoral was severely impaired. Furthermore the victory provided the Fund with a source of revenue on which it could depend for a number of years. Finally, it furnished the Fund a new means of income which did not violate the avowed principle of "the theatre taking care of its own" inasmuch as the money had derived from the theatre owners themselves. Its effect on Mr. Palmer personally was to intensify his conviction that theatre was elevating to the human soul; particularly the souls of children. So earnest was he in this conviction, that at one of the early annual meetings of the Fund he arranged for a choir of youngsters to recite poetry and sing choral numbers to show the audience what a healthful effect such activity could have on young people. Thereafter he proceeded with an action which he felt sure would consolidate the gains of his victory. He saw to it that Mayor William R. Grace, Edward E. Loew,

Robert Nooney and Adolph L. Sanger—all of whom sat on the Board of Estimate and Apportionment—were elected to honorary memberships in the Fund.

It is difficult to realize today that in the 1880's actors and others engaged in the theatrical profession could seldom receive help from established church charities. Theatre people were habitually refused admission to their hospitals and homes for the aged because they were still regarded as belonging to that class of person designated as "rogues and vagabonds," even though such legal classification had never been incorporated into the American body of law which had otherwise inherited so much from English law. Of course, the classic case of church prejudice aaginst actors was that which is recounted in Joseph Jefferson's autobiography. In it Jefferson tells how in 1870, on learning of the death of George Holland, a dear friend and highly respected actor, he visited Holland's widow immediately. Mrs. Holland's sister asked Jefferson if he would undertake to see the pastor of her church and request him to officiate at the service for Holland. The sister also expressed Mrs. Holland's desire that the service take place in the church, inasmuch as the house in which the family lived was too small to accommodate the large gathering that would be likely to assemble in view of the fact that Holland had an extraordinary number of friends and, according to Jefferson, was extremely beloved among them. Jefferson set about his mission at once, which he describes in the following passage:

> I at once started in quest of the minister, taking one of the sons of Mr. Holland with me. On arriving at the house I explained to the reverend gentleman the nature of my visit, and the arrangements were made for the time and place at which the funeral was to be held. Something, I can scarcely say what, gave me the impression that I had best mention that Mr. Holland was an actor. I did so in a few words, and concluded by presuming that probably this fact would make no difference. I saw, however, by the restrained manner of the minister

and an unmistakable change in expression on his face that it would make, at least to him, a great deal of difference. After some hesitation he said that he would be compelled, if Mr. Holland had been an actor, to decline holding the service at the church.

Jefferson was shocked and angry. Above all he felt a deep hurt for Holland's young son whose eyes began to fill with tears. He concludes his account of the episode in these words:

> I rose to leave the room with a mortification that I cannot remember to have felt before or since. I paused at the door and said: "Well, sir, in this dilemma is there no other church to which you can direct me, from which my friend can be buried?" He replied that "there was a little church around the corner" where I might get it done; to which I answered: "Then, if this be so, God bless the little church around the corner"; and so I left the house. The minister had unwittingly performed an important christening, and his baptismal name of "The Little Church Around the Corner" clings to it to this day.

Jefferson's autobiography was published in 1890—twenty years after Holland's death. It is highly unlikely that he could have foreseen that the Church of the Transfiguration, at 1 East 29th Street in New York, would be listed in the Manhattan telephone directory as "the Little Church Around the Corner," one hundred years after his encounter with the bigoted clergyman.

Prevailing conditions of rank prejudice against people of the theatre certainly angered many of them. Yet they had, as individuals, very little strength with which to combat them. Certainly, none of the predecessor organizations to The Actors' Fund had been effective in reducing discrimination. Palmer, with the salient victory over the Society for the Reformation of Juvenile Delinquents fresh in his memory, and with his abiding interest in children, attempted for many years to have

The photograph of The Little Church Around the Corner was taken around 1895. This endearing name has clung to The Church of the Transfiguration for more than a century. The name emanated from the refusal of the pastor of a nearby church to allow funeral services for the much beloved George Holland, because he was an actor. Joe Jefferson, who was trying to arrange the services, asked the prejudiced pastor what might be done under the circumstances. The cold reply was: "There's a little church around the corner . . ."

the Fund establish its own orphanage. In this he never succeeded. But his continued efforts in this direction did, indirectly, eventually lead to establishing an Actors' Fund Home for the aged in the theatrical profession.

More and more, as the name Actors' Fund, became preeminent among the theatrical charities, arguments would arise as to whether the Fund could rightfully assist other than actors within the profession. It seems to have been very quickly forgotten that the appellation "actors' fund" was adopted, (without very much forethought it might be said), as a carryover from the *Dramatic Mirror*'s handy epithet used in its two-year campaign to get *some kind* of a fund together that would sup-

plant the ailing American Dramatic Fund. Of course, the incorporators of The Actors' Fund were perfectly well aware
that the legal language of the charter provided that there
should be no limitation which would restrict the Fund from
granting aid to others than actors and that the power to define
who are "members of the theatrical profession" (i.e. persons
eligible for financial assistance) lay solely in the "unrestricted
judgement and discretion of the board of trustees." Against all
attempts to limit assistance to those who were actors, President
Palmer stood like the Rock of Gibraltar. On this point, his
address to the membership at the Fund's eighth annual meeting
is particularly enlightening. He catalogued recipients of Fund
assistance during the fiscal year 1888-89 as follows: "Among
those helped were 249 actors and actresses belonging to the
dramatic, operatic and variety stage, 2 minstrels, 1 ballet girl, 9
dancers, 7 musicians, 4 stage managers, 5 circus performers, 3
wardrobe keepers, 3 door keepers, 9 stage machinists, 12
agents, 4 property men, 1 gas engineer, 2 dramatic authors, 4
managers, 1 captain of supers, 3 scenic artists, 2 widows of
professionals and 2 magicians." Surely a very comprehensive
cross-section of theatrical occupations! Further on in his report, Palmer went on to drive the point home: "The plan on
which the Fund was founded . . . was that everybody, from
the manager and the star actor down to the usher and the call
boy, was to contribute free and willing service to the benefits
which support it and that all alike were to receive its help
when help was neeed."

Apart from burying the dead and relieving those who were
destitute and infirm, the Fund did carry on certain activities
in those early days, under provisions of the charter and by-
laws which declared the objectives of the Fund to be, among
other things, "to advance, promote, foster and benefit the condition and welfare, physical as well as intellectual, of the members of said corporation, and of other persons belonging to
the theatrical profession and their families, in such a way and
manner, and at such time or times as may be provided in the

by-laws and regulations of said corporation." A reading room was established in the Fund's headquarters; an "actors' exchange" was conducted where information as to job-opportunities was posted and a "Ladies' Hospital Committee" was activated. Brander Matthews, the eminent Professor of English Literature at Columbia University was particularly helpful in getting the volumes assembled for the reading room and in the conduct of it. The "exchange" was supposed to be a self-supporting operation, its income to be derived from modest fees to be paid by actors who secured jobs through information gained at the "exchange." But in the long run, it had to be discontinued. Whether its demise was justified by those who carped at the manner of its operation or whether it posed too much of a threat to the incomes of people in the business of being actors' agents, is difficult to assess from this distance. "The Ladies' Hospital Committee" survived to a much later date than the other two activities mentioned. It was the function of this committee to arrange for visits by stars and the wives of theatre managers to invalid actresses who were in hospitals under the Fund's care. In making their rounds, the good ladies distributed books, periodicals and food delicacies. Palmer had grandiose plans for an Actors' Fund House, in which these and other functions could be carried on. He envisioned a sizeable structure in which there would be a large meeting room, in addition to office space for The Actors' Fund as well as for such kindred organizations as the Actors' Order of Friendship and the American Dramatic Fund. Before laying plans to acquire or build such a structure before a membership meeting in 1887, in characteristic fashion, he had previously gotten assurances of some financial contributions towards its realization. But the proposal seems to have evoked nothing more than extended arguments among the membership as to whether such an expansion was not beyond the scope of what the Fund was basically set up for. Since Palmer was not a man to move in any direction where he had less than full support, he did not pursue the matter further.

Instead, he concentrated his attention on efforts to expand the membership rolls and increase attendance at annual meetings. He inaugurated a practice of offering what were called "commemorative exercises" which would follow the business portion of each annual gathering. The first of these programs was held on Tuesday, June 5, 1888, at the Madison Square Theatre. The program included musical numbers played by the combined orchestras of the Casino and Madison Square Theatres, a vocal number by Lillian Russell, and speeches by Col. Robert G. Ingersoll and Dion Boucicault. Notables who entertained or adressed subsequent annual meetings included Chauncey DePew, William Winter, ex-President Cleveland, Lawrence Barrett, Joe Jefferson and Generals W. T. Sherman and Daniel Sickles of Civil War fame.

A notable event in the year marking the tenth anniversary of the Fund took the shape of a great bazaar, or fair—a form of fund-raising which was a departure from the typical theatrical "benefits" which had been so successful in launching the Fund, but which had, in subsequent years, fallen far behind the financial goals anticipated for them. In organizing for the Fair of 1892, an amalgam of theatrical and social "notables" was created which had an electrifying effect. And the success achieved was positively brilliant. The net proceeds from this outstanding event amounted to $167,500. Immediately, several trustees were encouraged to think that such fairs could become annual occasions and would thereby resolve the Fund's financial problems for all time. Palmer, very wisely, discouraged such thinking. He was too aware of the prodigious amount of energy that would be required to repeat the effort and that it would be almost impossible to generate the same kind of excitement on a year-after-year basis.

Nor was the success of the 1892 Fair an altogether unmixed blessing. The publicity attending it gave rise to a substantial increase in applications for assistance from the Fund. Over the span of the first ten years of its existence, the Fund's disbursements for relief had gradually increased from $12,349 in the year ending June, 1883, to $22,965 in the year ending June, 1892. The annual increase for relief disbursements had rarely exceeded a jump of $1,000 over the previous year. Suddenly, for 1893, the jump was in excess of $6,500. Similarly, the building of a capital fund had progressed in a steady, but relatively modest series of steps, from $43,249 in 1882-83 to $75,081 in 1891-92. The addition of the $167,500 gained from the fair skyrocketed the capital assets to $243,782. It is only natural that many who had witnessed the small beginnings of the Fund were quite overwhelmed at the thought of its being worth almost a quarter of a million dollars. Consequently, it is quite understandable that the impression of seemingly limitless wealth would stimulate a host of unexpected demands. In addition to the rising number of applications for relief, there was also the matter of administrative costs becoming ever greater. These had risen in approximately the same ratio as the disbursements for relief and burials, so that by 1892, total Fund expenditures had more than doubled in a ten year period. Although the president was properly proud that administrative expenses "continued to be less in proportion to the amount of money disbursed than those of any other American charity," Palmer felt the time had come to apply the brakes.

The thing that had apparently been most disturbing to him was a spirited discussion which arose in the annual meeting of 1892. The discussion centered on the question of expanding the scope of the Fund to rescuing whole companies that were left stranded on tour. The official response to such a suggestion was this: "While the Fund might agitate reformation of the state law in such a way as to make it possible to get hold of men who deceive actors and actresses by false representations as to their reliability and responsibility, and take them on the road . . . as the Fund laws are at present constituted they prescribe that we shall confine our relief to those who are sick and to the burying of the dead." (It is interesting to note that this matter of actors being stranded away from home continued to plague the profession for another quarter of a century;

that it became a primary factor in creating an actors' union and was not finally settled until the strike of Actors' Equity Association in 1919, when a firmly established Standard Minimum Contract for actors was finally achieved, and with it the requirement that managers post a cash bond to insure the payment of all obligations undertaken.)

In 1893 Palmer felt the necessity of speaking out more forcefully than ever before on the matter of the Fund's scope. His remarks to the general membership are worth quoting in full, not only because they became rather permanent guidelines for his successors but because they undoubtedly reflect the philosophy of most charity as it was practiced in that day:

> Large as the list of our beneficiaries appears (it was 695 persons assisted and 72 burials in 1893) it represents only a portion of those applying to us for help. With the increase in our means which we secured last year through the Fair has come an avalanche of applications for relief, based on all sorts of reasons and from all sorts of people. Some of these cases are unworthy and may be dismissed without a regretful thought. Many of them, however, are worthy, and your officers heartily wish they had the means to afford them relief.

> It is often hard for us to refuse temporary help to a worthy actor, who through stress of circumstances for which he is not responsible is in distress as real and poignant as are those who are sick; but, except in a very few instances, we are obliged to refuse, for the reason that the sick and the dying exhaust our available funds. It is a thing greatly to be hoped for that our Fund may some day be rich enough to give a helping hand to these well but unfortunate members of our profession who often find themselves, through no fault of their own, stranded in the middle of a season in some distant city, or having at the end of the season to face a long summer of enforced idleness with no money with which to support themselves or their families.

Let me not be misunderstood. I would not place a premium on shiftlessness or extravagance. Many actors who can command excellent salaries are often guilty of these faults, and bring distress upon themselves, for which they deserve to suffer. It is not for them I plead. But there are many others who though willing to work can get employment only at irregular intervals and at small salaries. There are others who, in order to earn even a small salary, are obliged, in the present deplorable methods of the theatrical business in our country, to travel from the Atlantic to the Pacific, and from Maine to Florida, living in bad hotels, traveling all day and working at night, and being obliged to purchase every little necessary comfort at rates which absolutely preclude the possibility of saving. Often, too, they have to share with an unfortunate or an over-venturesome or (in too many cases, alas!) a dishonest manager, the consequences of bad business; and a season's work is, in these cases, done for a half season's pay. Distress among such people resulting from such causes comes almost weekly to the attention of those who are in charge of the administration of the Fund, and it is a never failing cause of regret that we cannot respond favorably to their appeals, not in the way of charity, but in temporary relief, which could be extended in such a manner as not to sacrifice the independence of the recipient, and not to permanently deplete our treasury.

In a never ending search for other means of revenue that would be fairly constant, and would not require free services from theatre people, the Fund became intrigued by a proposal made by the eminent German manager, Heinrich Conried. His plan was this: to get the managers of 200 leading theatres throughout the country to levy a tax of ten cents on each complimentary ticket issued during the forty week season—the normal length of a season in that day. Conried conjectured that if 200 theatres would agree to the plan, the resulting income would be $48,000. The project was put to the test for a twelve week period in a few theatres; two in New York, two in Brooklyn and one in Denver. In the experimental period the five theatres contributed $700 to the Actors' Fund treasury, and President Palmer optimistically reported to the membership at the June 6, 1893 meeting: "If 200 theatres could be induced to join these five and would make returns equally as good, the annual income to the association from this source would amount to $93,360." Genuine efforts were made to put Conried's plan into operation. Notwithstanding, there was never any more than a tiny fraction of this number of theatres that agreed to the plan and would then be conscientious about following through. Although some money was collected from the ticket tax each year for the next twelve years, there was never any substantial sum derived from it and the plan was finally abandoned.

Of more far-reaching importance to the theatre in general, was the stance that The Actors' Fund took with respect to children performing on the stage. It was only to be expected, given Palmer's general attitude about theatre as a cultural force, and given his particular interest in the welfare of children, that the Fund would take a strong position against the stringent restrictions that prevented children from appearing on the stage. In 1893 the matter had become one of widespread debate. Here is what the Fund, speaking through the voice of Mr. Palmer, had to say about it: ". . . dancing children can earn from thirty to fifty dollars a week. And yet here in our virtuous metropolis if they should turn this gift which nature has given them to the material advantage of themselves or their parents they would be arrested and punished almost as criminals."

The following year ushered in a general business depression. The increase of demands for assistance from the Fund was enormous. Still bound by the rule precluding the Fund from aiding indigents who were not also ill, there was little direct action it could take. But the Fund lent whatever cooperation it could toward raising a separate and special fund (largely contributed by the theatrical profession through the *New York Dramatic Mirror*) which was disbursed by a committee composed of The Actors' Fund executive committee, and members of the Edwin Forrest Lodge of the Actors' Order of Friendship. The committee concluded its work in April of 1894, having afforded relief to 517 actors and actresses and paying out $8,155.96. A balance, amounting to $1,554.59 was "turned into the hands of our regular executive committee where it remains a separate and independent fund devoted to the relief of those members of our profession who, though in bodily health, find themselves in most desperate straits." In time, of course, the limitation that an applicant had to be ill, as well as being "broke" was removed from The Actors' Fund set of rules—just as the laws were eventually changed, however slowly, to permit children's performances so long as certain precautions with respect to their education and the safeguarding of their earnings were maintained.

Although Palmer continued as president of the Fund until 1897, by the time the last decade of the century had begun, another strong influence on Fund policy was beginning to be felt. It appears to have been traditional—at least during the first years of the Fund—that the first vice-president should also be chairman of the executive committee. In 1889, Louis Aldrich, who had been elected to the board of trustees two years earlier, was elected first vice-president. According to precedent, he was then made chairman of the executive committee. But what is of particular significance about the arrival of Aldrich on the scene, is the fact that he was an actor—and a fairly prominent one as well. For some unaccountable reason —or at least for reasons that do not appear anywhere in the available records—all of the original trustees who were actors disappeared from the board at the same time. After 1885, Booth, Barrett, Harrigan, Jefferson and Wallack, all of whose names had shone so luminously on the original roster of trustees, were missing from the rolls. Only one actor from among those who were original trustees, ever returned to serve the Fund in such a capacity. This was W. J. Florence. Although he too went off the board in 1885, he came back in 1887 to serve for two more years. Within the fifteen year span, between 1885 and

1900, the number of trustees who were also prominent actors became drastically reduced. Other than Louis Aldrich, DeWolf Hopper and F. F. Mackay were the only performers to sit on the board of trustees for terms of any considerable length during the last decade and a half of the nineteenth century.

Aldrich's influence on the affairs of The Actors' Fund was, however, very substantial. As an actor it was only natural that he should be concerned about the exorbitant number of "benefits" that actors were called upon to play for innumerable "causes." While it was true that many other elements of the theatre world would periodically air their complaints about abuses in this area, Aldrich was determined to do something about it. He saw The Actors' Fund as the only theatrical organization strong enough and sufficiently unified to accomplish his purpose. And, instead of approaching the problem with the negative proposals—which had proven so ineffective over the years—of entreating the profession to turn down requests for benefit performances, he succeeded in getting the Fund to adopt a scheme which became known as the "Aldrich Percentage Plan." Under this plan any benefit performance played for any organization other than The Actors' Fund, anywhere in the United States, would be required to turn over 25 percent of its profits to the Fund. To implement the plan, the Fund solicited pledges from actors and managers all over the country not to participate in any benefit in which performers were to volunteer their services unless The Actors' Fund percentage was agreed to in advance. The plan was inaugurated in the season of 1893-94. That it did not become the panacea for the illness it was supposed to cure may be adduced from the following excerpt from the president's report to the membership in June of 1894: "Something like 1300 pledges were given by actors and actresses not to act in benefits, and by managers not to permit benefits to be given, unless The Actors' Fund should receive 25 percent of the profits derived from the same. These are all on file at our office. Yet, so difficult does it seem to be for us to put our own charity before all others that these pledges have been violated or evaded, or begged off from, in more instances than they have been kept." The treasurer reported $890.65 as being received from the "Aldrich 25 percent plan." Thereafter, receipts from this source were only sporadically reported, and never in an amount in excess of $1,000. But, in spite of the plan failing to become the bonanza that might have been hoped for it, it did lay the groundwork for two very important subsequent developments. The first was that it established a principle that survives to this day, namely, that The Actors' Fund would have a preferred claim on actors' unpaid services on behalf of the Fund. The second was that it foreshadowed the creation of Theatre Authority. This organization, founded at the invitation of the Fund, was later to be regulated by the various theatrical and entertainment unions; they being in a stronger position to stipulate and police conditions under which professional services for a charitable purpose would be permitted.

In the last ten years of Palmer's presidency, and particularly in the last eight years of it, Aldrich's voice was to be raised very frequently on various issues—and not always in support of Palmer's policies. Nevertheless, they maintained attitudes of mutual respect for each other, no matter what their differences were. One endeavor in which Aldrich ardently, albeit unsuccessfully, persisted, was to create what he termed a "preferred membership" within the Fund. In his capacity as chairman of the executive committee he was privy to the names and details of the circumstances of all those who were appealing to the Fund for aid. And he was concerned that there were too many "free-loaders" looking for easy "hand-outs" from the Fund. As early as 1884, three years before he held any office in the Fund and five years before he became chairman of the executive committee, he propounded the idea in the pages of the *Dramatic Mirror* that the Fund should receive its major financial support from a small percentage of an actor's salary which the manager would collect and turn over to the Fund. At the third annual meeting of the Fund (June 1884) he had been asked to explain his idea to the membership. In doing so he reasoned: "It (the percentage) would average about three dollars for each person. Out of six or seven thousand actors not more than 4 percent send a subscription (i.e. annual dues) and many decline to play a benefit. Now this plan will cut both ways. If any actor declines to assist he will not be entitled to the assistance of the Fund." William Henderson countered the Aldrich suggestion by stating: ". . . this Fund is for the purpose of rendering assistance to sick and destitute people only, in order to provide them with immediate relief. Mr. Aldrich's scheme bars out certain people. Now, we cannot do that. If a person is in immediate want, and perhaps dying, we cannot inquire whether he or she has contributed to the Fund or not. They are in want, and that is enough for us." Aldrich argued that he had been misunderstood by Henderson. He conceded he did not wish to interfere with the "charitable objects" of the Fund and that these must be left "to the discretion of the trustees." But, he nevertheless asserted: "I look on my plan as a kind of cheap insurance. . . . I calculated recently that there were about sixty-eight combinations, the weekly salaries of which would aggregate over $68,000. If each member of these companies had been taxed five per cent, it would yield all the money required." The matter, while being favorably received by the membership attending the meeting, was referred by vote to the board of trustees. The latter did not accept it, but they had not heard the last of the subject from Mr. Aldrich.

After 1892, the year of The Actors' Fund Fair, memberships in the Fund spurted upwards, at least temporarily. And so did general interest in the Fund. But the increased interest in the Fund's affairs was not devoid of a certain amount of criticism. The wisdom of the executive committee was occasionally called into question as to whether a particular case was justified in receiving help from the Fund; likewise the reverse situation as to people who had been denied assistance. In 1895 President Palmer found it necessary to refute, publicly, some of the adverse allegations. He did it in this fashion: "The number of persons to whom relief has been extended since our last meeting is 524. In 1894 the number recorded as relieved was 903. This comparison shows a falling off in our beneficiaries of over 40% for the year. I wish to remark in explanation of this, however, that the year 1894 was an exceptional one in the depressing conditions surrounding our profession. . . . Numerous instances of complaint against the Fund have no other basis than a refusal on the part of the Executive Committee to make it a dumping ground upon which these 'worthy persons' may unload burdens which they themselves should bear. Acting for a Fund benefit once in four or five years surely does not entitle one to claim that a protege should be kept in a hospital at the expense of the Fund year in and year out, and just as certainly it does not justify anyone, when the proper officers at last feel that the limit of expenditure for a single individual has been reached, in indulging in reproaches and in public declarations that the Actors' Fund is a humbug and a delusion." Other forms of criticism manifested themselves in the calling of special meetings to change the by-laws and the manner in which the officers were elected and in the number of trustees and the terms of their respective offices. The net result of a very complex series of parliamentary maneuvers was to strengthen the general confidence that the profession had in the management of the Fund; the most important of the specific changes having been to increase the total number of officers and trustees from seventeen to twenty-one and to elect only one-third of the total each year so as to provide against abrupt changes in the over-all management and fundamental policies.

In 1897 Louis Aldrich was elected to the presidency. At this point he had put in ten years of service to the Fund—two as a trustee and eight as vice-president and chairman of the executive committee. During the two years prior to his election as president he had vigorously advocated a project for establishing a home for elderly actors. This put him increasingly at odds with Palmer whose primary interest was to explore all the possibilities of raising money to erect an orphanage to be run by the Fund for the benefit of orphaned children of the theatrical profession. While Palmer did not directly oppose the idea of a home for the elderly; he would constantly point out that the Fund did not have the means to embark on such a project; yet, whenever an opportunity arose he would give hints that money might be available for an orphanage.

Another episode occurred in the year 1896 which put Louis Aldrich further in the limelight of Actors' Fund affairs. Charles Dickson, who was chairman of the nominating committee for that year proposed a resolution to the effect that "the Board of Trustees be instructed to employ an officer in addition to the Assistant Secretary who shall be known as the Executive Officer of the Fund, said officer to be paid a salary of not less than three nor more than five thousand dollars." This resolution followed in the wake of spirited discussions that had gone on for more than a year, which generally extolled Aldrich for the depth of his concern about the Fund, and, at the same time deplored the fact that he was unable to assume greater responsibilities and devote more time to things that many thought were not receiving the attention they deserved. The pro-Aldrich faction had particularly singled out his determination to discourage benefits which would not adhere to the "Aldrich 25 Percent Plan" and to encourage more performances to be given for the sole benefit of The Actors' Fund. The resolution to establish a paid executive officer carried with it the implication that Palmer was not fulfilling his obligation as president to the fullest extent. Such implication was clearly resented by Aldrich, who in debating the issue, vigorously opposed the resolution and with great forthrightness declared, ". . . it was the intention of a member of the Board of Trustees, in view of the work which I have done, that I should be made a salaried officer. . . . I ask no salary and won't take any, and I hope the members of the Fund will think very seriously before taking an action of this kind." The motion was finally tabled.

In 1900, about three years after Louis Aldrich became The Fund's president, the intersection of Broadway, Seventh Avenue and 45th Street was ripe to become the center of theatrical activity. The entire area was then Longacre Square. This view, looking south, shows the Hotel Pabst—soon to be replaced by the Times Building. In 1905 the three-block section to the south of 46th Street was renamed Times Square.

The problem confronting Aldrich was the same then as that confronting actors today who sincerely desire to work for the betterment of their profession. If the actor is out of work he has the time which he can devote to activities outside of performing, but only at the sacrifice of actively seeking work to sustain himself. When he is performing, he frequently cannot maintain the continuity of effort required for effective volunteer work, and its value is consequently diminished. While the same conditions may prevail for others not categorized as actors, in the theatrical world, those in a managerial or business capacity can usually dispose of their time with a greater degree of flexibility. Nevertheless, the time eventually came about when the Fund would have to employ a paid, full-time executive officer, albeit when such a post was finally created it carried the title of "General Manager."

Louis Aldrich's term as president was relatively short, lasting only until 1901. Nevertheless, during this term he forged ahead with his dream of a home for retired actors and actresses. Palmer remained on the board of trustees after his retirement as president and it must have been a source of real gratification to Aldrich to realize that Palmer would now lend his support to the "Home Project." In Palmer's "farewell address" he said: "We have discussed almost regularly for the past ten years the propriety of founding an actors' home and hospital. . . . So far we have been able to do nothing practical in this direction, but I have good reason for believing that in the near future such a home may be provided. This will be done, I think, without entrenching in any way upon the Fund's present investment. A special fund will be created for the purpose, toward which a large sum has already been pledged." There can be little doubt that to Palmer's practical mind, the fact of a sum of money having actually been pledged for a "home"—whereas nothing concrete had ever been offered for an orphanage— despite his ardent campaigning for the latter idea—was the factor which determined his switch. It is sad that Aldrich did not live to see The Actors' Fund Home a reality. But there is ample evidence, which will be set forth in detail in the section dealing with the Home, the major credit for its realization justifiably belongs to Aldrich.

Other matters claimed much of his attention. Foremost among these was how to find another source of assured income to replace the annual $11,000 to $13,000 which the Fund had been receiving from the City of New York. In 1900 that revenue was entirely cut off. Van Wyck was then mayor of New York; the first one to hold that office under the Charter of Greater New York; that is since the five boroughs were amalgamated as one entity. The new charter was very emphatic on the powers of the mayor to exercise "home rule." Legislation which had passed at Albany about two years prior to the issuance of the new charter had made it mandatory for the city to give a clear half of the license monies from theatres to The Actors' Fund. Indeed, Palmer had been instrumental in getting that legislation before the legislature because he felt it would be a safeguard against any local maneuvering to reduce The Actors' Fund share. But Van Wyck had espoused the principle of home rule so vehemently, that he felt he had no alternative but to veto it—even though he declared that it was not because of any prejudice he had against the Fund. Nevertheless, from then on, the Fund nevermore received a penny of financial assistance from the City of New York. And, in passing it might be noted that although Van Wyck may have had an expressway named for him, he remains one of the few New York mayors who held that office subsequent to the creation of the Fund, who was not elected to honorary membership.

On June 17, 1901, Louis Aldrich died, following a brief illness. His successor was Al Hayman. As general manager of the Klaw and Erlanger interests, he was both wealthy and powerful. It was he who had responded so generously to Louis Aldrich's personal appeal for money for the Home. But Hayman was oriented almost exclusively to the business side of the theatre. The Klaw and Erlanger syndicate had achieved a near monopoly of all the theatres in America and was commonly referred to as "The Trust." It operated with great efficiency and can properly be credited with having replaced chaos with order in the matter of bookings. It also gave the theatre a financial security on a wide scale that was hitherto completely unknown, for it became the first theatrical enterprise to operate on a multi-million dollar basis. And Al Hayman was in no small measure responsible for its remarkable growth. But its grip on the over-all picture of the theatre was so powerful that it revolutionized both the artistic and business side of theatrical production. One after another, the great stars, instead of ven-

turing forth across the land as "soloists" playing their great
roles as "guest artists" of a resident stock company, became
"employees" of the Trust. And bit by bit they lost their
artistic independence. Hayman was so fully absorbed in the
day-to-day operations of Klaw and Erlanger, that he could
devote very little time to the Fund. But his pledge of $50,000
toward a fund to build The Actors' Fund Home was widely
publicized. Being a man of fierce determination, and one of
intense personal loyalty, it is not surprising that he was anxious
to have the "Home Project" turn out to be a success. In all
likelihood, when the presidency of the Fund was offered him
he saw in it an opportunity to fulfill an implied obligation to
the memory of Louis Aldrich—and to the enhancement of his
own public image. In all truth, it cannot be said, however, that
he showed any vital interest in the over-all affairs of the Fund.
He was president from 1901 to 1904.

Fortunately for the Fund there was a man waiting in the
wings, so to speak, who had evinced the greatest possible interest in every aspect of the Fund's operations. This was
Daniel Frohman. He was one of the incorporators, the first
secretary of the Fund—an office which he filled again from
1894 to 1898—first vice-president from 1901 to 1904, and continuously a trustee in the twenty-two years that intervened
between 1882 and 1904. It would have been almost impossible
for the nominating committee to by-pass his name when Mr.
Hayman decided to relinquish the office of president. Thus it
was that Mr. Frohman was elected president in 1904 and was
destined to hold that office for an unprecedented length of time
—thirty-seven years. Furthermore, his continuous service and
sustained interest spanned an almost incredible fifty-nine years.

Inasmuch as Palmer and Frohman together dominated the
Fund for all but a very few of its first sixty years, it is hardly
surprising that its permanent course should have been shaped
by them. While Frohman's background was somewhat different
from Palmer's—Frohman having never been involved in anything but theatre from his early teens on, as against Palmer's

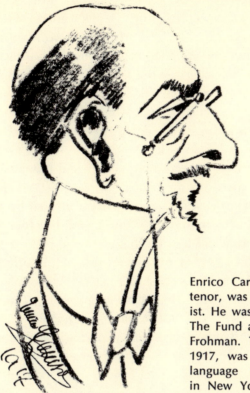

Enrico Caruso, the great Italian tenor, was also a gifted cartoonist. He was both a benefactor of The Fund and a friend of Daniel Frohman. This sketch, made in 1917, was done for an Italian language newspaper published in New York.

legal education and prior experience as a librarian and in the political arena—the outlook of the two men vis-à-vis the Fund was remarkably similar. Each was concerned with investing the image of the Fund with all the glamour possible by encouraging participation in its affairs, not only by the stars of the theatrical firmament, but also those who held high positions in the political, social and business worlds. Both were bent on bestowing the aura of respectability to the theatre and its people. And both men felt that the Fund was an instrument well adapted to achieving this goal. Being men of cultivated taste, they were in an ideal position to do this, for they were identified in the public's mind more with the artistry of the theatre than with its commercial side. Under the circumstances, the short term during which Hayman, who was regarded as the epitome of "commercial theatre," held office did little to disturb the image that was created by Palmer, continued by Aldrich and intensively carried on by Mr. Frohman.

But for all his idealism, Frohman was not unmindful of the essentiality of sound financing for the Fund. One of his major objectives was to achieve a million dollars in capital assets for the Fund. That he was eminently successful in this objective is attested to by the fact that at his death the capital worth of the Fund had risen to $2,365,944.40.

Of course, a man with the enormous energy and imagination of Daniel Frohman could not be content with the status quo. While stoutly believing that the essential pattern created by the founding fathers had been soundly conceived, and therefore not subject to revolutionary change, he did not hesitate to bring about many innovations within the framework of the original constitution and by-laws. He established a category of membership designated as "associate." This enabled persons in rather substantial numbers, who did not qualify as "honorary," to join the Fund notwithstanding their lack of professional credentials. They paid the same dues as the regular members, whether on an "annual" or "life" basis. They were not permitted to vote, but they could come to the annual meetings, receive the annual report and in all ways were encouraged to increase their potential for personal involvement. This enlargement of the arena affording personal identification with the professionals of the theatre was responsible for many subsequent bequests and sizeable donations from people who loved the theatre but who were not "of" the theatre.

By 1910 the list of honorary life members had also been expanded to include such names as Stanford White, William R. Grace, Marcella Sembrich, Ignace Paderewski, Walter Damrosch, William Howard Taft and Henry Huddleston Rogers. The list of regular life members had risen to embrace almost every notable name in the theatrical galaxy. "Physicians to the Fund," who charged no fee to professionals referred by the Fund, numbered fourteen in New York and Brooklyn alone, and extended to one or more doctors in some forty cities across the land! An impoverished actor in need of medical attention, could, on recommendation of The Actors' Fund, be treated at no charge in such unlikely places as Winfield, Kansas; Decatur, Illinois; Parkersburg, West Virginia; Mt. Clemens, Michigan; or Moberly, Missouri.

A network of corresponding secretaries was maintained in key cities from Boston to Los Angeles and from Buffalo to Galveston. Worthy of note is that the corresponding secretary in Buffalo was one P. C. Cornell, M.D. He was the father of Katharine Cornell. In addition to his medical practice, Dr. Cornell was involved in the management of Buffalo's Star Theatre.

In May of 1924 annual disbursals for relief had reached $140,000. This was $12,000 less than the total income for the year. Mr. Frohman and Sam Scribner, the treasurer, had become concerned as to the financial ability of the Fund to meet the constantly expanding needs. Mr. Frohman declared that expenses were frequently outrunning income by as much as $25,000 a year. One of the greatest drains on the Fund's resources came from the Los Angeles area where the motion picture industry was attracting hordes of newcomers to the entertainment field. All of these people—for the most part totally inexperienced—hoped for stardom. But they rarely found themselves cast as anything but "extras"; that is providing they could even so much as find any employment at all within the gates of a motion picture studio.

The Fund had inaugurated a motion picture branch a few years earlier in an effort to take care of relief cases that were applying for help in Hollywood. But the requests had become totally disproportionate to the Fund's ability to satisfy them. Therefore, legal steps were required to insure that the Fund's purpose, as originally chartered, could and would be safeguarded. Accordingly, at a special meeting called in New York on December 3, 1924, the membership unanimously endorsed a change in the by-laws which empowered the trustees, "in their sole discretion" to decide what persons were to be defined as members of the theatrical profession and thereby eligible for Actors' Fund assistance. The effect of this action was the immediate activation of the Motion Picture Relief Fund. Articles of Incorporation for the new agency "designed to take over film relief work formerly carried on by The Actors' Fund of America" were filed in Sacramento on December 30, 1924. Prominent among its incorporators were: Mary Pickford, Douglas Fairbanks, Charles Chaplin, Cecil B. DeMille, Jesse L. Lasky, William S. Hart and Rupert Hughes. They announced the incorporation with a statement that: "Both branches, The Actors' Fund and the Relief Fund will work in harmony and cooperate with each other." Jesse Lasky was a trustee of The Actors' Fund at this time and remained so until 1926.

Undoubtedly the greatest test of the Fund's powers of endurance came during the depression years of the nineteen-thirties. Nothing could be a greater credit to the wisdom and steadfastness of Daniel Frohman than the manner in which he conducted its affairs during that decade. Those were years when the income of the Fund was drastically reduced at the same time as its obligations were being just as drastically increased. There were some within the profession who had misgivings about the Fund's ability to cope with the dimension of need that the economic cataclysm forced on the country in general and on the theatre in particular. As a consequence, there came into being an organization called the Stage Relief Fund. Some people closely connected with the Fund tended to resent the intrusion of newcomers. No matter how well intentioned they might have been, they were without the experience and know-how which The Actors' Fund had accumulated over the years. Certainly it could be, and was, argued that instead of creating a new and separate entity to pursue exactly the same objective as the Fund's, these people of good-will should have lent their energy and given their money to strengthen the Fund in a time of sore distress. But Frohman, always sensitive to the egos and individuality of theatre people, astutely chose to welcome their efforts. With true statesmanship he established a decent rapport between the two organizations which lasted during his lifetime. Although the Stage Relief Fund was initiated to fill the need of an acute national emergency and presumed to deal only with "emergency cases," it persisted as an organization until 1951. When, in that year, it eventually "closed up shop," its remaining assets of $5,842.22 were turned over to the Fund.

With the passing of Frohman in 1941, the spirit which had imbued the "founding fathers" understandably came to an end. With many of them the establishment of the Fund was an act of procreation rather than an act of creation. Although the three presidents who succeeded Daniel Frohman in the thirty years following his death have all been dedicated men, their relationship to it could not possibly be quite the same as one who had been instrumental in actually giving birth to the Fund and who had seen it grow from infancy to become a healthy, mature and highly respected institution of the American Theatre. Daniel Frohman was the last of the "founding fathers."

No telling of The Actors' Fund story is really possible without bringing into it the intimate association which links it to Actors' Equity. It will be remembered that, from time to time, the plight of actors in road companies which were "stranded" would be brought to the attention of The Actors' Fund. But no matter how much sympathy there might have been for the people caught in such misfortune, a provision in the Fund's Articles of Incorporation, and other limitations imposed by the by-laws, limited the trustees to assisting those who were either "destitute" or "sick." And the word "destitute," as interpreted by the executive committee, seemed to imply a state of almost permanent impoverishment. Apparently, being "stranded on the road" was a temporary condition and one of the normal risks of the business against which the individual actor was supposed to be prudent enough to protect himself. Besides, the Fund, governed as it was by a group primarily drawn from the ranks of responsible managers, was loathe to being put in the embarrassing position of having to "bail out" irresponsible members of the managerial fraternity.

With the growing power of the Theatrical Syndicate, the average individual actor became increasingly helpless in mastering his own fate. This gave rise to the formation of a group who called themselves the Actors' Society. Louis Aldrich played an important role in its creation and development. (It should be noted that the Frohmans—but particularly Daniel's brother Charles—played major roles in the functioning of The Syndicate. Nevertheless, it is a measure of the outstanding integrity of these men, as well as most who served on the Fund's governing board, that they never permitted whatever interests they may have had outside the Fund to interfere with their dedication to what they felt to be in the best interests of the Fund itself.) The function of the Actors' Society was to attempt to regulate, and if possible standardize, contractual obligations as between actors and managers. In the decade between 1895 and 1905 the Society grew in membership and prestige. But after 1905, it seems to have entered a period of slow but steady decline. Perhaps the loss of Louis Aldrich as a leader had something to do with this. At any rate, by 1910 its failure to achieve its goals had become increasingly apparent. At The Actors' Fund annual meeting of 1909, Joseph Grismer, then first vice-president of the Fund, advanced the proposal that the Actors' Society be consolidated with the Fund. Later on in the meeting, Thomas A. Wise, president of the Society, was called on to express his view of Grismer's proposal. Wise had only been recently appointed, as an interim replacement, to the Fund's board of trustees. He did not go beyond promising that the proposal would "receive profound consideration from the officers of the Actors' Society." In the 1910 meeting, the subject was again brought forward. At this point

Wise was to retire as a trustee of the Fund, but he was called on to speak by Mr. Frohman. Now his attitude was quite negative to the proposal of any merger, inasmuch as the Actors' Society was then attempting to obtain a charter from the American Federation of Labor. Had it been successful, its obvious course would have been to become militantly involved, as a labor union, in getting a standardized employment contract from theatrical employers. But, being unsuccessful in this endeavor, the Actors' Society went into rapid decline. It is plain to see that it would have been most unfortunate for the Fund to have become aligned with the Society and, in ensuing years, (which were fraught with struggles by actors to correct the abuses practiced by some managers) to have had its own ranks torn apart by those bitter struggles. Also, it was surely considerate, as well as discreet, for Tom Wise to relinquish his post as a Fund trustee, knowing—as he must have—what lay in store. Because of their import for the future, it is worth setting down Wise's final words, addressed to the membership of The Actors' Fund in the meeting of May 24, 1910—and particularly the exchange that followed:

> MR. THOMAS WISE—I think the nature of the two societies are so far apart—the Actors' Fund is to take care of the sick and helpless—the Actors' Society is to look after the well ones. The motto of the Actors' Society is "equity." It is their desire to establish an equitable contract, equitable for the actor and equitable for the management. It is to look after the actors' side; it looks after the actors who have been ill treated by what are termed bogus managers, and to help them fight their cases; in fact, to benefit the well actor in every way. . . . I do not think the two societies could come under one head.
>
> MR. DICKSON—There is nothing in what you mention but what is good for the actor. Why can't the Actors' Fund do as well.
>
> MR. FROHMAN—We cannot go into argument now. When

Mr. Dickson comes on the board we will accept the firebrand * and see what we can do and pour upon the con-
gregation some of Mr. Wise's common sense.

On December 22, 1912, one hundred members of the Actors'
Society of America met to decide whether or not it would
be worthwhile to try to continue. The consensus of opinion
at that meeting was that it would not. But that same meeting,
which heard the death sentence pronounced upon the Actors'
Society, witnessed the birth of a new organization which was
to become Actors' Equity Association.

There were times in the six years between Equity's formal
organization in 1913 and its "coming of age" with the strike
of 1919 when the leadership of the Fund may have been hard
put to maintain a strict neutrality between the newly formed
actors' group and the Producing Managers Association. But
there is little formal documentation for any tensions that might
have arisen. However, certain inferences may fairly be drawn
from certain unassailable actions that were taken which, in all
probability, were taken for the very purpose of maintaining
an equilibrium between the two opposing associations. To begin
with, in 1913 the Fund recruited Francis Wilson again as a
trustee. He had previously been on the Fund's board for four
years, 1898 to 1902. When he was later re-nominated, and
elected, he was one of the leading advocates of a revitalized
actors' association, and did, in fact become the first president
of Actors' Equity. It is impossible to escape the conclusion
that he was placed on the board to redress the balance on a
board that was preponderantly representative of the managerial
group. Another "sign of the times" was that there was extended
discussion at the annual meeting in the spring of 1917 about
having a woman elected as trustee. The result was a motion,
offered by Mrs. Millie Thorne, and seconded by Nora Bayes,

* (Mr. Dickson had been elected as a Trustee at the same meeting and
had stated earlier: ". . . I shall be a firebrand.")

recommending that should a vacancy occur during the coming year that it be filled by a woman. Joseph Grismer, actor and playwright, was first vice-president of the Fund at the time. He skillfully intervened in the proceedings to aid the ladies in getting their motion in proper parliamentary form. The significance of the move to get a woman on the board of trustees is that Equity had found it necessary to accord women of the stage their "equal rights," thus setting an example which it would have been difficult for the Fund to ignore. In consequence, Miss Bijou Fernandez's name appears on the roster of trustees for the year 1918—the first woman's name to so appear. In 1919 the name of Mrs. Edwin Arden appears in addition to that of Miss Fernandez. And in 1920, although Mrs. Arden's name had disappeared, the luminous names of Blanche Bates and Ethel Barrymore brought the count of female trustees to three! Miss Barrymore had been a commanding and active figure in the Equity strike. It is not far-fetched to assume that her selection as a trustee did not entirely rest on the grounds of her sex or her renown as an actress, but rather because of her prominence in Equity affairs. This assumption is reinforced by the fact that since Francis Wilson ceased to be a trustee in 1917, nothing could be more appropriate than to elect a lady who, in 1920, had just become Equity's first vice-president.

In the following year, still another "balancing act" was performed by the Fund's nominating committee. At the time of the Equity strike, George M. Cohan had reached the peak of his almost unparalleled success in the triple capacities of author, actor and, in partnership with Sam Harris, producer. As an influential member of the Producing Managers Association he was in constant consultation with its officers. On one occasion, when they were discussing strategy, Cohan said: "I'll put $100,000 on any table around which you'll gather a representative organization of actors and I'll give up the rest of my life to it—but it can't be Actors' Equity Association." This remark received widespread publicity. George M. Cohan was

Left to right: George M. Cohan, Daniel Frohman and William Collier, Mr. Collier, on behalf of the Actors' Fidelity League, presenting Mr. Cohan's $100,000 check to Mr. Frohman, president of The Actor's Fund of America. August 30, 1919.

a man who was always very jealous of his public image. The $100,000 offer, he repeatedly maintained, was made only for what he considered to be in the best interest of actors—all actors. Nevertheless, Equity's rival organization never saw fit to accept it. But Cohan did not wish to be regarded as a "piker." So, in a flourishing gesture that was typical of him, he donated the money to The Actors' Fund. It was the largest donation ever to have been made to the Fund by an individual during his lifetime. In 1921 Mr. Cohan was elected to the board of trustees of the Fund, and he continued to embellish it until his death in 1942. Miss Barrymore, on the other hand, disappeared as a trustee as soon as she had completed the second year of a three year term. Her second year overlapped the first year of Mr. Cohan's first year on the board. One cannot help but wonder if there is any significance to those facts. But the spirit of the Fund is best exemplified by remarks that Mr. Frohman made at a Fund meeting which took place around then. He said: "The Actors' Fund, of course, stands aloof and apart from all professional tangles. Our business is charity for all with malice toward none. We want everybody's help. And when our Board meets—our Board which is made up of members of Equity, of the Fidelity, managers and actors—there is but one consideration, and that is charity to those who are entitled to it."

In 1919 Equity sent Howard Kyle to the Fund's annual meeting to affirm Equity's willingness to promulgate Louis Aldrich's long–cherished dream that no benefit performance would be played unless the Fund were to receive a percentage of the revenue. However, Equity felt that the burden of turning down a charity, or of explaining the requirement of reserving a share of the proceeds for the Fund should not fall on the shoulders of the actors alone. He pleaded Equity's argument that the Fund itself could and should do more to make the policy more widely known. Eventually, however, it was not until Theatre Authority came into existence many years later that this phase of the thorny "benefit question" was ever adequately resolved.

The need was great for an agency which could effectively resist the countless appeals which charitable organizations were in the habit of making to individual actors and managers for free services in fund-raising events for many worthy, and some not-so-worthy causes. It could be a serious embarrassment to a highly placed individual in the theatrical firmament to have to refuse such appeals—particularly those coming from recognized and worthwhile charities. But there always lurked the question of whether a given appeal was to aid a bona fide organization or a none-too-scrupulous person or group. The typical performer was not equipped to make a discreet but necessary investigation before any decision was reached. Furthermore, most frequently the appeals would devolve unfairly on a few just because the shows involved were hits or the stars were enjoying momentary spells of great popularity.

Despite all attempts of the Fund to regulate the practice and to intervene on behalf of those who were being particularly put-upon, it did not possess the means for completely effective action. The Fund stayed with the problem and, once Equity was formally established and recognized, the Fund was able to call on the union to collaborate in creating that separate agency, Theatre Authority Inc., which eventually put the enforcement powers of all theatrical unions behind it. Since the establishment of Theatre Authority there has been effective "policing," on a nationwide scale, of any and all "benefits" which seek to call upon any element of the entertainment world to donate professional services on a gratis basis.

A giant step forward toward assuring the Fund a steady income from the voluntary services of actors was taken when in 1924, at the urging of Mr. Frohman, Equity and the Producing Managers Association agreed to specific contractual conditions under which both actors and management would be required to give special performances in which neither the actors would be paid nor would the theatre owner or producer derive any profit. These conditions would apply to any production playing under the Equity Standard Contract either on Broadway or on the road. And the Fund was given the prerogative of designating which productions would be called on for the extra performances. This clause in the Basic Minimum Agreement applied uniquely to The Actors' Fund. It not only had the advantage of assuring the Fund of an adequate number of performances in any given season, but it allowed the Fund to earn money on the performances without increasing the established box-office price for tickets to any attraction it chose to call on. Although the details of this provision of the Equity contract have been modified from time to time over the years, the principle has remained intact. Even with today's diminished number of Broadway and road productions from

1924 ushered in a new era of "benefit" performances. The new basic contract between Equity, theatre owners and producers granted exclusively to The Fund the privilege of calling for an extra performance of any production playing on Broadway or the Road. And it became mandatory that such performance be given without revenue to the producer, theatre owner or Equity members of the company. The Theatre Guild's production of "Porgy" was the first to be given under these conditions. Since then, the term "benefit" has been eschewed in announcing Actors' Fund special performances.

which to choose, the Fund still is able to count on this source for a sizeable part of its income albeit the difficulties of scheduling such performances and obtaining cooperation from all concerned seem to grow with each passing year.

The man who followed Daniel Frohman at the helm of the Fund was Walter Vincent. Although he arrived on the New York scene only seven years after the founding of the Fund, he did not become closely identified with it until the Fund was entering its thirtieth year. Almost immediately, he was put on the executive committee where he functioned with wisdom and devotion until he was elected secretary in 1921. Thereafter, he successively occupied the chairs of second vice-president, first vice-president and, in 1941, president.

In all that he did for the Fund he was unsparing both of his time and his money. But the thing to which he addressed himself with the greatest energy was the building of a new Actors' Fund Home in Englewood. Even though very advanced in years when he undertook the project—he had already passed his eightieth birthday—he overcame many obstacles that confronted him, including considerable opposition from within the Fund itself. He realized that the necessary money would have to be gotten without dipping into current income or assets. Therefore, to give it one of its earliest and most important forward thrusts, he prevailed on the council of Actors' Equity to pledge $150,000 towards its construction. He was able to enlist the ardent support of Jacob Goodstein, Herman Bernstein, Emil Friedlander and Warren Munsell—all of them trustees who concurred in his belief that a new building was essential. So they put their shoulders to the wheel to help him with the technical and financial problems which were formidable, but not insurmountable.

Walter Vincent's wife, Eva, formerly an actress, was also devoted to the Fund. Between gifts made during their lifetime and bequests specified in their wills, the Fund has received more than $250,000 through the generosity of Walter and Eva Vincent. Of this amount, $100,000 went to the new building in Englewood, the completion of which they were unfortunately not spared to see, as had also been the case with Louis Aldrich in whose fertile mind the dream of a residence for retired people of the theatre had originated so long ago.

Vinton Freedley's tenure in the office of president for the decade 1959 to 1969 reflected the conservatism that imbued his political and economic philosophy. It might even be said that he regarded his responsibility as president of the Fund primarily as a fiscal one. Perhaps it was inevitable that his concept of the office would be shaped in this fashion as the result of

Annual meetings of The Fund are held each May. Traditionally they take place in a Broadway theatre; the board of trustees on the stage and the members in the audience. The 1972 meeting took place in the Booth Theatre. The stage-set is for "Butterflies Are Free." Octogenerian humorist Harry Hershfield is the speaker.

Members of the present executive committee are arrayed beneath portraits of Booth, Katharine Cornell, Charles Dillingham and Charles Frohman, (below Miss Cornell) Otis Skinner and Sarah Bernhardt which hang in the reception room of The Fund's offices. The committee members shown are: William P. Adams, Mrs. Martin Beck, John Alexander, Nedda Harrigan Logan and Warren P. Munsell.

the eighteen years of service he had rendered in the capacity of treasurer prior to his election as president. In addition, he was the first president to have "graduated" from the treasurership to that of the Fund's highest office. Moreover, he had had the immense satisfaction of seeing the net worth of the Fund increase from $2,346,813, when he first took over the financial reins, to $3,615,939, when he yielded them to his successor, Herman Bernstein. Inasmuch as Freedley had achieved this financial growth of 54 percent without resort to any financial innovations such as "fairs," special events or concentrated "drives," such as had been introduced from time to time under previous leadership, it can be said that Vinton Freedley accomplished his result primarily by the application of a principle of strict prudence to all of the Fund's financial affairs. As treasurer he exercised his considerable influence in keeping expenses at a minimum while, at the same time, he watched over the portfolio of investments with an eagle eye with the objective of increasing its capital worth and income yield to the maximum extent consistent wtih the greatest possible security. That his outlook as president was carried over from his lengthy term as chief fiscal officer—second only in length to that of his predecessor, Sam Scribner—is attested to by noting that the curve of the Fund's prosperity continued its steady upward trend all during the ten years that he presided.

The next president of the Fund, Louis Lotito, had had sixteen years service as a trustee and five as treasurer when he was elevated to the presidency. As this is being written he has been at the helm only two and a half years. Thus, it is too early to evaluate what his total impact on the Fund may turn out to be. But it is not too soon to detect that while he is appreciative of the tremendous legacy of stability and compassionate assistance to thousands which had been left by his eight predecessors, he is also aware that the socio-economic conditions in the United States are vastly different from what they were a century ago and that conditions in the entertainment world are nothing short of revolutionary if they are viewed from the perspective of 1882. Consequently, he is acutely aware that if The Actors' Fund of America is to continue as a viable institution in the future, its principles and its practices will have to be carefully examined to ascertain how it can function most valuably in the light of today's realities and the reasonable prospects for the future.

II

Profiles of Presidents

LESTER WALLACK

THERE IS LITTLE ROOM for doubt that Lester Wallack was made the first president of The Actors' Fund, not only because he was the most glamorous actor of the day but because he was the shining descendant of one of the most brilliant theatrical dynasties of English origin ever to bridge the dramatic distance between London and New York. He proved himself to be an astute manager, far more so than Booth, whom many regarded as vastly his superior as an actor. In addition, he was recognized as a very able playwright.

Wallack was born on West Bleecker Street, New York at midnight, on December 31, 1819; (later he adopted January 1, 1820, as his birthday, thereby giving the appearance of being a year younger). He was baptized John Johnstone Wallack. His grandfather, William Wallack, had been a successful English actor in the eighteenth century and his grandmother, Elizabeth Field Granger, had been the great Garrick's leading lady. But the fame of William's second son, James William Wallack (born in London in 1795; died in New York in 1864) would far outshine that of the father. The boy's stage career started when he was four and when he was only twelve he came to the attention of Sheridan who placed him at the Drury Lane. There he remained for the next two years, until that theatre burned down on February 24, 1809. It was after the re-opening of the Drury Lane in 1812 that James Wallack's star really began to rise. The first role to bring him recognition was Laertes to the Hamlet of Charles Lamb Elliston. Rapidly James

Lester Wallack,
First President.
The Actors' Fund of America.
1882 - 1884.

Wallack became more and more prominent in leading roles as
Petruchio, Mercutio and Benedick. In 1817 he married Susan
Johnstone. Susan brought with her a handsome dowry of
£20,000. She was the daughter of John Johnstone, a popular
Irish singer. James Wallack and his wife Susan named their
first and only child John Johnstone Wallack. In 1818 Susan
and James Wallack ventured to New York where he made his
first appearance on the American stage at the Old Park
Theatre. Although his range was remarkably varied, he was
particularly well received as Hamlet, Romeo, Macbeth and
Richard III.

Born in New York, the infant John was taken to England
where he was reared, and where he received his earliest training
under his brilliant father. That he did not think he was pre-
destined for a theatrical career is evidenced by the fact that he
spent two years in the British army, serving as a lieutenant.
But all his family—his Uncle Henry and his Aunts Mary and
Elizabeth, and Henry's three children were actors. So perhaps
there was no escape.

His first appearance in the United States was under the
name of John Wallack Lester (earlier he had called himself
Allan Field, using his grandmother's surname). It is obvious
that he wanted recognition on his own and not because of his
father's enormous prestige. Yet, in his choice of names he did
not exclude identity with his forebears of theatrical distinction.

His first American appearance was literally a "disappear-
ance." It occurred when, as Sir Thomas Goldstream, in a play
appropriately called *Used Up*, a trap door unexpectedly gave
way and he fell through it. This was at the Broadway Theatre,
on September 17, 1847. In 1848 he played Cassio to Forrest's
Othello. Later, on Christmas, 1848, he was the first in America
to produce Dumas' *Count of Monte Cristo* in dramatic form.
This played for 100 nights and literally saved the Broadway
Theatre from bankruptcy. In 1851 his father, who had been
shuttling across the Atlantic for the past dozen years (during
which interval he had acquired the management of the New

York National Theatre) decided to settle down in America, devoting as much time to the acquisition and management of theatres in New York as to acting. In these undertakings his son, now well known as Lester Wallack, was intimately connected.

On September 8, 1852, the senior Wallack opened the first Wallack Theatre to be so called. He did this by re-building the Old Lyceum Theatre, which was located on Broadway and Broome Street. In 1861 the elder Wallack ventured further north to Broadway at 13th Street, where a new Wallack's Theatre was opened. But from then on he became relatively inactive as an actor until his death on Christmas, 1864. In the earlier development of Lester Wallack's career he had the unusual experience of playing Mercutio when Charlotte Cushman played Romeo to her sister's Juliet. In this unlikely performance Lester Wallack received enormous praise from the reigning tragedienne, who spoke of him "as the coming young man." That, of course, was in England before he had made his debut on the American stage.

It was in 1849 that he established himself as a playwright, following his pronounced success as producer and actor in *The Count of Monte Cristo*. He continued in romantic roles with *The Three Guardsmen* and *The Four Musketeers;* both pieces examples of his own skill in dramaturgy and in writing roles for himself which endeared him to the public. The house on 13th Street continued under his management until 1881 when it closed. On January 4, 1882, Lester Wallack opened a new Wallack's Theatre. This was the same year as the Fund was established. He remained active as a manager of the theatre and occasionally acted there until his retirement in 1887.

Following his retirement, in May, 1888, a benefit was given for Lester Wallack with what must have been the most remarkable cast ever to have been assembled in the American theatre. It was at the Metropolitan Opera House and was sponsored by Augustin Daly, A. M. Palmer, Edwin Booth, Lawrence Barrett and Joseph Jefferson. The play was *Hamlet*, with Booth in the title role. Others in the cast were: the Ghost, Lawrence Barrett; Polonius, John Gilbert; King Claudius, Frank Mayo; Laertes, Eben Plympton; Horatio, John A. Lane; Rosencranz, Charles Hanford; Guildenstern, Lawrence Hanley; Osric, Charles Kochler; Marcellus, Edwin H. Vanderfelt; Bernardo, Herbert Kelcey; Francisco, Frank Mordaunt; First Actor, Joseph Wheelock; Second Actor, Milnes Lavick; First Grave-digger, Joseph Jefferson; Second Grave-digger, W. J. Florence; Priest, Harry Edwards; Ophelia, Helena Modjeska; The Queen, Gertrude Kellogg; The Player Queen, Rose Coghlan.

After the second act Lester Wallack was called on for a speech. In closing he said, "With these few sincere words I bid you a respectful goodnight and leave the stage to Hamlet."

Prior to his being officially elected as president of The Actors' Fund in July of 1882, he had served as its provisional president from the time of its early organization in March of that year. He continued as the first president of the Fund until 1884 when he retired from this position. But he continued for another year as a trustee.

Despite Lester Wallack's interest in the development of The Actors' Fund, unfortunately there is no record of his addressing any of the meetings which were held during his presidency. But that interest must certainly have been of more than passing importance. For it is recorded that the earliest meetings of the Fund took place at the Wallack Theatre and there can be no doubt that his influence, his prestige and collaboration with A. M. Palmer were of inestimable value in getting The Actors' Fund off to a most propitious start.

HENRY CLAY MINER

By ELECTING Henry Clay Miner to succeed Lester Wallack as
second president of The Actors' Fund, there was established
a tradition of awarding that office to a member of the profession exclusively identified with the "business" side of the field
rather than the performer side. This tradition was subsequently
broken only once and that was when Louis Aldrich was elected
president following the lengthy tenure of A. M. Palmer.

Henry Miner was born in New York on March 23, 1842.
His father was a civil engineer of considerable repute. Since
his early training was that of a pharmacist it is, perhaps, only
natural that during the Civil War he became a "medic" with
the Federal Army. In 1864, when he was twenty-two years
old (and presumably still in the army because hostilities had
not yet concluded) he married Julia Moore. This marriage produced thirteen children, of which only four survived. These
four were all sons and as they grew up they joined their father
in a multiplicity of enterprises which he was constantly devel-
oping. After he was mustered out of the service his first business venture was as representative of a certain Prof. de Courcey,
a lecturer on medical subjects. Later he became an advance
agent for a Signor Blitz who was a magician and an exhibitor
of trained birds. For a brief spell Henry Miner then joined
the New York Police with the thought that such experience
would propel him into a political career, which he seemed to
desire. However, he left the force very shortly to become advance man for "Buffalo Bill." From this time forward his

Henry C. Miner
Second President
The Actors' Fund of America
1884-1885

career proceeded in the field of theatrical management. It was in the year 1875 that he became manager of the Bowery Volks' Garten. In 1879 he acquired the lease to another New York theatre, the American, located on Third Avenue. This he did in partnership with Thomas Canary. In 1881 these same two men built the Eighth Avenue Theatre which became a very successful variety house. During the decade of the 1880's Henry Miner seems to have concentrated on the building or acquisition of theatres. He built one called the People's Theatre. Although it was a replica of the Grand Opera House it was devoted exclusively to variety performances.

By the time Miner was fifty years old (and by this time he was eminently successful) the urge toward politics once more overtook him. In 1892 he was elected United States Representative in Congress from the Ninth Congressional District in New York City. At this time, besides being president of the Springer Lithography Company, he owned a chain of drug stores, a theatrical cosmetics firm, and had large interests in various mining ventures. But the desire to expand his career as a man of the theatre persisted. In 1895, along with J. H. McVicker and Joseph Brooks, he established a sort of theatrical syndicate. Its object was the presentation of attractions of all managers in their own theatres on an interchange basis when the houses were not otherwise occupied. At this time he was in a position to exercise influence because he controlled six houses, four in New York, one in Brooklyn and one in Newark. It was also in these houses that he established the practice of instituting "amateur nights" and it was from these performances that the legendary phrase "get the hook" was actually born. On one occasion an amateur with what was called a "near-tenor voice" had been determined to continue his singing despite jeers and catcalls from the audience. Miner's son, Tom, who was managing this house at the time, tried desperately from the wings to motion the culprit off the stage. As the tumult in the audience increased, Tom suddenly spotted a prop walking cane which had been left backstage by a previous performer. He quickly had the cane lashed to a long pole and, extending the "crook" of the cane so that it encircled the amateur's neck, he unceremoniously pulled the performer off into the wings amidst the cheers, applause and peals of laughter from a now delighted audience.

The third annual meeting of The Actors' Fund, the occasion on which Henry Miner was elected president, was held at Wallack's Theatre on the afternoon of June 3, 1884. At this meeting Henry Miner distinguished himself by showing that he had a comprehensive and detailed knowledge of the Fund's financial affairs. Although he declared that he was satisfied with the way that the books were being kept, he took note of the fact that for the year 1884 the Fund had paid out $13,717.91 and had received an income of only $11,705.01. This, he said, should be of concern to all the members inasmuch as it had necessitated converting some $3,000.00 worth of securities into cash to "keep us going," as he put it. He then entered into a debate with Louis Aldrich who, although he agreed that depleting capital for current expenses was poor policy, had other ideas of how the Fund was to be financed. The debate wound up with Miner moving an amendment to an Aldrich resolution which had incorporated the latter's financing plans and which referred the whole matter to the board of trustees "with power to act." This amendment was seconded and carried. The effect of Miner's action was to establish a procedure whereby the complex task of deciding and executing financial policy remained within the board of trustees where it properly belonged. One of Miner's sons, Henry Clay Miner, Jr., served briefly as a trustee of the Fund in the years 1944-45.

Julia Miner died in 1894. She had been Henry Clay Miner's wife for thirty years. Two years later Miner married Annie O'Neill, at that time leading lady to W. H. Crane. He was then fifty-six years old. Six weeks before his death in 1900 the second Mrs. Miner gave birth to a son, John Lansing Miner. Henry Clay Miner died on February 22, 1900. Like his predecessor, Wallack, he succumbed to apoplexy.

ALBERT MARSHALL PALMER

A. M. PALMER had more to do with establishing the direction which The Actors' Fund was eventually to take than any of its founders. Among those who participated in establishing the Fund, Palmer had at best, a minor claim to authority in the theatrical field. Nevertheless, the force of his personality and his thinking could dominate such powerful elements in the theatrical world as P. T. Barnum, Lester Wallack, Ned Harrigan, Tony Pastor, Daniel Frohman, Harrison Grey Fiske and Edwin Booth.

Palmer was born on July 27, in 1838 or 1840—depending on which obituary notice you happen to believe in; the one in the *New York Times* or the one that appeared in the *Dramatic Mirror*. A third "authority" is the *New York Dramatic News* which states that Palmer had been born on July 20, 1838. Despite this lack of precision about his date of birth, it is definite that he graduated from the Law School of New York University in the year 1860. But he never practiced law. Instead, he joined the Republican Party organization and campaigned for the election of Abraham Lincoln. Thus began an association with Sheridan Shook, an established figure in the political field, who was collector of Internal Revenue for New York from 1861 to 1869. Shook made Palmer his chief deputy. However, Shook's career as collector of Internal Revenue came to a rather inglorious end when certain charges were made against him, and he was fired by President Grant. One biog-

A.M. Palmer.
Third President.
The Actors' Fund of America.
1885-1897.

raphy of Shook implies that Palmer assumed the blame for the
wrongdoings. In any event, in 1869 Palmer's political career
ended, albeit not his association with Mr. Shook. His next job
was that of librarian at the Mercantile Library which he held
until 1872 when his association with Shook reasserted itself.
It was during this period as librarian that he began an enduring
friendship with Richard Mansfield, which also developed into
a very important business relationship for him.

In 1872 his entrance to show business formally began. He
became manager of the Union Square Theatre. This theatre was
being operated as a losing proposition by Sheridan Shook. Palmer's latent skill for theatrical management soon became apparent. From the time he took over the management of the
Union Square it grew in importance. By far its most outstanding success occurred on December 17, 1874. This was the
opening of *The Two Orphans*, a production which became
legendary in American theatre annals. As is so often the case,
Palmer's acquisition of this melodramatic "gold mine" happened
almost by accident. His play reader, one Hart Jackson, read
the play in the original French. He reported that it was "a
Bowery melodrama, not suitable for the Union Square Company." Palmer told Jackson to get the play translated and try
to dispose of it for $1,500. But, by chance, during the course
of the translation Palmer read the prison scene. He was immediately struck by its power and thereupon cancelled the projected sale and set about to produce the work.

Other notable productions at the Union Square were: *A
Celebrity Case* (1878), *Lights o'London* (1881), and *A Pari-
sian Romance* with Richard Mansfield (1883).

In May, 1883, Palmer retired as manager of the Union
Square Theatre. Subsequently he became manager of the Madison Square Theatre in association with the Mallory brothers.
In 1885 he assumed exclusive control of the Madison Square
and continued in this position until 1891. His final production
at the Madison Square Theatre was a play called *Alabama*. It

introduced Augustus Thomas as a playwright and, incidentally, made a profit of $150,000. In the latter part of the 1880's Palmer also took control of Wallack's Theatre and changed its name to Palmer's Theatre. Its opening was an occasion of great prestige; it being *The American Beauty* with Constant Coquelin. It was at this theatre John Drew made his New York debut in *The Masked Ball* on the third of October, 1892. In 1894 Olga Nethersole made her American debut in *The Transgressor*. She later appeared at Palmer's Theatre in *Camille* with Maurice Barrymore in her supporting company. Despite the distinction of some of the productions at Palmer's Theatre, it did not prove to be a financial success. Palmer surrendered the lease on it in 1896. The final production under Palmer's management was a play called, *Roaring Dick & Company* in which Maurice Barrymore appeared.

Other theatres were leased by Palmer in the years between 1894 and 1897. None of them proved successful. So, in 1897 Palmer contented himself to manage the tours of Richard Mansfield. He continued in this capacity until 1902 when poor health forced him into an advisory rather than a managerial capacity with Mansfield. Early in 1903 his declining health forced him to give up even this advisory position and his complete retirement seemed imminent. Friends planned a huge benefit for him, to be given at the Metropolitan Opera House during the first week of May in 1903. Palmer reluctantly consented to the plan. At the last minute, the Metropolitan could not be available on the desired date. Palmer regarded this as good news and insisted that any plans for a benefit be postponed until the fall. He hoped that by then he would have recovered sufficiently to render assistance unnecessary. He remarked that the best benefit for him would be "work." His hopes were realized and the benefit was not needed.

In August, 1903, he was appointed manager of the Herald Square Theatre for Charles Frohman. He retained this post for the remainder of his life. His last active work in the theatre was a re-staging of his great success, *The Two Orphans*. This was at the New Amsterdam Theatre, on the twenty-eighth of March, 1904.

On the sixth of March, 1905 Palmer suffered a stroke of apoplexy while riding on an elevated train at 155th Street and Eighth Avenue. He died the following day (March 7, 1905) at J. Hood Wright Hospital.

Palmer was known for the deep love and respect he had for theatre people. His interest in the personal welfare of the actor was shown as early as 1878 when he established what was called a "Poor Fund" at his Union Square Stock Company. This led to the intense activity which preceded the formal organization of The Actors' Fund in 1882. He served the Fund in important capacities from its very beginning until his death. He was innovative and imaginative in his fund raising activities; so much so that he was quite frequently criticized by such periodicals as the *Spirit of the Times* and the *New York Dramatic Mirror* on grounds that his promotional methods were designed to attract more attention to A. M. Palmer than to the charitable purposes he was sponsoring. But it is rare that a forceful leader can wholly escape criticism from those who prefer to sit on the sidelines.

There is no question that his earlier activities, especially in the political field, had developed in him a fondness for power and the exercise of it. Only occasionally was he frustrated in realizing his ambitions—at least so far as The Actors' Fund was concerned. And there can be no doubt that The Actors' Fund occupied a central position in his range of ambitions and was to benefit thereby.

Palmer was buried after a public funeral service held at the Little Church Around the Corner, on the morning of March 10, 1905. He was survived by his wife, a son and a daughter, Mrs. Lyman Otis Fiske. In 1957 The Players acquired the complete archives of the Union Square Theatre for the years from 1872 to 1883. This record had been kept with the care of a skilled librarian. It includes clippings, photographs, lithographs, autographs of leading players, and playbills. The collection comprises twenty-one large portfolios and was given to The Players by Butler Davenport, who obtained them at the disposal of Palmer's estate in 1906.

LOUIS ALDRICH

In 1897, when Louis Aldrich became president of the Fund—being the fourth to hold the office—he was possibly more outstanding as a leader in the area of actors' organizations than as a star with universal public and critical acclaim. Seven years earlier he had been elected president of the Actors' Order of Friendship. Prior to this he had been one of the organizers within that body in establishing its second "lodge," the Edwin Forrest Lodge, which was chartered as the New York branch of this Philadelphia oriented association. The "Edwin Forrest Lodge" was established in 1888. In addition to these offices, during the last decade of the nineteenth century, he had been preeminently active in a group of actors concerned with "wages and working conditions" which was called the Actors' Society.

Aldrich was born Louis Lyon at a place called Ohio State Line on October 1, 1843. His first recorded stage appearance was as a child actor, playing initially the title role of *Richard III* in excerpts from that play given at John Ellser's Academy of Music in Cleveland. He essayed this malevolent character at the advanced age of twelve. That was on September 5, 1855. His performance met with such success that he was brought back the following week to do the entire play. Then followed *Macbeth* and some other very unlikely roles for a child of such tender years. However, the critics acclaimed him "the boy prodigy" and "the juvenile Roscius." This recognition in his early years led to his being engaged in 1858 as "the heavy man"

Louis Aldrich,
Fourth President,
The Actors Fund of America
1897 ~ 1901.

and "tragedian" by Robert G. Marsh, who had a successful troupe of juveniles which he took on extensive tours in the far west and across the Pacific. Marsh's troupe, besides playing its home base in San Francisco, also ventured to Australia, New Zealand and Vancouver. Thus, when Aldrich was a mere fifteen years old, he embarked on three and a half years of travel which took him halfway around the world. The Marsh Company returned to San Francisco. In 1863 it was disbanded. Either during the course of the tour, or subsequently in San Francisco, Aldrich married a member of the company, Clara Shropshire. The young actor and his wife remained in San Francisco until after the Civil War. He came East in 1866 to join the stock company of the Boston Theatre.

By 1873 Louis Aldrich had gained sufficient stature to be engaged as leading man in Mrs. John Drew's prestigious stock company at the Arch Street Theatre in Philadelphia. He stayed with that company for the 1873-74 season and immediately thereafter came to New York in the position of stock-star at Wood's Museum—later known as Daly's Theatre. In 1876 he scored a signal success in the role of "the Parson" in a play called *"The Danites"* which he played for two consecutive seasons and for a total of 542 performances. He achieved national fame in this role, after he toured in it for forty weeks. Then followed another brilliant success—the part of Joe Saunders—at the Union Square Theatre in New York in a play by Bartley Campbell called *My Partner*. In addition to playing the part of Saunders, Aldrich also produced the play. This play established Campbell as a leading American playwright. However, it was A. M. Palmer and Aldrich who reaped the enormous financial rewards which ensued. Campbell received an outright payment of $500 for the piece and thereafter a "royalty arrangement" amounting to $10 a performance. Aldrich toured in the Campbell piece for six years! Shortly after this he both produced and toured in *Kaffir Diamond* and *The Editor*. Both of these were rated personal successes for Aldrich but they were not financially profitable. It was during an engagement of *The Editor* in Syracuse, N.Y. when Aldrich was trapped in a disastrous fire at the Leland Hotel. He sustained injuries which compelled him to abandon the tour. These injuries appear to have produced a pronounced instability in Aldrich's personality. He was determined to make a success of *The Editor* and brought it to Hammerstein's Opera House in New York. On May 24, 1890, the *New York Spirit of the Times* had this to say about him and the play:

> Extremes meet: It is but one step from the sublime to the ridiculous. Last week, in spite of criticism, Louis Aldrich announced "THE EDITOR" for an unlimited run. This is its last week but one. We said that we could see no place here for Mr. Aldrich and his play and the event has verified our judgment. By way of satire, he has been elected President of the so-called Order of Friendship, which all real friends of the profession think should be merged in the Actors' Fund.

Then, in an interview appearing in the *New York Dramatic Mirror*, dated November 22, 1890, his manager, Edwin Knowles, said: "Between you and me, he is a very sick man . . . especially since the Syracuse hotel fire. He is suffering from Nervous prostration and though the excitement of his work keeps him up when he is on stage, as soon as he gets off it he is like a limp rag."

Aldrich doesn't seem to have had any great success as an actor betwen 1890 and his elevation to the presidency of The Actors' Fund. Despite his obvious poor health he was very energetic when it came to matters concerning The Actors' Fund in which he had been vitally interested and on whose board of trustees he had served for two years prior to his being elected first vice-president in 1889. He was determined that the Fund should provide a permanent home for retired actors and actresses who were in need. There is no question but that he encountered very real opposition from Albert M. Palmer, his predecessor who was equally determined that The

Actors' Fund should first establish an orphanage for the off-
spring of members of the profession. Even though Aldrich did
not live to see the fulfillment of his dream, the momentum he
created in the direction of a retirement home propelled that
idea to its final achievement a few years later.

Louis Aldrich's last public appearance was at the Academy
of Music, which engagement lasted from February 13 to
March 25, 1899. He died on June 17, 1901, while summering
in Kennebunkport, Maine. Services for him were held in Boston
on July 20. His body was cremated at Forest Hill in Boston,
where the ashes remain.

An obituary notice summed him up as follows:

> As an actor he just escaped being great. He was talented but
> was not a genius. He lacked that indefinable something called
> "temperament" without which no player ever attained great-
> ness. Few players possess the art of "making up" better than
> he and a comparatively few could lose their individuality in a
> character as well. The excellence of his performance always
> called forth praise from his critics.

AL HAYMAN

AL HAYMAN WAS BORN in Wheeling, West Virginia, in the year 1847. He was known as the "father of the Theatrical Syndicate" and was acclaimed by many as the man whose business ability enabled the Frohmans to build up the artistic side of the stage to the pinnacle that the latter are acknowledged to have done.

In 1871 he was sent out as manager of a *Black Crook* company on tour to the Southern states, Mexico and Central America. While he was in Panama he fell in with one Harry Kellar who was a prestidigitator. Hayman managed Kellar's trip through South America. Subsequently he was engaged by M. B. Leavitt to manage Leavitt's interests in Australia. He remained in Australia for a year. Then he had his real start in 1882 when he was sent to San Francisco by Leavitt to manage the Bush Theatre. In 1886, when Charles Frohman took his Lyceum Stock Company to San Francisco, Hayman and Frohman got together to organize a booking agency to provide the theatres in the west with attractions and to assure the Frohman companies theatres in which to play.

At this juncture Hayman severed his connections with Leavitt and operated independently of him throughout the west. In retrospect, this association with Frohman can be viewed as "the seed" which later grew into the colossal monopoly control of theatres known as "The Syndicate."

In 1887 Hayman and Frohman purchased the play *Shenan-*

Al. Hayman,
Fifth President,
The Actors' Fund of America,
1901 ~ 1904.

doah. They made a fortune out of it. In fact, they were able to pay its author, Bronson Howard, over $100,000 even before the many touring companies were sent out.

Eighteen ninety-six saw the formal organization of The Syndicate. Its ultimate composition included Klaw, Erlanger, the Frohmans, Hayman (all of New York), and Nixon and Zimmerman of Philadelphia. Together they began to dominate the bookings of almost all theatres in the United States and they succeeded until their position was challenged, after the turn of the century, by the Shuberts.

A major accomplishment of Al Hayman was building the Empire Theatre, which he did together with Frank Sanger and William Harris. The theatre opened on January 25, 1893, with a performance of *The Girl I Left Behind Me*, by David Belasco. This play ran 288 performances and it established the Empire Theatre as the most elegant theatre in New York. It continued to be so regarded until its destruction in the 1950's.

When Hayman died on February 10, 1917, at the Waldorf Astoria, aged seventy years, he left a huge estate. In fact, the *New York Times*, in its issue of March 1, 1919, stated that Hayman's net estate was $1,692,815 and went on to compare this sum with the net estate of Charles Frohman. Frohman, who drowned with the sinking of the *Lusitania*, May 7, 1915, had left an estate amounting to a mere $451.

Hayman's major contribution to The Actors' Fund was undoubtedly in carrying out Louis Aldrich's dream of building a home for retired actors. In fact, less than one year after being elected as president, Hayman was able to announce very proudly that The Actors' Fund Home on Staten Island was to open its doors. He had worked very closely with Aldrich in raising the money for building the home. It was his statement to Aldrich that he would write a check for $10,000 as soon as $50,000 could be raised by popular subscription which initiated the most unbelievably successful and rapid fund raising campaign ever undertaken for a theatrical purpose. The full account of this extraordinary event is detailed elsewhere. Here it is appropriate to say that Hayman, in starting that campaign, laid the groundwork for a truly permanent monument to Louis Aldrich and he continued to devote himself with great modesty to it until the final result was achieved.

DANIEL FROHMAN

DANIEL FROHMAN WAS BORN in Sandusky, Ohio, on August 22, 1851. He was one of three brothers, all of whom had theatrical careers. Charles Frohman, his junior by nine years, became one of America's most outstanding producers and theatre owners. His brilliant career was cut short at its peak when he was drowned with the sinking of the Lusitania in 1915.

Daniel Frohman was married to Margaret Illington.

His association with The Actors' Fund in a position of leadership out-distanced that of any other individual—spanning almost sixty years. His death occurred on December 26, 1940, when he was on his way to attaining his ninetieth birthday.

THE GOOD MEN DO LIVES AFTER THEM—
by RUTH GORDON

The title is a quote from myself. I know the correct quotation, but I don't think so. I think the good lives after; the *evil* gets accepted. Or forgotten. Or becomes hearsay. The good lives on and does us all some good.

A lucky December evening in 1915 I came home to the Three Arts Club, from a day of "Would you have any part in a play I could do?"

ED. NOTE: The biographical sketch of Mr. Frohman, "The Good Men Do Lives After Them" was prepared for this history by Ruth Gordon and was subsequently elaborated on and incorporated in her book, *Myself Among Others*, published by Atheneum, 1971.

Daniel Frohman
Sixth President
The Actors Fund of America
1904-1940

Miss Maude Adams had told her stage director, Mr. Homer St. Gaudens, to try me out for the part of Nibs in *Peter Pan*. She also told him to try out two other girls for the same part. The tryout wasn't to find if we were wonderful actresses, but were we limber enough to do Nibs' pillow dance? And Monday I showed up at the Lyceum Theatre, West 45th Street, one of three to get a break.

"Come to the Lyceum Theatre," said Mr. Homer St. Gaudens, but *where* at the Lyceum Theatre? The Lyceum Theatre is a big place to one lately from 14 Elmwood Avenue, Wollaston, Massachusetts. The stage door seemed ideal, but the stage doorman said I couldn't come in. "Ask out front," he said, disinterested, and returned to his own pursuits.

Out front. What did that mean? The box office? People were lined up buying tickets for the holidays; the box office was hard to get to. "Excuse me." I squeezed up to the window. "Where is Mr. Homer St. Gaudens?"

"Rehearsal hall. Next?"

Rehearsal hall? In show business, you know where to go or you don't know where to go. When you find out, you're a professional. I spun around in the lobby until Box Office took mercy. "Up those steps," he shouted. "Next?"

Up I rushed. At the top was an elegant, carved wooden door. Would a rehearsal hall have an elegant, carved— It opened. A tall, tall, elegant man in a tall, tall, hat filled a small, small elevator. I was clearly nowhere again and worry overwhelmed me; I didn't mean to, but tears dripped down my nose. "I have to go to where Mr. Homer St. Gaudens is rehearsing and I don't know how to. Or where." A frantic five-foot nothing in my Wollaston blue winter coat my mother made me, I looked ridiculous.

The tall, tall, elegant man held out his hand. "Step in," he said, "I'll take you."

My mother had warned me never to follow strangers, but that was Wollaston. A tall, tall stranger suggested I go with him and I accepted. Up we creaked, the elegant stranger running the elevator till we swayed to a stop. He opened the door and pointed, "There you are." I stepped out. "Good luck." The door closed, I was in the long, narrow rehearsal room with the sooty skylight windows, snow pelting against them, the piano player running over the pillow dance music for Nibs.

The stage manager looked at me with disgust, "Couldn't you walk up?" he snarled. "Did you have to bother Mr. Frohman?"

Could I believe my ears?

"If they tell you to come back here again," his tone implying that was unlikely, "*walk* up! Don't expect Mr. Daniel Frohman to run you up in his elevator."

Mr. Daniel Frohman had helped me find the rehearsal? Mr. Daniel Frohman of the Lyceum Theatre had said "Good luck" to Ruth Gordon, born Jones?

"Got your bloomers on?" The piano player went at it. And so did we. A Dorothy. A Mabel. And I. That night a Three Arts Club girl went to bed discouraged.

"Telephone for Gordon," somebody shouted down the eighth floor hall.

Into my lavender Japanese wrapper Mrs. Wetmore had given me as a going-away-to-become-an actress present and up the hall to the wall telephone.

"You're the worst dancer, but you got the job," said beloved stage manager, "the salary is thirty-five dollars a week."

Thirty-five dollars! I was staggered. What would I do with all *that?*

"Rehearsal hall, 10:00 A.M. and take the *stairs*, simp!"

"Good luck," said Mr. Daniel Frohman, and I had it.

When Daniel Frohman said good luck, he had a right to. He had it to spare. He was a man doing what he wanted to do. He wanted to be in show business and he was. He wanted to be a manager and he was. He wanted to own a theatre and he did.

Four years before he held out his hand to me, he wrote a book about things that interested him. "Chapter One."

"I used to come to New York once or twice a season from my youthful wanderings about America as advance agent of a one-night-stand show. Theatrical people are fond of the theatre, so on these homecomings I spent my evenings watching the splendid performances of Palmer's Company at the Union Square Theatre and those of Lester Wallack's Company, then at Broadway and 13th Street."

That's how Daniel Frohman began his book. Nothing boring, such as "I was brought up in Sandusky, Ohio. . . ." His "homecomings" were not to Sandusky; his homecomings were to 13th and Broadway. And Union Square. And not to pass the evening in a cosy apartment, but to see what Lester Wallack and Palmer's Company were doing. Daniel Frohman's book shows no interest in where he was born. "I used to come to New York once or twice a season. . . ." He was in show business and show business was in him. Sandusky, Ohio was a one night stand. A place you played and got out of and came "*home*" to Union Square. Sandusky, Ohio, he and his brother put up with, until Daniel could be an advance agent and lease and own theatres and his brother could become New York's and London's most admired manager. Did he mention their boyhood passed in Sandusky, Ohio? Never. In fact, he didn't even mention a brother until the end of "Chapter One." "I little thought I should pay E. H. Sothern $50,000 a year and later Charles Frohman would pay him $100,000 a year. And for two years." Was Charles his younger brother? His older brother? Did it matter? Did it interest him? What *did* interest Daniel Frohman was a manager who paid a star $100,000 a year. For two years.

May, 1882, they held a meeting on the stage of the theatre he used to visit on his "homecomings," Wallack's Theatre at Broadway and 30th. A lot of fine people showed up to found The Actors' Fund. Joseph Jefferson, William J. Florence, A. M. Palmer of the Union Square, Nedda's father Edward Harrigan —a lot of fine people. Wallack was elected president and Daniel

Frohman was elected secretary. "Everyone knew the secretary would have to do most of the work so I was unanimously elected."

Twenty years later, The Actors' Fund of America would establish The Actors' Fund Home. Toward it "Al Hayman gave ten thousand, my brother Charles gave five thousand and the players and managers all contributed." But Daniel's home now was the Madison Square Theatre which he was engaged to run. And later, it was the Old Lyceum and still later the New Lyceum. At eighty-nine he died in his rooms in a hotel. It was only a place he went till it was time to come back to his 45th Street Lyceum.

At the Old Lyceum, he was the lessee, Daly's the same, and after 1903, owner of his New Lyceum on 45th. And there were some in London "where the critics would sometimes say praiseworthy things, but nobody brought home any money."

Even the great Booth noticed it, "Did anybody ever know an American actor," asked Booth, "to bring home a profit?"

And John T. Raymond, the famous "Colonel Sellers" who arrived in London for his debut and said to his Shaftesbury Avenue agent, "Gillig, how do you send money back to America?" And after he had opened, whispered to the same Gillig, "How do you get money sent from America?" Mr. Daniel Frohman remembered things that interested him. It didn't interest him that he was born August 22, 1851. He took that for granted and forgot it. People are born Pisces, Libra, Scorpio, Sagittarius, he was born Virgo, but what he remembered was, you could get a great notice in London and come home with no money.

Some people enjoy going to a theatre, some people enjoy working in a theatre, some people enjoy leasing a theatre, the latter was Daniel Frohman. He leased the Old Lyceum at 23rd Street. And after he leased it, even though he had no play, he engaged an actor. Who better could The Actors' Fund of America have to be their first secretary?

The actor he hired was young Sothern appearing in Miss

A RUSSIAN HONEYMOON." MADISON SQUARE THEATRE. N.Y.— ACT II., CLOSING TABLEAU

PHOTOGRAPHED IN THE THEATRE AT MIDNIGHT, MAY 1ST, 1883, BY FALK. 949 BROADWAY — STAGE BEING ILLUMINATED BY BRUSH ELECTRIC LIGHTS, PUT UP BY WM. J. MAGRATH.

Daniel Frohman identified this photograph, taken at his Madison Square Theatre, on May 1, 1883, at midnight, as the first ever to be taken on the stage of a theatre.

Helen Dauvray's Company to whom Frohman leased his Lyceum until he found a play to put in it. Miss Dauvray's season closed in the early spring, so he said to his actor, "I'd like to keep the house open till hot weather, but I don't have a play." Ned Sothern said his father had left him some and had the old trunks sent up.

"I found one that appeared attractive," writes Frohman. "It was called *Trade*." The title didn't trouble him, he changed it to *The Highest Bidder* and to stage it, engaged another young man, Dave Belasco from San Francisco. Rehearsals didn't look too promising, but the first night surprised them and went off fine. "We had a right to be hopeful and during the first week we watched the performance and the box office." The end of the week he and Sothern were having dinner at the Ashland House across from the Lyceum. Suddenly Sothern pointed at the theatre. "Look!" he said excitedly, "There's a speculator!"

A few weeks later when they were playing to crowded houses, they had dinner at the Ashland again. "Can anything be done to stop those infernal speculators?" asked Sothern. Daniel Frohman ended "Chapter One" with that. "Chapter One" didn't tell us where he came from or how old was his brother, but it told us he knew a tag when he heard one. When his leading man asked "Can anything be done to stop those infernal speculators?" he knew that was the laugh. No need to add, "I hope not."

The Highest Bidder was a hit, but what Daniel Frohman wanted for his Lyceum was a splendid company in residence. Like Wallack's or Palmer's. He engaged a company, then hired two authors: "Write a good part for everybody," he said and gave them a list that was to make his Old Lyceum Stock Company a part of theatre history. No wonder that in 1903 The Actors' Fund of America made him their president for all those years to come. Like *Trelawney of the Wells,* he "loved the players." For fifty-one years he would occupy himself with the problems of the Fund, so when he started his own company, why wouldn't the new lessee of the Old Lyceum order, "Good parts for everybody?"

Henry Miller was the Old Lyceum's leading man. Matchless actor, matchless director and so successful a producer he was able to build his own theatre, the Henry Miller on West 43rd Street, his legacy to his son Gilbert.

The great Charles S. Dickson. Later generations saw him in *The Great Gatsby* listlessly wave his palm leaf fan to temper the heat as he drove a knife into Gatsby's future. Daniel Frohman sought the best for his new stock at the Old Lyceum and Charles S. Dickson was the best.

Grace Henderson near the end of her theatre days played my mother in a play. Someone asked her "Was it true she had acted with Lionel Barrymore?" "Acted with him, I *slept* with him," she said, contemptuous of such ignorance.

Mrs. Thomas Whiffen and the Old Lyceum Stock Company admired one another. When Henry Miller put on *Just Suppose* at the Miller Theatre, Mrs. Whiffen played the grand lady of Virginia who welcomed the Prince of Wales and his friend Bubbles, played memorably by Leslie Howard.

William Faversham. He played second fiddle to Henry Miller and understudied him. The years went by and, at Charles Frohman's Empire Theatre, he became the acknowledged matinee idol of the town. Elegant, handsome, charming, a real heart-throb, he filled the Empire's coffers. The boxes and orchestra seats rustled with taffeta to see the dazzling Faversham.

Faversham, the matinee idol of New York had been Daniel Frohman's choice for second business and understudy. In the end he once more was beholden to Daniel Frohman. He retired to the Percy Williams Home, on whose board of directors Mr. Frohman was a member.

"Write a good part for everybody!" He had the company who could play good parts and the writers went to work to write for it. They were Henry De Mille and Dave Belasco. Belasco had directed *The Highest Bidder*. He would also direct this new one. De Mille and Belasco liked the theatre as much as Daniel Frohman. Presumably they lived somewhere, but where they chose to write a good part for everybody was on the stage, after or before the performance. Their method was as unique as their locale. They wrote it without dialogue. "Putting in the dialogue was the most difficult part of their labors," writes the new manager of the Old Lyceum Stock Company. And as soon as the play got the dialogue in it, Belasco would direct. He had never been further than Sacramento, but Daniel Frohman heard about the bright boy at San Francisco's Baldwin Theatre and brought him east. A useful fellow for a new lessee to have around.

Prompter, actor, director and author, around the Baldwin, they said, Dave Belasco could make a play out of a "synopsis of scenes" from a theatre playbill. He could and he had. At the Baldwin Stock Company some week a play wasn't forthcoming, so their bright boy wrote one. Daniel Frohman had engaged him to be bright boy at the Madison Square Theatre and then, when Frohman quit the Madison Square, he brought him along to his Lyceum.

"Young, ambitious and hot tempered," remembered Mr. Frohman, "once in a fit of rage he brought his fist down on an iron safe with such violence he had to direct with one hand for a week." But one hand or two hands, Daniel Frohman saw he had a fine director.

And the De Mille–Belasco partnership worked. After he told them to write a good part for everybody, he said "a modern society comedy would be useful." Frohman figured the partnership this way: "De Mille was the literary man, Belasco was the dramatist." Working on the stage, before or after the current show, Belasco would act all the parts of their new play making up words appropriate to their dialogue-less scene and as he was improvising, the former bright boy of San Francisco's Baldwin and the Madison Square Theatre would time the length of the scenes, entrances and exits, so that De Mille, setting it down, would wind up with the play cut to measure. Daniel Frohman had an eye for talent. When he hired young David Belasco, he set in motion a legendary career.

The Old Lyceum Stock Company opened its first fall season schedule with as dialogue-full a play as one could want, which De Mille or Belasco or both of them called *The Wife*. On the evening of November 1, 1887, the curtain went up and stage fright was experienced by Henry Miller, Herbert Kelcey, Charles S. Dickson, Grace Henderson, Mrs. Thomas Whiffen,

William Faversham and numerous others. The legendary company's beginning did not meet with the success expected. The
critics praised the players, but found the play not consistently
good.

Daniel Frohman told his authors to get back to work. "By
excisions and revisions they got the show into more attractive
shape. Acts I and II became Act I and the part of a lame
veteran who limped slowly through the play was deprived of
his wound and his scenes like his game leg ceased to drag." The
bright boy of Baldwin's or the literary De Mille or the lessee
of the Old Lyceum knew what made show business; the play
ran a year at the Old Lyceum. "My old friend, S. S. Packard of
Packard's Business College bought 300 seats as a Christmas
present to his pupils." Daniel Frohman did not elaborate on
how Packard of Packard's became his friend. Indeed, he never
mentioned him again, but a friend is certainly somebody who
buys 300 tickets for a mildly wavering show. The lessee of the
Lyceum had proved his mettle: his cast was praised, his play
ran through the season, his friend bought 300 tickets. He could
be proud of his stationery:—

LYCEUM THEATRE, 4TH AVE. AND 23RD ST.
DANIEL FROHMAN, LESSEE.

A name in print is enjoyable. He enjoyed Daniel Frohman,
Lessee.

I enjoyed my name in print too. As soon as *Peter Pan*
opened, I ordered professional cards. The first time I used my
card was at Daniel Frohman's New Lyceum Theatre on West
45th Street at the Thursday matinee of Ethel Barrymore in
Our Mrs. McChesny. In the same lobby where I had been so
distracted, I offered the company manager, my:

RUTH GORDON
THE MAUDE ADAMS CO.
EMPIRE THEATRE

and used the lingo, "Do you honor the profession?" I asked.

He did. I saw Ethel Barrymore in *Our Mrs. McChesny* in Daniel Frohman's Lyceum Theatre, where the stationery read:-

LYCEUM THEATRE, WEST 45TH ST.
DANIEL FROHMAN, OWNER

In the second play at the Old Lyceum, Maude Adams had stolen the show. A wisp of a girl with a corner on charm and she was asked to *play* a *drunk* scene. A drunk scene was the last thing suited to the future Peter Pan, but after a glass or two, she waved a rose around so absurdly, so enchantingly that everybody knew she was smashed. And also, that she would be the biggest thing in show business.

Daniel Frohman bought the London hit, Pinero's *Sweet Lavender* for his Lyceum Company and felt confident. His New York opening night did not seem as though the London success was in the cards for the Old Lyceum. "The first night patrons were startled," writes Frohman, "to find the heroine was an illegitimate child." Startled first-nighters were not what Daniel Frohman was after. He cabled his London author to arrange the parental relations. Pinero grudgingly consented and while at it, expressed a dim view of the New York public. "But," writes the lessee of the Lyceum, "the success of the play was at stake and the revision made it run a season. And two companies toured it." The leading man was Henry Miller and the only American in the play was acted by the only Englishman in the company, Herbert Kelcey. Our Actors' Fund President not only "loved the players," he didn't believe in typecasting.

The years went by at the Old Lyceum. Fourteen of them. In the meantime, Daniel Frohman found time to nurse the Lyceum School of Acting, now the American Academy of Dramatic Arts.

The Ohian whose "homecomings" were to bypass Sandusky for New York helped pave the way for all of us and those to

Frohman (left), a vigorous 82 when this was taken, was the unquestioned "dean" of the American theatre. In his studio atop the Lyceum Theatre (below) he lived amidst an accumulation of mementos acquired during a long and distinguished career.

come. The American Academy of Dramatic Arts, The Actors' Fund of America, The Actors' Fund Home. He could see what was going to help the actors. Not only for that season, but for all the seasons to come. Our day is different, but our needs are the same, "A good part for everybody and the leading woman to appear in the big scene."

The London author of *Sweet Lavender* forgave him and the New York public and wrote Daniel Frohman another, *The Second Mrs. Tanqueray*. "I do not dare present so frank a play in the evening bill," he cabled the author, "but I would like to produce so fine a work at a series of matinees." Pinero trusted him again. Frohman did not produce it after all, he ceded the rights to the famous English couple, Mr. and Mrs. Kendal. *The Second Mrs. Tanqueray* was regarded as exceedingly strong meat, although in San Francisco where a play like that should find favour, *Mrs. Tanqueray* fell flat. The explanation was, the play carried no illusion for the Golden Gate audiences. The city, it was explained, was full of Mrs. Tanquerays. Philadelphia loved it and requested a return engagement.

He was reminded of Irving on the subject: "Sir Henry told me that his *Faust* had greater success in Philadelphia than any city in this country outside of New York."

After *The Wife* came other plays, all with fine titles, *The Maister of Woodbarrow*, *The Dancing Girl*. And as needed, other players were added. The ingenue for *The Maister of Woodbarrow* and *The Dancing Girl* was enchanting Effie Shannon—later to star with her beloved Herbert Kelcey.

Effie Shannon was a beautiful person and a beautiful actress. In the leaner years, after Herbert was gone, she played on into her eighties. And then she went blind. Time to retire to the Home. The Home was ready to welcome Daniel Frohman's Old Lyceum ingenue and thought how might they best make her feel at home. Her theatre-maid had stayed on with her, even after Miss Shannon played no more engagements. The Home wondered if Miss Shannon would like to bring her maid with her. Miss Shannon was pleased. The good men do lives after them. . . .

Arrangements were made, then Effie Shannon died. And with her went the love, admiration and respect of the profession. Can anyone ask for more?

Effie Shannon was the ingenue in *The Dancing Girl*, but the star was E. H. Sothern. Up to now Sothern had always played in comedies; *The Dancing Girl* was a Henry Arthur Jones drama, the great role was the Duke of Guisebury. Sothern was dubious about playing it. "I urged him to switch," writes Frohman. "I had invested $5,000." And all for the best. *The Dancing Girl* and E. H. Sothern as the Duke of Guisebury were a hit.

A good thing it was. Forty-one players listed. "And others," read the program. Our president loved the players and put on plays with a lot of players in them. A hit, a merciful hit! Sothern knew enough to listen to his manager's urging. Daniel Frohman had contributed a lot to him, to the players, to the theatre. And when Frohman needed somebody, he had the right to urge. "Good luck," he said, and had it to spare. Sothern listened. And Henry Arthur Jones gave his theatre a hit.

Well, he was eighty-nine and he died in a hotel. And he wouldn't think that worth remembering, but what is, is that the Lyceum he built on West 45th Street still has an outfront and a stage door and probably somebody is trying to get in it and somebody not letting them. And the steps are there and the elegant carved door. And Daniel Frohman's small, small elevator? Let us hope so. And let us hope somebody is telling somebody to get in and wishing them "Good luck."

The *good* men do lives after them. Who cares what's interréd with their bones?

WALTER VINCENT

WALTER VINCENT'S NAME is not generally known to the public, but he was an important "in-member" of the theatre, and a pioneer in the vaudeville and moving picture world.

His birthplace was Lake Geneva, Wisconsin, almost one hundred years ago. Following his secondary education, he attended Wheaton College, which he left to become a reporter on the *Denver Republican*. This was at a time when the West was "wild and woolly," but it did not deter Edwin Booth and Lawrence Barrett from playing an entire season at Tabor's opulent Grand Opera House in Denver. Young Walter Vincent was allowed to join their company, which he called, "one of the greatest experiences of my life."

Then, as now, the "theatre" was New York, where he arrived in 1889. After a few years playing small parts, he was noticed by Alexander Salvini, a famous Hamlet, who cast him as Horatio, a role that must have come easily to him, since all his life he was a most faithful friend to others.

His friendship with a young writer called Sidney Wilmer led to their collaboration on vaudeville skits, which Walter Vincent acted in. They also wrote plays; two were produced on Broadway and designated "hits": *A Stranger in a Strange Land* and *In New England*. In vaudeville there began his life-long friendship with George M. Cohan.

To provide a stage for some of their material, he and Sidney Wilmer took over the Majestic Theatre in Utica, the

Walter Vincent
Seventh President
The Actors Fund of America
1941 - 1959

first of the chain of theatres they eventually owned, extending from northern New York State down into Virginia.

They started on a "shoe string" and were their own janitors, sweeping out the theatre, minding the box office, and attending to any other odd jobs. They presented vaudeville acts in 1901, but moving pictures were on the way; a two-reeler was a big event. As innovations were made, the Wilmer-Vincent Circuit moved with the times; needless to say, they prospered. Walter Vincent was to become chairman of the board of Republic Pictures, and the friends were partners until Sidney Wilmer's death in 1941.

Walter Vincent was a "natural" as a business man and also had a genius for theatrical investments. A few of his notable choices were *The Children's Hour, Affairs of State, The Moon Is Blue, The Seven-Year Itch, The Solid Gold Cadillac, Wonderful Town, The Bad Seed, Witness for the Prosecution, Cat on a Hot Tin Roof* and *No Time for Sergeants.*

He had an attractive wife to share his success. In 1905 he married Eva Burnham of Boston and, as a former actress-dancer, she also shared his love for the theatre and helped to operate the American Theatre Wing in its wartime activities.

His fellow-members at The Players club and the Lambs Club, where he was known for his "card playing sense," remember him as a tall, fine-looking, white-haired man with courtly manners. He was active in sports until he was seventy-five, when he gave up golf, tennis and diving. "I'm getting along in years and a man should pace himself," he said philosophically, but he continued to walk several miles each day for the next ten years.

He was President of the Will Rogers Memorial Fund and one of the original directors of the Percy Williams Home. The organization that interested him most, however, was The Actors' Fund.

In ninety years of its history, The Actors' Fund has been fortunate in the calibre of its officers and trustees, and while its presidents have been men of varying personalities, all had in common the purposes of the Fund, and each left his imprint on its development.

To succeed Daniel Frohman, a man who had held the office of president for thirty-seven years was not easy. Quite naturally, during that long period certain practices had assumed the proportion of "traditions." Walter Vincent's unique ability was to "humanize" those traditions and bring them more in harmony with the radical changes in concepts of charity, which the depression years of the 1930's had forced upon America.

He resolved that a new and larger Actors' Fund Home should be constructed. The site was already available in Englewood, New Jersey, where the second of the Homes had been in use since 1928. To this project he brought to bear all his persuasive powers, which were indeed considerable.

Unfortunately, he did not live to see his resolve fulfilled. Two years after his death the beautiful new Home he envisioned was completed. He would surely have been gratified with the outcome.

Two awards were given him in 1958: The Actors' Fund Medal and the Kelcey Allen Award, both embodying the ultimate appreciation for his labors and achievements in behalf of the theatre. Walter Vincent died on May 10, 1959.

On May 13, 1959, Ralph Bellamy, then president of Actors' Equity and a trustee of the Fund, delivered a eulogy at the Madison Avenue Presbyterian Church, which was filled to capacity. He said, in part:

> . . . Walter Vincent had more friends than most of us. He has been the greatest friend actors have ever had. His friendship and concern for and his service to actors has been boundless and selfless.

> The measure of achievement of a man's life is the degree of service rendered to his fellow men. The mark of achievement

of Walter's life exceeds the measure. Actors' Equity Association, The Actors' Fund and all the people of the theatre will miss Walter profoundly, but we have the cherished memory of his friendship, his kindness and his warm understanding. We are privileged and proud that he was one of us.

VINTON FREEDLEY

VINTON FREEDLEY WAS A MAN of many talents, but best known as a theatrical producer and "starmaker." It would seem that to be a "starmaker," one would, oneself, have to be a "star," and he was; a Renaissance man of vigorous artistic and practical abilities.

Born in Philadelphia (a descendant of John Alden), by the time he was twenty-six in 1917, he had graduated from Groton and Harvard and received his law degree from the University of Pennsylvania. But, in spite of this gilt-edge background, he chose to become an actor.

A few months after his marriage to Mary Mitchell, of Philadelphia, he made his Broadway debut at the Playhouse in a long-forgotten play called *L'Elevation*. He appeared in seven other productions during the next six years (which included an interval in 1918-19, when he served as a sergeant in the United States Marine Corps). He produced his first Broadway play, *The New Poor*, with Alex A. Aarons as his partner, in 1924.

The real beginning was later the same year when he and Aarons brought in *Lady Be Good* with Fred and Adele Astaire, and the music and lyrics of George and Ira Gershwin; this was also the Gershwins' first hit show.

Between then and 1956 came a succession of musicals of legendary fame, many of them graced by the genius of the Gershwins and Cole Porter.

Vinton Freedley

Eighth President
The Actors Fund of America
1959 - 1969

The titles invoke nostalgia: *Tip Toes* with Queenie Smith and Jeanette MacDonald, and *Oh, Kay!* starring Gertrude Lawrence. The first production in the Alvin Theatre ("Alvin" being a combination of Alex and Vinton), was *Funny Face* with the Astaires and Victor Moore. Thereafter, they opened at least one show every year. In 1930 it was *Girl Crazy* with Willie Howard, Ginger Rogers and a then unknown Ethel Merman.

Producing alone in 1934, he drew raves for the unforgettable *Anything Goes* with Ethel Merman, Victor Moore, William Gaxton, and Cole Porter's music and lyrics.

Although he was a master of musical productions, Vinton Freedley was tempted twice by "straight" plays, both by Ferenc Molnar: a revival of *Liliom* with the young Ingrid Bergman and Burgess Meredith, and *Delicate Story* with Edna Best. Neither was well-received.

The successful *Red, Hot and Blue* with Ethel Merman, Jimmy Durante and the rising star, Bob Hope, was his third Cole Porter show; *Leave It To Me*, two years later, introduced Mary Martin proclaiming: "My Heart Belongs to Daddy!"

In his role of "starmaker" he encouraged Carol Channing, who understudied Eve Arden in *Let's Face It*, and she went on many times in the part. It might also be said he "discovered" a young actress called Jacqueline Susann. She had a small part in *Jackpot* in 1944, and was also well-publicized as a *Bond Date Prize*, meaning that a patriotic War Bond buyer could have the pleasure of her company for an evening on the town.

Vinton Freedley succeeded Florenz Ziegfeld as a judge of the "Miss America" contests, an annual event he enjoyed, being well-qualified as a connoisseur of beautiful women.

The years of theatrical success in New York were only a part of his life. The time he spent at Elmwood Farm, the estate he inherited from his grandfather in Pomfret, Connecticut, he claimed as the source of his inspiration, where he "raised ideas for musicals."

"My first step in a production," he said, "is finding an idea, and that generally comes to me at my farm. I'm a farmer half of every year, and while I grub around in the earth I mull over ideas for a show."

As well as raising musicals, he and his wife Mary raised two children, Vinton, Jr. and Eleanor; eventually there were seven grandchildren.

Of Mrs. Freedley, who died in 1955, it was said, "Her sageness and amiable counsel were a sustenance to her husband and friends." After her death he spent more and more time at the Pomfret estate. Towards the end of his life he only came to New York for special occasions, or the meetings of the numerous committees where he served or presided; notably The Actors' Fund meetings and its business, which absorbed him intensely.

He was "a lean and handsome man," always impeccably dressed. His admirers believed his clothes came from London's Bond Street, but he invariably patronized one excellent New York haberdashery, owned by his old friend, Earl Benham. In the city, a white carnation was delivered each day for his buttonhole.

It might seem that producing musicals and directing the activities of Elmwood Farm would not have left much spare time, but he was also a sports enthusiast; a tennis player, a horseman, a duck hunter and a dedicated fisherman, especially deep-sea fishing off Bimini.

He belonged to the Racquet and Tennis Club, the Lambs Club and The Players club, where he was made a director in 1962.

He was a devoted member of many theatrical organizations; on the board of governors of the League of New York Theatres for many years; on the board of directors of the American Theatre Wing from 1941-56; president of ANTA from 1945-51; a director of the Children's Professional Theatre from 1951. He founded the Council of Living Theatre in 1956, and was president of the Episcopal Actors' Guild for twenty-seven years.

He was also a most popular master of ceremonies on the television programs "Theatre, U.S.A." and "Showtime, U.S.A." between 1949 and 1956.

The affairs of The Actors' Fund gave him great satisfaction; first a trustee in 1937, then treasurer in 1941. He was elected president in 1959 when Walter Vincent died.

Unlike the popular conception of theatre people as extravagant, happy-go-lucky children, Vinton Freedley was a conservative; a man with instincts of thrift, which he no doubt inherited from his New England ancestors, and considerable financial acumen.

During his eighteen years as treasurer of The Actors' Fund he kept a sharp eye on its investments. His conservatism made him reluctant to consider anything but the "tried and true," but once convinced of a "good buy," he was delighted to follow its progress. In June of 1968 he wrote, "I watch our IBM with interest—up twenty one day, down ten the next—a butterfly on the wheel, but I believe good for us in the long run to make our successors say how smart we old folks were in bygone days. . . ."

As president of The Actors' Fund, he lent a glamorous image at the annual meetings, or producing its fund raising fetes. An exciting evening was the sixtieth anniversary of the Fund, on February 15, 1942 when the Shuberts loaned the use of the Imperial Theatre for the first Sunday Evening benefit.

"Against the set of *Let's Face It*, Vinton Freedley presented 'A Galaxy of Stars': Gertrude Lawrence, Sophie Tucker, George Jessel, Bill Robinson, Tallulah Bankhead, George Price, Clifton Webb, Bobby Clark, Walter Hampden, Ella Logan, Fred Waring and his Glee Club, and Elsa Maxwell. . . ."

Vinton Freedley died on June 5, 1969. If an epitaph were written for him, it could be said that he was a man of many images and interests, but first he loved the theatre, and everyone and everything connected with it.

LOUIS A. LOTITO

LIKE NEARLY ALL the eight men who preceded him as president of The Actors' Fund, Louis Lotito's entire life was spent in the theatre on the managerial side.

He was born on July 24, 1900, on Manhattan's lower East side. Thus he is the first of the Fund's presidents to have been born in the twentieth century. His early aspiration to become a civil engineer was thwarted when the necessity to help increase the family income took precedence over continuing his education beyond the high school level. He attended Stuyvesant High School from 1914 to 1917.

His theatrical career was launched modestly enough in 1917 when he landed a job as an usher at the Hippodrome. This was an immense ornate theatre which occupied the entire block front of Sixth Avenue between 43rd and 44th Streets. It stood there from 1905 to 1939 and was the scene of some of the most elaborate extravaganzas in American theatre history; presented on a huge stage replete with a tremendous tank to accommodate aquatic spectacles. Although the new usher in this prestigious establishment was chosen over a host of other applicants, it was a blow to his pride to find out that he got the job, not for any outstanding character traits or special ability, but only because he was the sole job-seeker who could fit into the available small-sized uniform.

The young man's next step up on the theatrical ladder came when he was chosen office boy in the Charles Dillingham office.

Louis A. Lotito
Ninth President
The Actor's Fund of America
1969 -

Mr. Dillingham was a truly great gentleman of the American theatre who combined good taste with keen business judgment in most of his ventures; ventures which included many distinguished productions, ownership of the Globe Theatre, and a managerial interest in several other Broadway houses. Louis Lotito could not have had a finer mentor than Charles Dillingham. That he was an apt pupil is demonstrated by his rapid promotion to second assistant treasurer, first assistant treasurer, and then treasurer of the Globe Theatre. Varying fortune, after 1929, sometimes saw him as manager or press agent for different attractions, both on Broadway and on tour. But from 1930 to 1934 he was treasurer of the famous New Amsterdam Theatre, original home of the Ziegfeld Follies, and many other glamorous musicals. Then from the New Amsterdam he went on to the newly built Center Theatre and was managing director of that luxurious house in the Rockefeller Center complex when it opened in 1934 with a production of *The Great Waltz*. In 1938 he was chosen to manage the fortunes of the Martin Beck Theatre.

Nineteen forty-three was a busy year for Mr. Lotito. In addition to producing Frederick Lonsdale's comedy, *Another Love Story* he not only became president of City Playhouses, Inc., but also was serving on the board of governors of the League of New York Theatres—of which he subsequently became vice-president and then president—as well as being a director of the American Theatre Wing. The City Playhouses group of theatres was the largest chain of legitimate playhouses, other than those under Shubert control, which had been put together in recent years. At various times the following theatres belonged to this group: Helen Hayes, Lunt-Fontanne (originally Mr. Dillingham's Globe Theatre but later completely remodeled), Martin Beck, 46th Street, Coronet (later the Eugene O'Neill), Morosco, ANTA, ANTA Washington Square, and the National in Washington, D. C. Mr. Lotito's prime responsibility was to keep these houses booked with the best possible attractions. That he did so, and brilliantly, is attested by glancing at a list of only a few outstanding productions during the score of years which followed his becoming President of City Playhouses. The attractions included: *Guys and Dolls, Damn Yankees, Bye, Bye, Birdie, Long Day's Journey Into Night, Death of a Salesman, Teahouse of the August Moon,* and *How to Succeed in Business Without Really Trying.* Mr. Lotito felt another, perhaps more important, responsibility to the theatre as a whole. In order to encourage theatrical productions he not only invested in the series of plays listed above which were booked into City Playhouses' theatres, but also invested in the following, which played at competitors' theatres: *Music Man, Most Happy Fella, Inherit the Wind, Detective Story, Chalk Garden, Can Can, The Bad Seed, Solid Gold Cadillac, Picnic* and *Two for the Seesaw.*

His career with The Actors' Fund began when he was elected trustee in 1949. He continued in this capacity until 1963 when, upon the death of Herman Bernstein, he succeeded to the post of treasurer. Six years later, when Vinton Freedley died, he was named to the presidency. Mr. Lotito has been the chief executive officer of the Fund for a relatively short period yet he has adopted a positive stand on certain things which he thinks particularly relevant. As the Fund approaches its nine-tieth birthday, he recognizes that certain precepts which were fundamental to a charity a century ago are in need of being re-evaluated in an age when social security, medicare, union pension and welfare funds, and modern geriatric concepts are filling needs which were formerly entirely within the province of "voluntary" charities. Therefore, he is concerned about exploring areas in which the services of The Actors' Fund can become most meaningful in the light of modern economic developments and social philosophy. That is his long-range objective. More immediately, he is taking steps to correct the prevalent misconception that the Fund restricts its assistance to actors when, in fact, its help is available to all professional theatre people regardless of work category. Recognizing that the title "Actors' Fund" is, and has been, a misnomer from the day of the Fund's founding, nevertheless, he is prepared to change that name if it proves to be the only way of correcting this long-standing but faulty image of the Fund. Inasmuch as the Fund has always dispensed its aid without regard to race or creed, Mr. Lotito has long deplored the duplication of effort which has arisen from the establishment of agencies on denominational or racial lines. These organizations came into being subsequent to the establishment of The Actors' Fund, and Mr. Lotito would like to convince them that they would serve the theatrical community more valuably concentrating on social functions rather than taking on relief burdens. Then they would not have to turn to the Fund for financial help, which happens when their own resources are insufficient to carry a relief case through to its conclusion. And, finally, he is determined to do everything he can to recapture for the Fund the vital financial support of those individuals who have made fortunes out of the theatre but who tend to neglect it and its people when it comes to making annual donations for charitable or income tax purposes.

It is often said that involvement in the theatre is so all-consuming that those who are successful in it find time and energy for nothing else. Louis Lotito's personal life is perhaps an exception to this theory, but it tends to give the lie to those who propound it. He has been happily married to Adeline Valerio for forty-six years and maintains a close family relationship with his son, Louis, his daughter, Theresa, and seven grandchildren. And despite his continued interest and activity in everything concerning the theatrical community, he still finds time to indulge in his two favorite hobbies—golf and coin collecting.

III

Notable Benefit Performances and Fund Raising Affairs

JEAN LOGGIE

To ATTEMPT TO DESCRIBE the hundreds of benefit performances given in behalf of The Actors' Fund in a single chapter would be impossible; the time span is nearly a century. The first forty years, from 1882 to 1922, when an endowment fund was finally made possible, were the challenging times when the largest and most interesting fund raising events took place.

The first benefits, of course, were certainly due to the persistent editorializing of the *New York Dramatic Mirror*. Harrison Grey Fiske never lost an opportunity to publicize the desperate need for a fund to care for ill or indigent theatre people, and he continually urged the profession to confine their benefit performances solely to the object of organizing and maintaining such a fund. But when would it happen?

Perhaps Miss Fanny Davenport provided the spark. On tour in the mid-west, she wrote an enthusiastic endorsement and promised to give a benefit, herself. Since she was the first star to support the idea, the publication of her letter in the *Mirror* was undoubtedly influential, but she did not write it entirely by chance.

Harrison Grey Fiske had been a friend and admirer of Miss Davenport since their first meeting on a shipboard crossing to England, two years before he became editor of the *Mirror*. Although he was still in his teens, he had already been a drama critic for the *Jersey City Argus;* she was apparently intrigued with the precocious (and rich) young man or, at least, willing to be charming to a drama critic. Her flattering attentions continued in London, where she went out of her way to introduce him to all the great personalities of the English stage. They stayed good friends and it was quite natural he should call upon her to support his pet project, an actors' fund.

Once the idea caught fire among theatre people, there was much enthusiastic planning; a date in early April was set for the first benefit. Miss Davenport was still on tour and did not have a chance to give the first one, but M. B. Curtis' *Sam'l of Posen* company at Haverly's 14th Street Theatre got ahead of everyone by giving its benefit on March 13.

The production netted something over $300, not a large sum, but the *Mirror*'s publicity on the event brought offers of benefits from actors in other parts of the country from Boston to San Francisco.

It was also on March 13 that Lester Wallack, A. M. Palmer and William Henderson met to organize the "super-benefit" which would take place on April 3. The managers of all New York and Brooklyn theatres had agreed that special matinees would be performed that day and the proceeds turned over to Mr. Palmer, who would act as treasurer until a "fund" was incorporated which, as yet, had no official name nor legal entity.

The list of theatres and their productions giving those benefits are now, for the most part, unfamiliar, but they should be mentioned with gratitude in a history of the Fund.

They were Abbey's Park Theatre playing *Divorcons*; Booth's: *The Mighty Dollar*; Daly's *Odette*; Germania's gave *Anonymous Correspondence*, *Full of Mischief* and *A Husband Locked Out*. The Grand Opera House presented Clara Morris in *Article Forty-seven*; Harrigan and Hart's: *Squatter's Sovereignty*; Haverly's Fifth Avenue: *A Celebrated Case*; Miner's Eighth Avenue: *A Variety Entertainment*; Miner's New Theatre (Bowery): *Variety Olio*; Madison Square Theatre: *Esmeralda* and *The San Francisco Minstrels*; Standard Theatre: *Claude Duval*; Tony Pastor's: *Variety Entertainment*; Thalia: *The Highwayman*, *For Nothing* and *Fitzelbarger's Reception*; Union Square Theatre: *The Lights o' London* and at Wallack's: *Youth*.

The proceeds turned over to Mr. Palmer amounted to a

substantial $17,595.80, not forgetting this was in 1882 when money had a different value than it has today. An "actor's fund" had happened!

The following year a Benefit Day was again performed and raised $16,000 for the now incorporated Fund. Mr. Palmer, the elected treasurer, told the annual meeting, "There has never been a charity in which the public has shown so much interest."

This was true, but there was also some criticism of the benefit, mostly about its organization. Ironically, it came from the *New York Clipper*, an arch-rival of the *Mirror*, which had always belittled Mr. Fiske's efforts in behalf of his favorite cause. They took it upon themselves to complain, "The benefits for the Actors' Fund at most of our local theatres on the afternoon of April 12 did not prove so successful as hoped for. The weather was inclement. No special effort seems to have been made to attract the public."

They pointed out that advertising was "loosely done," and that names of participating theatres had been omitted from the published lists until the last moment. Also, "No performances were given at Booth's, the Fifth Avenue or Cosmopolitan, which had been advertised. "

At the Fund it was admitted, that had it not been for the remarkable ticket-selling zeal of the New York police, the benefit day might have been a disaster.

The considered opinion was that perhaps a different approach should be made in the future, since a novelty no longer existed. Why should the public be urged to attend special performances of regular-run plays they could see at any time?

A new formula gradually evolved to make the special performances really "special" by presenting programs rather like "super vaudeville": something for everyone, where popular "stars" and performers appeared in excerpts of plays or musicals, which they might have made famous, or in roles to which they were particularly suited.

This made possible an infinite variety of attractions, something which the public would not tire of, where in one afternoon they could enjoy scenes from Lester Wallack's company of *Moths*, a dramatic version of the Ouida novel; dramatic moments from *The Hunchback* with Nat Goodwin and Maude Harrison, and arias from *The Gypsy Baron* sung by the Conried Opera Company.

At the Academy of Music in Philadelphia, a matinee was given with excerpts from *Princess Toto*, in which Leonora Braham had made her American debut, a dramatic recitation by Louis Aldrich, a music hall skit by Tony Pastor, and an act from *The Mikado*.

One of the most brilliant programs took place at the Grand Opera House in New York on December 1, 1887. An enraptured audience saw an act of Edward Harrigan's *Pete*, the Lew Dockstader Minstrels, the great Henry Irving in a scene from *Jingle*, Joseph Jefferson and Mrs. John Drew in an excerpt from *The Rivals* and, as a climax, DeWolfe Hopper and the fabulously beautiful Mrs. J. Brown Potter in a series of surprise "turns!"

The success of these variety programs as Fund benefits did not mean the public were never offered plays in their entirety. Hit shows were always popularly subscribed, and the casts were generous in giving Fund performances in New York and on tour, even in small towns with brief bookings.

Members of the profession thought it a great advantage to have benefits as single events, where they could attend great programs they might otherwise have missed, had they been playing in their own shows on a benefit day. Working actors had money to pay for tickets and were always eager to take a "busman's holiday" and go to the theatre; the same is true today, and as an audience, actors find actors the most appreciative in the world.

They had a unique opportunity when Constant Coquelin, the magnificent French actor (later to team with Sarah Bernhardt), made his American debut during the season of 1888-89, and played to his wildly enthusiastic colleagues of the American stage. The bravos, the encores and the seemingly endless ap-

Handbill (left) of an old-type benefit for The Fund. This one was for a matinee given on a December afternoon in 1887.

During his debut engagement in America (1888-89), the great French actor, Constant Coquelin (below), became the first of a great many foreign artists to perform for the benefit of The Fund.

plause were related as a legend by those who had been present at that incomparable performance.

By and large, in the first few years income outpaced disbursements by a comfortable sum, but the officers and trustees felt their scope was limited by not having more substantial capitalization. The beginning of this capitalization was the remarkable Actors' Fund Fair held in Madison Square Garden for six days in May of 1892, which realized the enormous profit of $163,087.63.

What must have been the most elaborate stage-set the New York public had ever seen, an entire "village" designed by Stanford White, was built on the floor of the Garden. A rendering shows an incredible melange of architectural periods: Grecian columns and an arch surrounding a plaza, a maypole reaching to the bunting-draped rafters, a Romanesque castle, a Tudor manor house, fanciful pavilions, and many other exotic edifices to delight the enthusiastic Fair patrons who thronged its "avenues."

Scores of booths displayed a great variety of merchandise and food and drink against colorful backgrounds. Costumed barkers shouted the side-show attractions, the circus and vaudeville acts, and other entertainments. Concerts were given each day and an elaborate and profitable souvenir program was made possible by dozens of advertisers.

Embellishing the program were photographs of leading actors and actresses of the time, such legendary names as Adelina Patti, Julia Marlowe, Mary Anderson, Edwin Booth, Ada Rehan, Lillian Russell, John Drew, Ellen Terry, Loie Fuller, Sarah Bernhardt, Edward DeRezske, Joseph Jefferson, Lily Langtry, Edwin Forrest, Tony Pastor, Edward Harrigan, Modjeska, Lawrence Barrett, E. H. Sothern and Richard Mansfield.

An elaborate autograph book in a velvet case with these signatures and many more, was auctioned off to the highest bidder. Eventually Mr. David Belasco acquired it and returned it to the Fund in 1931 with the suggestion that perhaps it might be auctioned again.

Also listed in the program were the names of men and women, The Actors' Fund members and theatre people, who had worked so hard to make the "production" a smash hit.

An interesting aspect of the fair was that it was the first occasion when the theatre had received overwhelming acceptance from society. The names of a few of these early patrons are still familiar today. Led by former President and Mrs. Grover Cleveland, there followed *the* Mr. and Mrs. John Jacob Astor, J. W. Auchincloss, George F. Baker, Cornelius N. Bliss, O. M. Bogart, Andrew Carnegie, Chauncey M. Depew, A. J. Drexel, H. C. Fahnestock, J. H. Flagler, J. W. Gerard, R. W. Gilder, George J. Gould, T. Havemeyer, Thomas Hitchcock, C. P. Huntington, Robert Ingersoll, Adrian Iselin, A. D. Julliard, Charles Lanier, G. deForest Lord, Ward McAllister, Ogden Mills, J. Pierpont Morgan, Herman Oelrichs, Russell Sage, William Steinway, Anson P. Stokes, F. K. Sturges, Robert Stuyvesant, H. McK. Twombly, Cornelius Vanderbilt, K. Van Rensselaer and A. R. Whitney.

At the annual meeting a month later, President Palmer said, "The benefits arising from this great effort, so successfully carried out . . . are not to be measured by dollars and cents. . . . More important is the great moral gain of having brought the vast public into a new and pleasant relation with members of the profession. . . ."

It was the largest and most profitable single fund-raising event the Fund had ever held. The first decade ended triumphantly.

A severe business depression in 1893 was catastrophic for theatre people.

At that point the fund had disbursed almost $267,000 from the half-million dollars which had been paid into its treasury since its founding. The total number of people who had been helped financially in those eleven years were 4,669 and burials were given to 763. Between June, 1893, and June, 1894 doctors in New York and Brooklyn had treated 4,226 Fund patients free of charge.

BIRDS EYE VIEW
of the
INTERIOR of the MADISON SQUARE GARDEN-ACTORS FUND FAIR.

Stanford White transformed the interior of Madison Square Garden into a fascinating and highly eclectic "village" to house the various activities of the first Actors' Fund Fair—an event that continued for six days in May of 1892. It celebrated The Fund's tenth anniversary and raised over $165,000.

Many of the most celebrated leading ladies of the day pitched in to tend the booths at the Fair. Pictures of some of them embellished the Art Supplement of "The New York Commercial Advertiser," May 7, 1892.

More than eighty signatures of internationally prominent personalities were collected and bound into a book auctioned at the Fair. In 1933 David Belasco reacquired it and turned it over to Mr. Frohman to be sold again. The latter put it in the safe to await a more favorable market. It is still in The Fund's safe.

Autographs of Benjamin Harrison and Caroline Scott Harrison.

Autograph of Charles Gounod.

Autograph of Thomas Edison.

The benefits continued during 1893 at a better pace than before, spurred, no doubt, by the increased suffering brought about by the economic plight of the country. In Chicago, Sir Henry Irving, Ellen Terry and Mrs. Bartlett Davis gave a benefit which raised $7,000. In New York, Richard Mansfield offered a program of exerpts from *Beaucaire*, *A Parisian Romance*, *Beau Brummell* and *Dr. Jekyll and Mr. Hyde*, which sold out at seat prices ranging up to $500 each and brought in $8,500 for a single matinee.

A performance of Paderewski's opera *Manrù* starring Madame Sembrich sold out on the same basis and raised $11,000. William Brady and DeWolfe Hopper arranged a performance at the Academy of Music, which contributed over $2,000 to the cause, and there were many other donations from theatre people and the interested public.

Benefit performances had been the very life blood of the Fund, especially in the years before its capital fund was sufficiently established to be counted on for any sizeable and assured income. By the twenty-fifth anniversary in 1906, a million dollars in charity had been disbursed. Aside from a few bequests and donations, this large sum had come from benefits and the Fair of 1892; the men and women of the theatre giving their time and talent to make the events successful. In 1907 a second Fair was essayed, It was installed at the Metropolitan Opera House from May 6 through May 14. The net profit from it came to $63,941.69.

However, their efforts have not always been for the Fund or for themselves. Notably, $125,000 was raised for the relief of victims of the San Francisco earthquake.

And, at the annual meeting in May, 1919, Daniel Frohman said, "During the progress of the War the dramatic profession has written its imperishable record of activities on the annals of our country. The work of the profession was something to be very proud of. The motion picture, the vaudeville and the dramatic people, with all their wonderful ramifications and affiliations, secured for Uncle Sam, as shown by the records in

A benefit of Paderewski's "Manru," starring Marcella Sembrich, raised $11,000 for The Fund. Both Paderewski and Mm. Sembrich were made Honorary Life Members of The Fund.

Washington, $200,000,000 from their efforts alone. This is official. "

It is evident that, other than the hard work involved, the most valuable attributes the profession brought to these fund-raising events were their enthusiasm and ingenuity.

As Charles Burnham, the general manager of the third Actors' Fund Fair in 1910, said, "People no longer go to fairs because they are charities, but because they provide a novelty."

At an expenditure of $50,000 that year, with 4,000 people assisting, the fair was most certainly novel. A replica of the Gardens of Versailles was constructed in the Seventy-First Regiment Armory, and it was described as "less a salesroom than a spectacle!"

The main floor was the garden area. In its center, among the brilliance of the flowers, rose a snow-white Court of Honor, illuminated, and reaching the dome of the hall. Within was a pergola hung with flowers and vines, a hundred feet in diameter. Here were a dozen booths tended by the "beauties" of the stage, and the flower booth, which authenticated the theme of the Fair with the most exotic and beautiful blooms that private greenhouses could contribute.

Again, Society gave generously to support the theatre. Mrs. James Speyer was chairman of the flower booth, assisted by elegant and gracious ladies from prominent families: Mrs. Cornelius Vanderbilt, Robert Goelet, Philip M. Lydig, John H. Drexel, William Jay, Stuyvesant Fish, William D. Sloane, Nicholas M. Butler, Miss Anne Morgan, Lady Paget and Countess von Bernstorff.

Also within the pergola were four platforms partially screened by evergreens, as enclosures for the popularity contests, where enthusiastic fans bought votes for their favorite actors and actresses, and played at games of chance.

Extending over the entire upper part of the hall were two other pergolas, each 200 feet in length, supported by white Doric pillars topped by huge urns of flowers. On this level the booths were open and the public, entering from the 34th Street side, had an unobstructed view of the entire scene.

The largest booths were built below the galleries of the great hall and extended around its four sides. They were separated by lattice-work covered with vines which climbed to the balconies. The one hundred booths on the main floor sold everything from automobiles to taffy, which was made and pulled by pretty chorus girls dressed as French maids.

The most prominent supporter of this fair was the President of the United States, William Howard Taft. Months earlier, a portrait bust was commissioned and Mr. Taft sat for the sculptor, Robert Aitkin, in his office in the White House. Mr. Aitkin described the president as "the handsomest man in public life," and the finished bust was given to the fair to be auctioned.

He came from Washington for the opening ceremonies on May 9, and was a great attraction. "Twelve girls of the rarest beauty strewed armfuls of flowers in his path" as he made his way to the court of honor, which apparently embarrassed him to the blushing point.

One of the twelve girls of "the rarest beauty" was an American Indian, and a publicity release announced that "her grandfather was a scalper, but not the low-browed Broadway sort." Another, was reported to be "a grand-daughter of the Emperor of Brazil," but, of course, celebrities were more common than not: John Barrymore served ice cream at the soda fountain.

The Barrymores participated in force. The first diamond mined in the United States was split by Ethel Barrymore, as she held a chisel and tapped it with a golden hammer; the resulting stones were then auctioned. Miss Barrymore also sat for a portrait, which was sold to the highest bidder, and although she longed to buy it herself, it went to one of her admirers.

A sampling of articles for sale was eclectic, indeed, ranging from a bullet sent by former President Theodore Roosevelt, which had killed an African elephant, to a linen blouse worn by Beethoven shortly before his death; it had loose sleeves, a soft collar and was embroidered with his name. Also for sale was a dwarf donkey, less than three feet high, called "Fritzi Scheff"; she had gold shoes and was valued at $500. All the prominent authors of the day gave autographed books to be sold.

Dolls were very popular, especially those dressed by Lillian Russell, Mary Garden, Madame Nordica and one from the great Tetrazzini, which held a concealed phonograph that played one of her arias. California offered gold nuggets and articles made of gold; beautiful "belles" from Louisiana sold pralines and live alligators.

If looking at the booths and exhibits were not enough, there was plenty of entertainment. The well-known producer, Martin Beck, who was at that time general manager of the Orpheum Vaudeville Circuit, organized a play-writing contest for "the best one-act play ever written," with a prize of $250. One thousand eight hundred fifty-three plays were submitted and six were produced at the fair. The winner was Francis Wilson, first president of Actors' Equity, and an extremely popular actor. He may have also been the artist who painted Ethel Barrymore's portrait, since the name was the same, but it is doubtful that he actually wrote "the best one-act play ever written."

Other attractions were Ruth St. Denis performing her Oriental dances, and circus features from Barnum & Bailey and the Hippodrome; Colonel "Buffalo Bill" Cody brought his Wild West Show, complete with cowboys, Indians and a rifle tournament. the Lambs Club, the Players, the Green Room, the Friars, the Twelfth Night Club and the Women's Professional League offered full dramatic programs every afternoon and evening.

If patrons stayed too late they could have their shopping lists filled at the country grocery store by Fred Stone and his assistants dressed as clowns in overalls and jumpers. Or they could dine at the huge cafe overlooking the "Stage and Society Circus." There were other eating places, but this was a favorite.

The Fair of 1910 was, indeed, a "many-splendored thing" and it netted The Actors' Fund $126,500, much good-will and the satisfaction of another project successfully accomplished.

In 1915 the Fund was disbursing $70,000 a year to maintain the Actors' Home and in relief for the needy. The administration was considered the most economical in the country, spending only $3,000 annually on salaries and rental; its board of directors, then as now, served free of charge, but the lack of sufficient capitalization loomed as a dark cloud threatening the future of the Fund.

It was essential to have an endowment and the goal was set at $1,000,000, which would alleviate the constant danger of disintegration. A national campaign was proposed that would include the moving picture industry with its 10,000 players and 20,000 movie houses.

The committee was headed by Mrs. Florence R. O'Neil and its offices were in the Astor Hotel. Patrons included President Woodrow Wilson, the governors of New York, Illinois, North

Carolina, Kansas, Wyoming, Montana, Arizona and North Dakota, and many of the prominent society people mentioned as sponsors of the various fairs.

"What Do You Owe The Actors?" a *New York Journal* headline asked; then answered its own question: "Laughter— Which Means Health! Emotion—Which Helps Thought! Pay Part Of What You Owe!"

The New York Times noted "Motion Picture People To Help . . ." and went on, "Samuel Goldfish has accepted the invitation of the committee in charge of the campaign to raise a million dollar endowment for The Actors' Fund, to become chairman of a special committee to interest moving picture people in the movement. Mr. Goldfish will organize . . . representatives of leading producing and distributing companies as its members. Jesse L. Lasky will supplement the work of this body. . . ." Samuel Goldfish, of course, became most celebrated by the name of Samuel Goldwyn.

"$100,000 Raised The First Week," was the caption in *Billboard* on December 1, 1915. The moving picture people were determined to raise at least $500,000 in fifteen weeks by a country-wide appeal.

The publicity campaign was remarkable and the newspapers more than generous in their coverage. What went wrong is hard to ascertain, but there was no mention of $100,000 in the Fund financial statement the following May. Perhaps British war relief benefits took away contributions that would normally have gone to the Fund.

In any case, Hollywood persisted and 40,000 people attended an open-air production of *Julius Caesar* in Beachwood Canyon with William Farnum as Mark Antony. Shakespeare was credited as the author, but there were definitely changes in the script. It had "a cast of thousands" and some of the additional characters were "Cleopatra," "Cleopatra's Son," "A Barbaric Dancer" (none other than Mae Murray), opposing armies and hundreds of dancing girls "gyrating madly in leopard skin robes." The crush for admission to the illuminated scene was enormous and it was discovered, among other difficulties, that there were 1,500 counterfeit tickets. When the expenses were paid there was only $15,000 for the Fund.

In the meantime, and in spite of World War I, it continued its benefits and fairs and managed to carry on the work of charity. There were always individuals and groups who, although they could not raise "a million," never ceased their efforts for the Fund. Mary Pickford danced at the Hippodrome, Diaghilev and the Ballet Russe performed and Geraldine Farrar sang *Madame Butterfly*. *The Lambs' Gambol* brought in $22,000 and E. H. Sothern raised $15,000; these were just a few of the loyal benefactors.

The Fair of 1917 was in aid of the Actors' Home and its underlying theme was one of patriotism. President Wilson touched a button in the White House, activating a circuit in Grand Central Palace in New York, which unfurled all of the Allied flags; this officially opened the ceremonies, as Madame Louise Homer sang "The Star Spangled Banner" and was cheered by the 10,000 people present.

The declaration of war was still new and it was an opportune occasion for recruiting. The Army, Navy and Marines each had booths, draped in red, white and blue, filled with "The Most Beautiful Girls On Broadway" offering kisses in exchange for enlistments. Today, it may be hard to imagine a young man being persuaded into military service with such a small inducement, but 1917 was still within the era of "courtly love"; the girls were very successful.

John Philip Sousa came out of a twenty-five year retirement to conduct the Navy Band in a rousing evening of patriotic marches. The old gentleman wore the decorations which had been presented him in years gone by, the Victorian Order, the Palms of the French Academy, the Corps Devices of the Sixth Army Corps, and also a citation conferred on him by the United States Navy. On the final evening of the Fair, he conducted the Women's Orchestra through his "Washington Post March," which was considered a fine stroke for equal suffrage.

ACTORS NATIONAL MEMORIAL DAY DEC 5th 1919

To The ACTORS FUND OF AMERICA

From Howard Chandler Christy

December 5, 1919, was proclaimed Actors National Memorial Day. Financing The Fund during World War I days had been difficult. The entertainment world was busy selling War Bonds and Thrift Stamps. The business world and the politicians recognized this so they undertook a huge program in which, on one single day, theatres all over the country were to give special peformances. Howard Chandler Christy lent his talent by creating this poster which was widely distributed.

The net profit was about $80,000 and Daniel Frohman, the Fund president, said that it would support the charity for a year. "We are highly gratified," he said. "The results have surpassed our expectations in view of the existing circumstances."

Perhaps Mr. Frohman coined the expression "one more time"; it was his decision that the Fund should try again for the million dollar endowment in the spring of 1919. He was able to persuade a group of nationally prominent business men and politicians to sponsor the plan, which was to be called The Actors' Fund National Memorial Day.

They agreed that since theatre people had done so much for the country, it was time for the debt to be acknowledged. Mr. W. H. "Big Bill" Edwards became chairman of the New York area. Others associated with him were John D. Rockefeller, Jr., H. P. Davidson, William G. McAdoo, George W. Perkins, Felix Warburg and Mortimer L. Schiff.

The idea was that major industries should buy up large blocks of tickets and distribute them, free, among their employees for matinee performances, which would take place on Monday, December 5, 1919, across the country.

In addition, pairs of tickets in prime locations at the hit shows were auctioned off, the novelty being that they were first autographed by various celebrities. Ethel Barrymore was playing in *Declassée* at the Empire Theatre and a pair of tickets to the show was autographed by Edward, Prince of Wales, an unprecedented royal gesture which could hardly be matched today.

The trade papers, especially *Variety*, publicized the project enthusiastically. It was noted that Theodore Roosevelt joined the drive, that as much as $2,000 was raised at auction for a pair of gallery seats and $5,000 for two orchestra seats. The Memorial Day performances were arranged in 221 cities and New York alone scheduled forty-five of the special matinees.

But in spite of the excellent and varied publicity, the receipts were disappointing. Many of the New York performances played to half-empty houses, although the tickets had already been paid for. There were conflicting opinions as to why this had happened. Some said it was because "business men" were handling the details, rather than theatre people. Or it may have been that the public felt "left out" of the project and not as involved as they might have been if they had contributed their own money.

Daniel Frohman was obliged to make a specific denial to

Empire Theatre

Actors' National Memorial Day
DECEMBER 5, 1919
MATINEE

Contribution $ ....

Name ....
Detach before presentation at Door

BOX
GOOD ONLY ON
EMPIRE THEATRE
FRIDAY, DEC. 5
B

ACTORS' NATIONAL MEMORIAL DAY
Empire Theatre-Matinee-December 5, 1919

Your contribution of $ .... is gratefully acknowledged.

Daniel Frohman, President.

SERVICE was the guiding sentiment that actuated the American stage during the war. Emulating that spirit in deed a record was emblazoned upon the theatrical firmament, which from the standard of achievement alone, glows in unrivaled splendor. That it may never grow dim, public spirited idealists designated December 5, 1919, as Actors National Memorial Day, as a testimonial and a tribute to the player and to erect in the hearts of the people a storied monument that will endure with time. It is the intention to have America write the closing chapter of the Actors glorious career, expressive of its warm appreciation, and to reward service with service.

THINK! THANK! HELP!

OFFICIAL CHECK
OF TICKET HOLDER

Name ....

Address ....

Obtained by ....

Name ....

Address ....

Trade ....

Amount $ ....   No. ....

BOX
GOOD ONLY ON
EMPIRE THEATRE
FRIDAY, DEC. 5
B

An unusual "gimmick" for Actors National Memorial Day was the auctioning of tickets autographed by celebrities. The one shown was signed by the Prince of Wales and reportedly went for $5,000. The ticket was for a box at the Empire Theatre where Ethel Barrymore was playing "Declassée."

rumors and suggestions that the whole affair was surfeited with graft. No more than 6 percent of the money collected had been spent on administration; it was most unpleasant to have the scrupulous integrity of The Actors' Fund put in doubt.

He stated that the stage-hands and international unions had been very co-operative, working free of charge, but that on local levels there had been exceptions, which cut into the anticipated profits. About the fact that some performances across the country had not taken place at all, he said vehemently, they had merely been "postponed and the Drive would continue," which it did.

The final figure in the annual report of 1921 was close to $400,000, which was not a million, but by no means a disaster.

At the annual meeting in April of 1922, Daniel Frohman

reviewed the work of the Fund since its founding: "If the originators of this organization had supposed forty years ago, when our expenses were $14,000 a year, that they would reach the gross sum of $100,000 in annual disbursements, they would have been staggered and stupefied at the prospect."

He went on to enumerate the fund-raising activities which had taken place since those early days. The high point of his speech came when he spoke of George M. Cohan's gift of $100,000 the year before, and then the bequest of $200,000 from General Rush C. Hawkins, who had been a friend of Edwin Booth and a member of the Lambs Club.

The board of trustees had decided to transfer from the general fund the sum of $400,000, which added to these two gifts, made a total of $700,000. The endowment fund had finally happened.

"My duty is over," said Daniel Frohman.

IV

The Actors' Fund Home

CORNELIA OTIS SKINNER

THE FIRST THEATRICAL "Home" in this country was established by Edwin Forrest. In a verbose will the flamboyant and bellicose actor left the bulk of his estate—and it was a considerable bulk for he had amassed a vast fortune—to establish "an institution that shall be for the support of actors and actresses decayed by age or disabled by infirmity," the said "institution" to be called "THE EDWIN FORREST HOME" and established at my country estate called *Springbrook* in a section of what is now greater Philadelphia.

At the age of sixty-five the fiery Forrest had tamed some of the combative nature such as led to the Astor Place riot and was attempting to put on a show of respectability. In a late desire for community status he chose a distinguished list of directors, stipulating that the mayor of Philadelphia and certain city officials must always serve on the board during their terms of office. They do to this day.

The will goes on to specify that "the purposes of said EDWIN FORREST HOME are intended to be partly educational as well as eleemosynary and never to encourage idleness or thriftlessness in any who are capable of useful exertion." There was to be "a neat and pleasant theatre for private exhibitions and histrionic culture." The library from his Broad Street house was to be installed intact, as well as his collection of portraits, statuary and engravings (most of them depicting the great actor himself)—"these objects are not only intended to improve the taste, but to promote the health and happiness of the inmates. . . . The gardens and grounds are to be made productive of profit, as well as health and pleasure, and, so far as capable, the inmates . . . shall assist in farming, horticulture and the cultivation of flowers in the conservatory." Further along his high-minded document states that "The Edwin Forrest Home must promote the love of liberty, our country and her institutions . . . therefore, there shall be read therein to the inmates and public by an inmate or pupil thereof, the immortal Declaration of Independence as written by Thomas Jefferson, without expurgation, on every Fourth of July, to be followed by an oration under the folds of our national flag." A further ceremony was to take place every twenty-third of April, the birthday of "the great dramatic Bard."

The first "inmate" entered the Edwin Forrest Home in 1876 and the "institution" is still flourishing albeit in a much larger, baronial house (beyond the far end of Fairmont Park). The "inmates" have been dignified by the name of "guests," but the unexpurgated Declaration of Independence continues to be read every Fourth of July and on April 23 due homage is paid to the Bard.

The Actors' Fund Home was not established until 1902. For that matter, The Actors' Fund itself was instigated as late as 1882. The third president of the Fund was A. M. Palmer, a brilliant manager and a distinguished gentleman. He was also a deeply scholarly man, his scholarship having been self-taught through hours of omnivorous reading when he'd been employed as chief librarian in the Mercantile Library. Later Palmer's interest turned to the stage and it was due to his management that the Union Square theatre housed the most noted stock company of the day. The same success came to his Madison Square Company when he started it in 1884, a daring venture, for Madison Square was considered to be far north of the main theatre district. Palmer, a man ahead of his time, foresaw the days when New York's "Rialto" would gradually move uptown. This man was a great humanitarian, generous and kind to his actors, meticulous when it came to the rights of authors. At that period there still existed a fair amount of prejudice against the theatre which, in the eyes of the over-pious, exuded an odor of sin. Fanatical preachers occasionally fulminated against "the devil's workshop" and many people had the curious attitude that the acting profession contributed to the delinquency of minors, an attitude which Palmer, himself the son of a Baptist minister, deplored and combatted. His original idea, which he put before the board in 1891, had been to establish an orphanage for the children of actors. This was never carried out due to lack of funds.

Louis Aldrich, well-known as the star of Bartley Campbell's *My Partner*, was the first actor to become seriously interested in the administrative affairs of the Fund, although many gave generously of their time and talents in benefits and for fund raising events. The Fund's obligations were now expanding considerably. Eleven elderly actors were being cared for at various retirement homes in New York and one in Chicago. In 1895 a Mrs. Eldrege urged that the same charity be extended to elderly actresses, a suggestion which Aldrich enthusiastically endorsed, although he cautioned the Fund against "encouraging improvidence or intemperance." Perhaps he had the notion that old ladies in retirement homes were inclined to tipple. The following year he reported that a place was about to be found where "the indigent female members of the profession might spend their declining years."

Palmer retired as president of the Fund. In his farewell speech he talked hopefully about establishing an orphan asylum for children of the profession. It seems to have been constantly on his mind. Today this strikes one as a curious obsession. Or maybe actors and actresses died off more frequently then, leaving their children parentless. In addition to making a pitch for the orphanage, he went on to speak of the necessity of founding "an Actors' Fund Home and Hospital, where the super-annuated among our beneficiaries might find a pleasant retreat."

Louis Aldrich, who succeeded Palmer as president, made the even more eloquent appeal for establishing "a home for the aged and helpless of our profession who, through no fault of theirs, old and feeble, can no longer find employment and must perforce be turned out to die."

Aldrich, an energetic man, worked tirelessly on the project. Already the Fund was paying for the care of some forty-eight beneficiaries in other institutions. Why not, he argued, create an Actors' institution for them and other professional unfortunates? He remembered that Al Hayman, the fabulously successful manager and originating spirit of the powerful Theatrical Syndicate, was interested in The Actors' Fund. Aldrich called on Hayman and asked if his interest were serious enough to contribute some money toward an Actors' Fund Home. Hayman, who was about to depart for Europe and must have been in an expansive mood, gave Aldrich a written promise that if the Fund could raise $50,000 he would donate an additional $10,000.

Al Hayman then made the brilliant suggestion that if properly approached, the *New York Herald* might be willing to help in a fund-raising drive. Aldrich's approach must have been not only proper, but highly persuasive, for the newspaper's managers took to the idea at once and launched a campaign which caught the imagination not only of the profession, but of the general public. In less than three weeks, Hayman's stipulated $50,000 had been reached and passed and at the annual spring meeting, President Aldrich had the satisfaction of announcing that a total of $70,305 was deposited in the Knickerbocker Trust Company with late contributions still coming in.

The board of trustees found an ideal location at New Brighton on Staten Island, where they purchased the country estate of a wealthy and recently deceased Colonel Richard Penn Smith. It had some fourteen acres of cultivated land with well-kept gardens, wooded walks and gentle hills sloping down to a fine view of the Hudson. The house, a three-story stucco building, must in its day, have been the epitome of rural elegance with wings whose facades were decorated in an Elizabethan beam-and-plaster motif, gables and wide rustic porches. The house was so large that only a few additions were needed. The

The first of three successive Actors' Fund Homes for retired theatre folk was this mansion at West New Brighton, Staten Island. It was purchased in 1901. An imposing country estate of fourteen acres of woodlands, cultivated fields and gardens, it was maintained until 1928 when New York City acquired the land as an addition to an adjacent public park.

Joseph Jefferson was the main speaker at the official opening of the Staten Island Home on May 5, 1902.

The parlor at Staten Island was bright with sunshine, flowery carpets and wallpaper.

This guest bedroom at Staten Island is replete with personal belongings. The calendar above the desk indicates that the photograph was taken in November, 1910.

Cribbage and solitaire would appear to be the favorite games played by the men in their card room at the Staten Island Home.

The kitchen of the Actors' Fund Home, Staten Island.

interior paint and papering work was finished and handsome
furnishings from R. H. Macy were installed. The ground floor
had a number of salons, a spacious dining-hall, a billiard room
and a parlor set up with card tables. On the second and third
floors were some fifty bedrooms, many with private bath.

The Home was officially opened on May 8, 1902, with
Daniel Frohman as master of ceremonies. The main speaker was
that beloved perennial Joseph Jefferson who, being by then
seventy-eight, might have qualified for admission himself, except
that he had amassed his own sizeable old-age pension mainly
from the profits of *Rip Van Winkle*. In his voice of gentle
humor he announced that this was "an auspicious occasion and
a very noble one, and being noble, it behooves the speaker to be
careful what he says and how he says it."

A flowery description of the Home and its current guests
appears in a 1904 copy of *The Theatre Magazine* (and what a
crying shame that we have no equivalent today of that priceless
periodical!). The article, which is headed "The Actors' Home
on Staten Island" bears the none too cheering sub-title "Where
the Player Awaits the Last Call."

> In the midst of the garden patch of Greater New York,
> situated in a picturesque valley, surrounded by a huge amphi-
> theatre of majestic and well-wooded hills . . . dwell these old-
> time mummers . . . galled by no restraint and enjoying the
> utmost freedom and liberty. For the Actors' Home is a home
> in every sense of the word. There is no suggestion of the
> theatrical almshouse in this refuge where the inmates form
> one huge happy family. They live a life of plenty, almost
> luxury. They may be likened to guests at a hotel where all
> have tastes and sympathies in common, where there are no
> transient guests and no bills to pay.

The accompanying photographs show the guests all looking
cheerfully comfortable. Sitting on an open porch we see Mr.
and Mrs. Leon J. Vincent. He had been stage manager at

Niblo's and in 1866 had been responsible for that sensational spectacle, very questionable at the time, *The Black Crook* with its breathtaking scenic effects and its chorus of fifty pink-tighted ballet girls "damning to the soul to see." On a bench by a large hydrangea bush is John G. Bauer, the "old man" of the Home, known as "Daddy" Bauer, a lovable soul with a shock of white hair and a passion for flowers. He delighted in taking long walks about New Brighton. The neighbors all knew him and they'd call him into their gardens and give him fresh cuttings, or he'd wander the woods and come back laden with wild flowers to make into arrangements throughout the house. Under a large shade tree stands Harry Langdon, once a prominent member of both Edwin Booth's and John McCullough's companies, and a star on his own when he appeared in what must have been a gem called *The Stage-Struck Barber.* Seated before him is Fernando Fleury, known in his day as "the celebrated double-voiced vocalist," while on an adjacent chair is Sidney Cowell. She had come from a well-known British acting family, and as an ingenue had been the darling of the Charles Wyndham Comedy Company. Later, in America, she was a big hit in Steele MacKaye's *Hazel Kirke.* In the photograph she still looks lively and adorable, the eternal soubrette aging with dignity. "Of the women guests," says the article, "Miss Sidney Cowell easily ranks as leading lady. She it is who presides at the pianoforte each evening or sings dreamy sweet songs to the melody of her guitar upon the piazza." In a further illustration Harry B. Hapgood, an ex-manager, and John Foster, once a popular circus clown, are shown playing a game of pool.

From all accounts life was leisurely and enjoyable. In those pre-radio and TV days there was plenty of time for reading and a commodious library offered the choice of over a thousand books as well as newspapers and periodicals. The guests were free to do as they liked and, being actors, what they liked best was to put on a small show every few Sunday nights before an audience of invited visitors and local residents. There were no particular restrictions. Clothes were provided according to his or her individual taste, and for pocket money each received the heady sum of fifty cents a week.

The atmosphere was rather that of a luxurious theatrical boarding house where nobody had to pay board. Morale was excellent. It is easy for persons living alone to become sloppy in their habits and attire. Here the old boys and girls took pride in their appearance. For each it was a far better existence than that of having to live with relatives—and undoubtedly far better for the relatives. Here they could and did talk shop to their elderly hearts' content. It is a matter of conjecture as to how attentively they listened to one another's reminiscences, but at least they weren't boring the daylights out of non-professionals.

Since upkeep money for the Home came chiefly from other people in the theatre, none felt a vestige of "over-the-hill-to-the-poorhouse" humiliation. As Daniel Frohman said at the opening of the Englewood Home: "Don't think for a moment that you are here on charity; it's what we owe you."

That was in the spring of 1928. The Staten Island building was beginning to show considerable wear, and rather than go in for major repairs, the Fund purchased seven acres in Englewood, New Jersey, on which stood the former residence of Hetty Green, the Hackensack millionairess. It was a large white frame house designed by Stanford White, surrounded by green lawns, flower gardens and its own vegetable patch. The interior was the essence of comfort, with plenty of sitting rooms, a well-stocked library, a special men's lounge with easy chairs, pool and card tables, a frigidaire for snacks and soft drinks and eventually a TV set. There was also a handsome grand piano, a gift from Enrico Caruso. The ladies had their own sanctuary, very feminine in a Gay Nineties decor, with pink tufted sofas, glass-globed chandelier and small marble-topped tables on which tea was served every afternoon. The bed-rooms were commodious and attractively furnished.

As in Staten Island, there were few rules and regulations.

In 1928, when the Staten Island Home had to be vacated, The Fund bought the former country estate of Hetty Green. Designed by Stanford White, the house stood on more than six acres of landscaped grounds in Englewood, New Jersey.

The entrance hall, Actors' Fund Home, Englewood, N.J.

The sitting room at Englewood boasted a grand piano that was the gift of Enrico Caruso.

The library at the old home in Englewood.

The dining room at Englewood looks clean and comfortable—if not exactly charming.

The billiard room at the old Englewood Home was popular with the gentlemen guests.

Residents were free to come and go as long as they notified the manager of the hour of their expected return. The owners of the local movie houses presented the Home with season passes and groups would "go dutch" on taxis (that fifty cents per week pocket money had by now been considerably increased) to town to see what films they fancied. Every year the manager of the Palace gave a matinee party sending out buses for transportation and presenting corsages to the ladies and boutonnieres to the gentlemen. S. Jay Kaufman's annual contribution was a variety show complete with lights, sets and first-rate performers.

Undoubtedly, as in any close-living community, there were bound to arise a few cliques and occasional tensions. They would not have been old pros if certain former stars or leading actors didn't instinctively assert priorities on billing and feel that perhaps others should allow them precedence into the dining room. It would be interesting, for example, to see a flash-back of the grand mealtime entrances of Madame Fanny (or Franciska) Janauschek, the imposing, drapery-laden German tragedienne who in 1867 had come to this country to play Lady Macbeth in her native tongue to Edwin Booth's English-speaking Macbeth. Later she mastered our language, but never the accent. My father, in his memoirs, recalls his youthful apprenticeship in the Philadelphia Walnut Street Stock Company when Madame Janauschek played an engagement "trailing across the stage in a repertory of plays both awesome and exacting. Gloom sat in her train for four weeks." During his first brief scene with her he played a messenger and when the massive lady, her eyes blazing, thundered "How now, Sirrah, vot noos?" young Otis Skinner was so terrified, he fled speechless from the stage. Janauschek, for all her years of success, never saved her money and in 1904, at the age of seventy-four, was admitted to the Staten Island home.

Over the years many theatrical celebrities have been residents of this comfortable house of refuge. Rose Eytinge, a popular star of her time—and her time went back to the sixties and seventies, ended her days there as did Virginia Earle, a musical comedy favorite and hit in the title role of *Sergeant Kitty*. The dimpled "Queen of Burlesque" and revue, Fay Templeton, merry partner of Weber & Fields, who immortalized the song "Rosie," was a guest at the Home. By this time the dimples must have been covered in layers of fat for the record shows that Fay Templeton then weighed 450 pounds! Another celebrity was Effie Shannon, the blue-eyed, golden-haired darling of the Daly Company who later, with Herbert Kelcey, put the team of Kelcey and Shannon on a par of prominence with Sothern and Marlowe; Myrtil Tannehill the partner of George M. Cohan in *Broadway Jones;* Irene Franklin of vaudeville and musical comedy; Lizzie Hudson Collier, cousin of Willie Collier and a Shakespearian star of the Middle West; Bobby Barry who played Pappy Yokum in *Li'l Abner*. One big name actress was Nance O'Neill. When first she'd come into prominence, one enthusiastic critic proclaimed her to be "a legitimate successor to Charlotte Cushman," which strikes one as a sobering thought. After *Magda* and *Hedda Gabler* she appeared in those spectacular biblical plays which seem to have been popular—*Judith of Bethulia, The Fires of St. John* and further long-robed roles. Belasco starred her in *The Lily* and in 1920 she played the sultry lead in *The Passion Flower*. In 1927 she was the partner of Elsie Ferguson in *The House of Women* and was still going strong as late as 1937. What financial security Nance O'Neill had was dissipated—how is never asked—and she retired to the security of the Home. In her will she left all of her possessions to The Actors' Fund. The "possessions" turned out to be a reclaim ticket for a diamond ring she had been obliged to pawn.

One surprising name on the list of pensioners is that of Anne Nichols. Whatever happened to the profits she must have accrued from the 2,327 performances of *Abie's Irish Rose?*

Occasionally, when there is no vacancy in the Home, an applicant is sent to the Percy Williams Home in Islip, Long Island. This is an independent theatrical charity, not run by The Actors' Fund, but willing now and then to take in someone whose upkeep is paid by the Fund. Such was the case with Kitty Gordon, the auburn-haired, statuesque beauty whose perfect back was said to have been insured for one million dollars. Looking at a 1910 photograph of her in *Alma, Where Do You Live?* wearing a lavishly embroidered chiffon gown that clings alluringly to her voluptuous figure and is, of course, cut to expose that million-dollar back, one can't imagine her in any setting other than Delmonico's or a Mayfair mansion. Five years earlier she had first arrived on Broadway as the prettiest of the English principals of the "Veronique" company, and the society columnists had rapturously written her up as being "the wife of the Hon. H. W. Horsley Beresford, son of Lord Decies and therefore related in marriage to the Dowager Duchess of Marlborough." Kitty Gordon apparently severed her connections with British aristocracy, for she entered the Percy Williams Home as a Mrs. Ranlet. Besides the persons who once made it to the top of show business, there have been those who never made it to the first rung.

In our Home there have been cliques, friendships and occasional enmities. There have been saintly characters and a few "enfants terribles." While no mental cases can be admitted (the Fund supports them in other institutions) there have been one or two eccentrics. A certain old boy well in his eighties and becoming a bit forgetful wandered vaguely into a bedroom under the mistaken idea that it was his own. There was a scream from the occupant, a giddy girl of ninety, who immediately reported him to the management as being a sex fiend.

Another eccentric, and a very touching one, was an octogenarian actress who, while perfectly aware of the sad fact that her days in the theatre were over, was sure that a brilliant career awaited her in moving pictures. It was a fixed obsession with her. Every now and then, she'd wander off the grounds, hail a bus and ask the driver if his destination was Hollywood. Or she'd get into a car parked on the main street and when the owner returned, request please to be taken to California. A pleasant soul, lucid in other respects, she got to be known in the community and someone always drove her, if not to Hollywood, at least back to the Home. The obsession became worse and worse until eventually the poor woman was gently eased out and into another sort of institution where, let us hope, she ended her days under the happy delusion that she had become a leading film star.

Besides the friendships, cliques and the infrequent enmities, there have arisen gentle, twilight romances. In 1956 Royale Thayer, aged ninety-two, was seen so constantly in the company of Alice May Tuck (she'd been on the stage over sixty years and was one of the first actresses to play Ibsen). They were affectionately referred to as "Romeo and Juliet."

The Lambs Club in one of their yearly "gambols" put on a charming skit—fictitious, of course—of a love affair that might some day take place at the Home. A new boarder, a lady well along in years, arrives just in time for lunch. Sitting opposite her is a gentleman boarder also well along in years. Their eyes meet and they immediately realize that some fifty years before they had been bedfellows for a brief but rapturous period. After lunch the other residents retire to their respective rooms for their customary siestas. The two also retire, only to a secluded portion of a drawing room, and not for any siesta. Unfortunately, some official of the Home happens upon them during their interlude of dalliance and reports this elderly misconduct to the board of governors who are thrown into a state of perplexity as to how to handle the delicate situation. It is decided to summon the amorous pair to the New York offices of the Fund, where they duly appear before the board, and the skit ends with the two announcing that they have just got married that morning and they'd like to be moved into one of the double rooms.

One pleasant element of life at the Home is that few persons have died there. This is because no regular infirmary is connected with it. If someone becomes a chronic invalid, he or she is moved to a nursing home which has medical facilities. Anyone showing signs of rapid decline and obviously has only a short time to live is usually taken to the Englewood Hospital.

Most boarders have regarded the Home as a permanent residence for the remainder of their lives. A few, but only a very few, have left to go live with relatives. The entrant who holds the record of the shortest stay was an elderly actress who, for a number of years, had been a member of Katharine Cornell's company. Although she was still vigorous, she could no longer remember lines and she knew she was of no further use in the theatre. Moreover, she had never saved any money. Miss Cornell, a vice-president of The Actors' Fund, arranged for her to be admitted to the Home, sent her out to Englewood in a taxi, and gave instructions for the office to pay the fare when she arrived. She arrived, told the driver to bring in her bag and wait. The manager and his wife were there to welcome her and the first words the old girl uttered were, "Where's the bar?" On being informed that there was no bar, she turned to the driver and shouted, "Pick up my bag and take me straight back to New York!"

Quite obviously there could be no bar in an institution such as this, nor could there be liquor served in the lounge or dining room. But there are no restrictions in regard to the guests having drinks in their rooms. Often friends coming out to visit will bring a present of a bottle, or as the residents each receive $50 a month for spending money, they're free to go into town and purchase their own.

Even a house once belonging to Hetty Green can become outdated and eventually it was decided to build a new and more practical one right on the same site and tear the old Home down. During the year and a half of its construction, the Fund pensioners had been taken care of in other establishments.

It is a beautiful one-level modern structure. There is nothing to suggest anything institutional about the building, which is airy, spacious and rambling, with a number of ells and outgoing wings, each with a screened-in porch, for units of eight bedrooms apiece. There is room for thirty-six guests and individual accommodations give more the impression of a private sitting-

An aerial view of the Actors' Fund Home, Englewood, N. J. In 1959 the old white frame house was razed and in 1961 the present structure, built on the same site, was opened. During the construction, the guests were relocated in nearby nursing homes and other quarters.

The lounge of today's Actors' Fund Home is an airy bright modern room of generous proportions.

The solarium is to the south of the lounge. The terrace garden may be seen through the glass solarium wall.

The attractive dining room is on the same level as the guests' bedrooms and the other guest facilities—occupational therapy room, day rooms and dispensary.

A typical guest living-bedroom. Each has its own lavatory and toilet.

The kitchen, presided over by housekeeper Katie Morris, is a model of efficiency where truly delicious meals are prepared.

room than something essentially bed-roomy. The guests have
tables and desks on which to place their personal photographs
and bric-a-brac. Quite a few have hung up oil or water-color
pictures which they themselves have painted, for there is an
art department and a professional instructor holds classes once
a week. Pottery is also encouraged as further pleasant therapy.
There is a kiln and another instructor and the guests enjoy
displaying their works, some of which are remarkably good.
Each room has comfortable armchairs, excellent lighting, and
private toilets. Each has also a television set, the gift of Richard
Rodgers. This is perhaps a mixed blessing. After meals the
guests no longer mix sociably in the big lounge, but usually
rush off to their rooms for their favorite program. And that
loss in the social amenities is mitigated by the loss of acrimony
there used to be when one TV screen in the main lounge had
to suffice for the elderly viewers who had varying preferences
for varying programs. There would arise moments of heated
argument and even sometimes an occasional cane (there are
quite a few in the Home) would be flailed for emphasis.

Not every resident is a TV fan and one who openly
deplores the idiot box is Joe Smith. He will be remembered as
the partner of Charles Dale, the popular vaudeville team of
Smith & Dale. Joe Smith, whose real name is Joseph Sultzer,
just as Dale's real name is Marks—the subsequent title came
through the erroneous billing of some small-town theatre manager, and it stuck—is a gregarious fellow who likes to talk.

There is much that he can talk about, amusingly and with
justifiable pride—of his seventy years' partnership with Charles
Dale, of their beginning days as a couple of boys from the
Lower East Side, creating their comedy act, playing Bowery
saloons, any place where they could acquire an audience, getting jobs between times in Child's Restaurant to make ends
meet, of their gradual rise to becoming Vaudeville headliners
and the main attraction at the Palace where season after season
they delighted their fans with their joyous nonsense, especially
their "Dr. Kronkite" bit. On April 16, 1968, the Lambs devoted

to them a special Tuesday night tribute and the grand old comedians, Smith at the time eighty-four and Dale a spry eighty-six, responded with their old-time humor and gusto. They appeared the following March on the Ed Sullivan Show. Dale, who since the death of his wife in 1969 rejoined his partner, and Smith, whose own wife died in 1967, now both live in comfortable retirement at the Home. Out at the home, Joe Smith finds happy distraction in painting, and paints very well to judge by the oil canvasses hung on the walls of his room. Besides which, he reads a great deal, and reading is made easy for the guests as every Tuesday a delegation from the Englewood Woman's Club arrives with a mobile lending library. Joe Smith's comment about life in the Home is "I'm comfortable here. I'm content."

A more rapturous guest is Patricia Quinn O'Hara, widow of the popular actor Fiske O'Hara. She entered the Home in February of 1956 and was four and a half years in the old building. I recently called on her in her present quarters in the new—a cheery place filled with personal souvenirs and family photographs, including several of her handsome husband. A lively, pretty lady, Mrs. O'Hara talked joyously about life in the Home. "I adore and love this place," she said, "I wouldn't leave if you offered me a million," and she added that she thanks God every morning and evening for being there. Her friend, Beatrice Hendricks, who has been a resident for seven years, dropped by just then and corroborated her sentiments, saying with keen enthusiasm, "I love every stick and stone here."

Although private income of a guest must be turned over to the Fund, each is allowed to keep his or her Actors' Equity pension money. Then at Christmas, they all receive presents of $20 apiece from the Fund, as well as $25 by the will of John Golden. This, in addition to the monthly $50 makes for pleasant spending money and, of course, nobody has any expenses.

The meals, all supervised by Katie Morris, who has been

Visits by trustees and reigning Broadway stars to the Actors' Fund Home have been frequent over the years. In 1917 (left to right) Mr. Frohman was accompanied to Staten Island by Ina Claire, Elsie Ferguson and Marjorie Rambeau.

Ethel Barrymore visited at Staten Island in 1919 to pin admittance ribbons on guests who were invited to journey to Manhattan to see some of the performances being given for Actors National Memorial day.

Shortly after Lillian Gish became a Fund trustee she went to Englewood to lunch with the guests there. Here she is chatting with Joe Smith (of Smith and Dale fame). To her left is Trustee William P. Adams. President Lotito is at her right.

Celeste Holm is taken in tow by The Fund's Secretary and General Manager on the occasion of her visit to the Home with Keith Baxter and Wesley Addy in 1970.

During her engagement in "Butterflies Are Free" (1971) Gloria Swanson made the trip to Englewood to see the guests and the Home. Standing to her left are Louis Lotito and Cornelia Otis Skinner. The guests, seated in front of Miss Swanson, seem to enjoy an anecdote she is relating.

housekeeper and cook for ten years, are excellent. I happen to serve on the executive committee which passes on the many applications for financial or medical assistance referred to the Fund. There is always handed around the board table a memorandum of the daily meals for the week that Katie Morris has provided. As our meetings are at noon every Thursday, it seems almost unfair to read these mouth-watering items prior to our own lunch times.

Existence in the Home is not only comfortable but actually luxurious. Visitors are always welcome. I'd advise all members of the theatrical profession to take the bus to Englewood and go see for themselves. They might be tempted to stay.

V

The Blood Bank

NEDDA HARRIGAN LOGAN

THE BLOOD BANK:
A PERSONAL ACCOUNT

ONE DAY IN 1954, I met John Golden on the street in the Times Square area. I'd known him for many years, and as we stood chatting, he casually suggested that I lunch with him at Sardi's. When we entered the restaurant, in an equally casual way, he told me he was expecting Eleanor Roosevelt to join him. I had never met Mrs. Roosevelt and although I was aware of what a warm and gracious person she was, I was understandably nervous about the prospect of meeting her so unexpectedly.

Perhaps to dispel the awe which kept me tongue-tied from the moment Mrs. Roosevelt entered, or perhaps by way of justifying (at least to himself) his sudden impulse to invite such a guest as me to the feast, John launched into the story of his first meeting with my father, Edward Harrigan, of Harrigan and Hart. In his autobiography, *Stage Struck,* he describes this occasion and I believe it is worth recounting here because in a strange, fateful way it resulted in the Blood Bank of which I want to tell you.

Contractors "Horgan and Slattery" had prepared the building plans for a new theatre which my father was about to erect. He was going to name it Harrigan's Theatre and in it he was going to present the repertoire of plays he had written for his Harrigan and Hart company. These included the *Mulli-*

The celebrated team of Harrigan and Hart. Edward Harrigan was a founder of The Actors' Fund.

gan series, *Squatter Sovereignty* and many others for which he had written both book and lyrics and for which the music had been composed by my maternal grandfather, David Braham.

In his book, John writes: "One of the outstanding experiences of my life [he had not yet turned fifteen] was being sent to the home of Ned Harrigan, with a set of blue prints for his new theatre. I can still conjure up the feeling of almost unbelievable exaltation that came with the realization that I was about to meet in person that super-man, that great actor, that sacred name—Ned Harrigan! For years afterwards I bragged of having been in conversation with Harrigan. I had been. He had said, 'Come in, boy, and sit down,' while he wrote some memoranda concerning the plans.

"He lived at 14 Perry Street in the Greenwich Village section of New York, and I remember as I came along there was a little boy sitting on the front steps, about whose head was an invisible aura. I recall a feeling of disillusion and disappointment when closer inspection revealed that the scion of so great a house should permit his nose to betray such obvious symptoms of a common cold. Perhaps right then I ceased to believe in scions. I hope this early unlaundered portrait does not offend a good actor on the stage by the name of William Harrigan. However, I was thrilled and delighted when, by a wave of the hand and a 'hello,' this privileged being acknowledged my existence and invited me to play with him, which I unfortunately could not do, being there, as I explained, in a big business capacity."

John finished the story that day in Sardi's by reminiscing that subsequently the contractor gave him a job laying bricks and that it was in this same Harrigan's Theatre that The Actors' Fund had been established. (His memory was faulty. It was another earlier theatre of my father's, the Theatre Comique, at 728 Broadway, which had become headquarters for the Fund after an initial organizing meeting in the Union Square Theatre.)

John turned to me, and I imagined that he intended to include me in the anecdote. (I fleetingly thought how much easier it would have been for John if I had been the one sitting on the front steps with my nose running. However, he really would have had to stretch things a bit, for I wasn't born until thirteen years after the theatre opened with *Reilly and the 400*.) Instead, as he looked at me, John suddenly shifted from the past to the present, and with great emphasis, said, "Nedda, you of all people should be on the Board of The Actors' Fund of America."

Perhaps at that moment he was seeing, as I so vividly re-member it, the three-story stairway in our home that was lined with pictures having to do with the theatre. One of the largest was of Harrigan's Theatre. Near it was the framed certificate of my father's charter membership in the Fund. On the oppo-site wall was a picture of my mother, looking regal and beautiful, among other fascinating leading ladies. The picture was called "Leading Ladies of The Actors' Fund Fair." It had been taken in May, 1892, when these actresses had manned sales booths at a gigantic bazaar in Madison Square Garden, which had been organized as the first of a memorable series to raise money for the Fund.

The theatre was our life and our heritage. Working for the Fund had been as natural a part of that life as putting on greasepaint. Of course, I had always been active in various capacities. But now I wasn't at all sure that I would be well-cast as "a board member." Nevertheless, I had to admit to myself that there might be some dramatic value in my sitting on the board, where the gavel in use was the self-same one that had called those first meetings to order in my father's theatre almost three-quarters of a century earlier. To be at the heart of one of the warmest and most personal of all philanthropies was an honor too great to refuse. When I received the formal notice of my election from the Fund's president, I was truly delighted.

During the first meeting I sat silent, respectful—although I confess a little emotional. I had firmly made up my mind to listen attentively and learn all I could about the workings of this august body.

But during a routine report on expenditures when I heard mention of sixty pints of blood for a dying actress at a cost of $30 a pint, I suddenly heard myself saying aloud, "Good heavens!" I had done some fast mental arithmetic and I con-tinued, "When there are at least twelve thousand members of Equity, we're paying $1,800 for *blood* for one person!"

In no time at all, I found myself heading a new committee.

I was forthwith appointed chairman of the "Actors' Fund Blood Bank"; as the "Entertainment Industries' Blood Bank" is more familiarly known—inasmuch as it was organized and is operated by the Fund.

It became quickly apparent that the symbolic virtue of being "blood brother" to one's fellow actor was more appealing to me than to anyone else. In spite of a prestigious committee, headed by Mrs. Dwight D. Eisenhower as honorary chairman, an enormous amount of work, and the cooperation of all the unions, our first drive yielded a paltry 360 pints. Of this one third automatically went to the Red Cross.

I realize now it is easier to get money than blood from actors. True, they had given generously to the blood banks during the war. But now, they were not about to regard it as a way of life. Not only was it unglamorous and undignified, but it was a little frightening. And, as one old friend very reasonably pointed out: "On the day of a performance, Nedda darling, what is in my veins is water, of absolutely no value to anyone."

We tried again the next year, with John Effrat working tirelessly and continuously. He appealed to some non-professionals, offering them two tickets to a New York play in return for a pint of blood. We even gave them a spot of brandy—but we only upped our take by five pints, for we had no means of reaching the non-professionals en masse.

Finally, in 1962, Alexander Cohen offered a Sunday night benefit performance of *Beyond The Fringe*. The only "currency" acceptable at the box office for this special performance would be a validated receipt for a pint of blood. This would be an event—something that could be publicized. I asked the Red Cross to furnish a Bloodmobile outside the theatre. And we used all the theatrical tricks we knew. We arranged for nurses to serve coffee, and large arc lights to light up the street. We began receiving many pledges from donors. It became clear now that showmanship could get blood. So we stepped up our "show biz" efforts.

Trustee Alexander H. Cohen. He devised the plan for increasing donations to the Actors' Fund Blood Bank (which serves the entire entertainment profession in the Greater New York Area) by giving a pair of free tickets to a Broadway attraction to everyone who contributes a pint of blood.

I asked the Shuberts for the use of Shubert Alley, and they responded gladly. There we registered those who agreed to give blood in return for tickets to the forthcoming special performance. The Red Cross parked a Bloodmobile in the Alley and we dramatically filled the stages of the Royale, Majestic and Golden Theatres with beds. We began to be a success. The benefit "sold out" and we had 736 pints of blood.

The next year we went further. Now we obtained tickets from practically all producers and theatre owners, and instead of limiting the seats to a single performance, we were able to procure tickets for performances covering a period of several weeks. We set up a gaily-striped circus tent in Shubert Alley. In it we installed a platform and a band. Sammy Davis, Jr., along with many others performed. And ever since then, top stars have made it a practice to come by on Actors' Fund Blood Bank Day to dance, sing or give autographs. Every year the musician's union (Local No. 802 of the A.F.M.) furnishes a band and all the unions of the theatre pitch in wholeheartedly. Since the untimely death of Jack Effrat (May, 1965) the task of making all the arrangements each year has fallen to Louis Simon, whose job of organizing has been miraculous. He and the officials of AFTRA enlisted the aid of Ed Sullivan, who received the Actors' Fund Medal in 1967 for his invaluable help in publicizing our annual event.

Blood Bank Day is now an established occasion every August in New York. Currently we need two days to handle all the donors—one day at Shubert Alley and one at Lincoln Center. In fact our growth has been so great that, at the annual meeting of May, 1972, I was able to report that 1,694 pints of blood had been collected—an amount that amply serves the needs of all the entertainment industry personnel in the Greater New York area and also provides substantial amounts for the general community.

Moreover, the day has achieved a gay Mardi Gras feeling to it that effectively disguises the grim needs we are forced to meet. And its gaiety keeps us from feeling too virtuous.

But sometimes we are made dramatically aware of just what it is that we are accomplishing with our foolery. For instance, not long ago an eight-year-old child of theatrical parents had to undergo open-heart surgery. In such a situation "fresh" blood must be used. So we made appointments, at proper intervals, for donors to go to the hospital to give direct transfusions.

We find ourselves in this situation many times at the Blood Bank. The little eight-year-old girl I mentioned was able to get the kind of blood she needed exactly when she needed it. And she lived. If John Golden had not once laid bricks for Harrigan's Theatre that child might now be dead. Destiny is indeed a tangled web.

VI

Special Purpose Funds
and Bequests

MANY PEOPLE, both within the profession and outside of it, have been benefactors of The Actors' Fund through substantial financial contributions. They have taken various forms—real estate, securities, cash, royalties and even jewels. Some have been gifts made during the benefactor's lifetime; some bequests. Occasionally, donors, having been generous during their lives, have also remembered the Fund in their wills. For the most part, contributions have been unrestricted. But a few have been made for special purposes, either for specific projects initiated by the trustees—the monuments in the two Fund cemeteries or The Actors' Fund Home, for example—or to carry out an idea of the donor which is acceptable to the trustees. The "Mandel Fund" is an example of the latter category.

Apart from the contributions made in the spring of 1882— prior to the Fund's being established—there has been a long and steady succession of benefactors. Among them are some of the most notable names in the profession; others are people who have aided the Fund very substantially but whose names would not be generally recognized by the public.

It is altogether fitting that Edwin Booth should have been the first person to give $500 soon after the Fund became a corporate entity. (He had also been very generous during the drive to establish the charity.) He made this second major contribution in February, 1886. The gift was duly acknowledged on February 8 of that year by Samuel Colville as treasurer and the original of Mr. Colville's letter was turned over to the Fund where it has been preserved ever since.

In June of 1886, Booth's example was followed by Denman

Thompson, a beloved actor of that day, and also by Emma K. Schley (otherwise unidentified) who "upped the ante" to $1,000. In that same year the first legacy to the Fund was recorded. President Palmer noted the fact at the annual meeting by stating: "The once celebrated danseuse, Norlacchi, has made a bequest from which it is expected that $2,000 will be realized." Apparently the estate of the danseuse was not settled for some three years and presumably the Fund was "residuary legatee"; in June of 1889 the sum of $1,000.63 was entered on the books as having been received from the Estate of Mme. Norlacchi. Then, when Mr. Booth died in 1893, he again demonstrated his generous feeling for The Actors' Fund. His will provided a bequest of $5,000—the second legacy to have been received.

Another early benefactor was the actress Agnes Ethel. In 1897 she became a life member. She must have thought that the $50 life membership fee was a niggardly amount, for along with it she sent another check for $500 together with a pledge to send $500 each year thereafter for as long as she lived. She kept her pledge faithfully until her death in 1903 at the age of fifty.

In 1911 the Fund received its first contribution for a purpose stipulated by the donor—in this instance Ettie Henderson, widow of William Henderson who had served the Fund variously as first vice-president, second vice-president and trustee within the years 1882–1890. Mrs. Henderson was a distinguished actress who had achieved success in company with her husband as well as in her own right both in England and America. She left $5,000 to endow a bed in a private room at the German Hospital (now Lenox Hill) to be available to The Actors' Fund in perpetuity. Later, Mrs. Henderson's idea was repeated by other donors at other hospitals in New York; notably by Marie Doro in the name of her mother Mrs. E. H. Stuart. And there was even a bed similarly endowed in a Boston Hospital.

Charles H. Hoyt, a playwright and manager, set the example for dramatic authors to remember the Fund in their wills. He was treasurer from 1895 to 1898, and subsequently a trustee, until his death in 1900. According to the terms of his will, royalties accruing to his estate were to be turned over to the Fund. In those days the life of a moderately successful play was considerably longer than it is today. What with the many stock companies that existed in hundreds of cities and towns, there was a ready market for a competent playwright's output, or a New York manager's productions, that in some ways can be compared to the voracious appetite of today's television. So it is not surprising that royalties, coming in steadily over the years, could amount to very tidy sums. In 1929, Daniel Frohman had some illuminating comments to make with respect to "special bequests we have received from playwrights, namely: from Charles H. Hoyt, which Estate is now closed, we received $75,000.00. From the Clyde Fitch Estate we have already received to date over $150,000.00 and we are still entitled to royalties on his plays, books, etc. From the Estate of Roi Cooper Megrue we have received on account $100,000.00 in cash. This Estate is not yet entirely settled. We have also received from the Theodore Kremer Estate $20,000.00. These men were all dramatic authors."

The monies received as royalties from the Megrue Estate, beginning in 1929, were, of course invested with the result that in 1972 the royalties themselves plus the money generated from their investment adds up to more than a half million dollars over the forty-three–year period. Since Mr. Frohman made those remarks in 1929 the name of another prolific and successful author, whose royalties provided a fortune from which the Fund benefits, should be added. The name is Winchell Smith. His will stipulates that certain sums shall go to The Actors' Fund to be disbursed for the assistance of needy dramatists and to be known as the Winchell Smith Fund. Besides having made Broadway history with *The Fortune Hunter* which established John Barrymore as the most popular matinee idol of the American stage, he co-authored *Lightnin* with Frank Bacon who also starred in it. Produced by John Golden, this play was the first to achieve a record of more than one thousand consecutive performances on Broadway.

A bequest which the Fund had to fight for—but one certainly worth the struggle—was contained in the will of one John Hoge of Zanesville, Ohio. Mr. Hoge, a successful soap manufacturer, died in June of 1917. On June 8, the *New York Times* reported the fact in rather routine fashion along with the information that his will provided that The Actors' Fund would receive a piece of property he owned on Fifth Avenue valued at upwards of $500,000. But the press in Zanesville was highly indignant that such munificence should befall an outfit comprised of theatre people in New York. Churches and civic organizations in Zanesville felt they had been slighted by the bachelor multi-millionaire, notwithstanding the fact that they had all been included in Mr. Hoge's will for amounts that the old gentleman obviously thought suitable. In short order the testament was challenged on the grounds that the codicil— which also left property to the Metropolitan Musuem of Art valued at over a million—was executed by a man who had become incompetent. The principal legatee, a nephew in Seattle, where Mr. Hoge also owned the *Post-Intelligencer*, did not join in the challenge, being astutely aware of a clause in the document which would immediately cut off any beneficiary who would challenge it. When the other challenges nevertheless went forward, an Ohio court very swiftly ruled that Mr. Hoge had indeed been of unsound mind. As it became known that the whole estate was valued at between $12,000,000 and $14,-000,000 the story became a sensational one of national proportion. At first any possible interest by Mr. Hoge in the theatre seemed to be shrouded in mystery. But very shortly it became known that Hoge had built the opera house in Zanesville, together with his brother-in-law Schultz (the theatre was known as Shultz's Opera House) and that he held the majority interest in a lithograph company which was an outstanding printer of theatrical posters, known throughout the entire country. It also developed that Mr. Hoge knew Mr. Frohman and had visited him in New York to disclose his intention of remembering the

Fund in his will. Frohman's account given at an Actors' Fund meeting is as follows:

> With regard to Mr. Hoge, he was a quaint old chap. Several of us had to go out to Ohio to fight the matter of the will, because they said out there he was crazy when he made his will; but we won the case very easily. He came up to see me one day and said: "I own the opera house in Zanesville, Ohio, that you used to rent and because I have had so much pleasure from the theatre, I want to leave it to the unfortunates of the shiftless thearical profession." I said: "Do not characterize the people of the profession as *shiftless*. How many weeks work a year do you give your operatives in Ohio?" He said: "Fifty weeks." I said: "If we could get forty weeks work a year for all in the theatrical profession the actor would not need a fund." I went on to explain the conditions of the profession, the short working year, the expenses and so on. So he changed the word "shiftless" to "precarious" which mitigated the situation.

The property, at 518 Fifth Avenue, was appraised at $600,-000 when the Fund received title to it in 1919. In the fifty-two years that the Fund has owned the land and building on it, this bequest has earned $2,106,792.61 in income! And of major importance is the fact that during the depression of the thirties, even though the lease on the building had to be revised, the rental from it gave the Fund its most stable income over those perilous years.

Among bequests that have been made to The Actors' Fund where the benefactor has not turned over a lump sum of money to the Fund but instead has instructed his executors to make continuing donations, are those specified in the wills of Frank and Isolde Mandel. Mr. Mandel—author, librettist and producer—whose name is associated with such renowned musicals as *No, No, Nanette!*, *The Desert Song* and *The New Moon*, set aside a sum of money for Christmas checks to be given to theatre people known by The Actors' Fund to be in straits where extra money at holiday time would be especially welcome. Over a period of years The Actors' Fund has dispensed at least $100,000 in accordance with Mr. and Mrs. Mandel's concept of an annual "Christmas Fund."

Perhaps the most unusual special fund which The Actors' Fund has to administer is known as the Conrad Cantzen Shoe Fund. In accordance with the provisions in the will of a little-known actor named Conrad Cantzen who died in 1945, some 750 pairs of new shoes are given annually to needy actors. Mr. Cantzen, by frugal living and shrewd management of meagre financial resources, posthumously startled the theatrical community when his will revealed an estate of $226,000 which stipulated that the major part of it be spent exclusively for shoes. He believed a producer would look to see if an actor were "down at the heels" and if he were, would offer a lesser salary than if the actor were well-shod.

Two prominent actresses of the nineteenth century accumulated sizable fortunes which, upon their deaths, were to be used for the benefit of actors and actresses. Charlotte Cushman had established "club residences" for theatrical women in Philadelphia and Boston. However, as time passed and conditions changed these residences became infrequently used. The Actors' Fund was particularly aware of this situation and in 1959 Katharine Cornell and Warren P. Munsell journeyed to Boston. They prevailed upon the trustees of Miss Cushman's will to sell the Boston residence. The corporation which had owned the property was converted to the Charlotte Cushman Charitable Foundation. As the building of the new Actors' Fund Home in Englewood was then being actively contemplated, the Cushman Foundation was appealed to. One hundred thousand dollars was thereupon given toward the new Englewood Home. This enabled the Fund to designate one of the wings of the building as the Charlotte Cushman Wing and also to do some landscaping, including a fountain, which has been suitably dedicated. Similarly, donations have come from the Lotta Crabtree

Estate. This fabulous actress, born in 1849, the year of the California gold rush, became immensely popular with the miners as a child actress and subsequently with the entire American public. She retired in 1891, having built up a huge fortune which she conserved extremely well. At her death, in 1924, she left an estate of some two and one-half million dollars—reported at the time to be second only, among theatrical fortunes, to that left by P. T. Barnum.

The memorial obelisk at The Actors' Fund plot in the Kensico Cemetery was paid for with jewels. For a good number of years after the second burial ground was acquired, the trustees wanted to erect a monument there similar to the one at the Evergreens Cemetery in Brooklyn. But they were loathe to use any money which they held in trust for the care of the sick, the aged and the needy in the profession. Then Walter Vincent put his imaginative mind to work. He remembered that in 1929 Edna McCauley Lewisohn Fox had bequeathed some jewelry to the Fund with the proviso that they were to be used by Georgie Caine during the latter's lifetime. Mrs. Fox, the daughter of a Brooklyn policeman, had flashed across the musical comedy stage briefly as Edna McCauley in the early 1900's. Her retirement came about when she married Jesse Lewisohn, copper financier and turfman. She inherited large sums of money from her husband and his father, Leonard Lewisohn. Subsequently she married a Mr. Fox who was a steel manufacturer. Georgie Caine was another charming musical comedy actress.

For a time, it seemed as if there was nothing the Fund could do other than insure the gems against loss while Miss Caine presumably sported the baubles. Mr. Frohman wasn't very happy about the situation and remarked rather dryly on one occasion: "It seems as if The Fund is in the jewelry business." Walter Vincent took it upon himself to make some arrangement with Miss Caine for possession of the jewelry. She cheerfully and generously relinquished all claims and turned them over to the Fund. But this was in 1931 when the market for jewels was

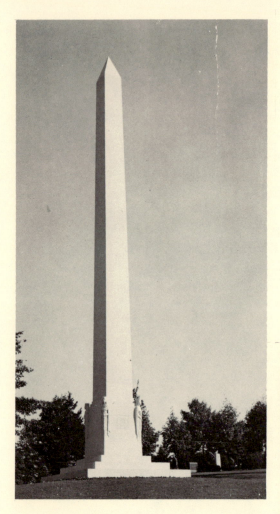

The obelisk at The Fund's second cemetery. This one is at Kensico, N.Y.

Setting the obelisk in place at the Kensico cemetery.

almost non-existent. So, until 1940 they reposed in the vault. Then they were reappraised and sold for a satisfactory sum and the money was applied to realize the dream of a monument at the Kensico Cemetery.

It would be futile to try to delineate the circumstances under which so many people have either left money to the Fund or have donated sizeable amounts. Accordingly, there follows a list of those who have benefited The Actors' Fund with very substantial bequests or gifts:

Sylvea Adams
Edward F. Albee
Mrs. Louis Anspacher
Dolly Belasco
Edwin Burke
Conrad Cantzen
George M. Cohan
Margaret Dale
Henry Dazian
Marie Doro
Paul Dulzell
Jeanne M. Edmonds
Clyde L. Fitch
Jessie Storms Foot
Edward Franklyn &
    Mary Lee Cole
Vinton Freedley
James K. Hackett
Rush C. Hawkins
Elizabeth Hayden
John Hoge
Charles M. Hoyt
Daisy Humphreys
Richard Hyde
Mary I. Jackson
Al Jolson
Boris Karloff
Leila Bennett Keough

Pauline Lord
Frank & Isolde Mandel
Fania Marinoff
Vera Maxwell
Roi & Stella Cooper Megrue
Gilbert Miller
Irving H. Niles
Edmund Plohn
Rachel B. Powers
F. F. Proctor
Georgene M. Proctor
Claude Rains
T. Arnold Rau
Rita E. Rawll
John A. Schwenk
Milton I. Shubert
Edward F. Silvers
Winchell Smith
Eugene Tompkins
Nellie F. Turner
Paul N. Turner
Walter Vincent
David Warfield
Clifton Webb
Edgar Monty Woolley
Cecil Yapp
J. Fred Zimmerman

VII

Appendix

WILLIAM BIRCH	1882-1885
EDWIN BOOTH	1882-1885
WILLIAM A. BRADY	1896-1904
EDMUND BREESE	1923-1929
DONALD BRIAN	1936-1939
JOSEPH BROOKS	1902-1918
A. O. BROWN	1930-1945
RUSS BROWN	1959-1965
JULES E. BRULATOUR	1942-1945
FRANK BURBECK	1908-1910
	1924-1931
CHARLES BURNHAM	1905-1920
R. H. BURNSIDE	1923-1933
ARTHUR BYRON	1931-1934
LOUIS CALHERN	1949-1952
HUGH CAMERON	1936-1937
ROBERT CAMPBELL	1922-1924
Secretary	1924-1955
GEORGE CHRISTIE	1931-1950
BOBBY CLARK	1944-1960
CHARLES DOW CLARK	1929-1932
	1935-1961
GEORGE M. COHAN	1921-1943
ALEXANDER H. COHEN	1963-
SAMUEL COIT	1927-1934
JAS. W. COLLIER	1883-1885
SAMUEL COLVILLE	1883-1887
Treasurer	1883-1887
HEINRICH CONRIED	1904-1910
HOLLIS E. COOLEY	1912-1919
JOHN COPE	1922-1924
KATHARINE CORNELL	
Second Vice-President	1940-
FRANK COTTER	1895-1900
WILLIAM COURTLEIGH	1910-1912
WILLIAM H. CRANE	1895-1902
	1904-1910
OWEN DAVIS, SR.	1933-1936
HENRY DAZIAN	1917-1937

PEDRO DE CORDOBA	1934-1937
ALFRED DE LIAGRE, JR.	1965-1969
First Vice-President	1969-
RALPH DELMORE	1906-1924
WILL J. DEMING	1924-1927
CHARLES DICKSON	1910-1918
I. M. DITTENHOEFER	1924-1929
ALFRED DRAKE	1960-1962
JOHN DREW	
Second Vice-President	1898-1899
First Vice-President	1899-1901
Board of Trustees	1901-1905
OSCAR EAGLE	1916-1922
HARRY EDWARDS	
Secretary	1883-1885
Board of Trustees	1887-1889
JOSEPH K. EMMETT	1882-1883
A. L. ERLANGER	1901-1905
EDWARD ESMONDE	1934-1935
MAURICE EVANS	1953-
GEORGE W. FAWCETT	1909-1910
GEORGE FEINBERG	1958-1962
BIJOU FERNANDEZ	1918-1936
HARRISON GREY FISKE	
Secretary	1885-1889
Board of Trustees	1889-1890
Board of Trustees	1894-1900
Board of Trustees	1912-1918
L. FLEISHMAN	1885-1888
W. J. FLORENCE	1882-1885
	1889-1891
JAMES FORBES	1901-1910
SAM FORREST	1938-1947
SAMUEL FORT	1885-1886
VINTON FREEDLEY	1937-1943
Treasurer	1942-1959
President	1959-1969
T. HENRY FRENCH	1886-1889
Treasurer	1887-1889
Board of Trustees	1895-1899

EMIL FRIEDLANDER	1944-1970
CHARLES FROHMAN	1894-1899
DANIEL FROHMAN	
Secretary	1882-1883
Board of Trustees	1890-1895
Secretary	1894-1898
Board of Trustees	1900-1902
First Vice-President	1901-1904
President	1904-1940
CROSBY GAIGE	1927-1933
	1940-1942
WILLIAM GAXTON	1962-1963
WILLIAM GILLETTE	1904-1906
MARGALO GILLMORE	1951-1963
E. J. GILMORE	1886-1889
LILLIAN GISH	1970-
JOHN GOLDEN	1945-1955
JACOB I. GOODSTEIN	
Counsel	1929-
Board of Trustees	1942-
NAT C. GOODWIN	1899-1901
MAX GORDON	1962-
RUTH GORDON	1950-1951
MAURICE GRAU	1902-1904
WALTER GREAZA	1956-1971
CLAY M. GREENE	1907-1913
JOSEPH R. GRISMER	1904-1905
First Vice-President	1905-1922
JAMES K. HACKETT	1900-1904
ROBERT T. HAINES	1922-1929
WALTER HAMPDEN	1950-1955
MARTIN W. HANLEY	1888-1895
EDWARD HARRIGAN	1882-1885
HENRY B. HARRIS	1903-1906
Treasurer	1906-1912
SAM HARRIS	1916-1919
WILLIAM HARRIS	
Treasurer	1900-1906
Board of Trustees	1907-1913
Treasurer	1912-1916

JOSEPH HART	1910-1912
HARRY HARWOOD	1899-1924
CARL HASWIN	1892-1896
J. H. HAVERLY	1882-1883
AL HAYMAN	1891-1898
President	1901-1904
Board of Trustees	1904-1912
ALF. HAYMAN	1905-1910
MARCUS HEIMAN	1941-1958
FRANK E. HENDERSON	1929-1944
WILLIAM HENDERSON	
Second Vice-President	1882-1883
Board of Trustees	1882-1889
First Vice-President	1883-1885
Second Vice-President	1887-1890
JOSEPH HERBERT	1921-1925
RICHARD HERNDON	1927-1942
CHRYSTAL HERNE	1934-1948
ALAN HEWITT	1971-
GUS HILL	
Secretary	1916-1921
J. M. HILL	1885-1886
R. M. HOOLEY	1886-1887
ARTHUR HOPKINS	1944-1950
DEWOLF HOPPER	1889-1895
	1898-1908
FRANK HOWE, JR.	1902-1907
CHARLES H. HOYT	1894-1895
Treasurer	1895-1898
Board of Trustees	1898-1901
WILLIAM INGERSOLL	1933-1937
JOSEPH JEFFERSON	1882-1885
EUGENE JEPSON	1893-1896
WALTER C. JORDAN	1922-1938
WILLIAM J. KELLY	1945-1949
MARC KLAW	1905-1931
EDWIN KNOWLES	1885-1895
Second Vice-President	1890-1898
Secretary	1898-1902
JESSE L. LASKY	1917-1926

EDWIN G. LAUDER, JR.	1945-1955
LAWRENCE SHUBERT LAWRENCE, JR.	1963-
JOS. LEBLANG	1930-1931
JACOB LITT	1899-1903
NEDDA HARRIGAN LOGAN	1955-
LOUIS A. LOTITO	1950-1964
Treasurer	1964-1969
President	1969-
ALFRED LUNT	1943-1946
LOUIS R. LURIE	1955-1972
BERT LYTELL	1946-1955
GEORGE D. MAC INTYRE	1905-1907
J. HERBERT MACK	1933-1947
F. F. MACKAY	1889-1910
Second Vice-President	1909-1923
M. H. MALLORY	1882-1889
FRANK MANDEL	1946-1949
RAYMOND MASSEY	1946-1949
CHAS. H. MC CONNELL	1883-1885
ANDREW A. MC CORMICK	1897-1899
Treasurer	1898-1900
THOMAS MC GRATH	1906-1910
FRANK MC INTYRE	1936-1942
FRANK MC KEE	1901-1903
Secretary	1902-1912
Board of Trustees	1918-1922
HARLEY MERRY	1892-1898
R. E. J. MILES	1886-1887
GILBERT MILLER	1942-1954
First Vice-President	1953-1969
HENRY MILLER	1914-1918
EDWIN D. MINER	1910-1912
Secretary	1912-1916
HENRY C. MINER	1882-1889
President	1883-1885
First Vice-President	1887-1889
Board of Trustees	1893-1896
H. CLAY MINER	1944-1945
HELEN STEWART MOORE	1932-1941
	1948-1953

WILLIAM MORRIS	1924-1934
HELEN STEWART MORRISON	1953-1961
WILLIAM H. MORTON	1888-1889
THEODORE MOSS	
Treasurer	1882-1883
Board of Trustees	1892-1893
WARREN P. MUNSELL	1937-1946
	1947-1955
Secretary and General Manager	1955-
CONRAD NAGEL	1964-1970
GEORGE H. NICOLAI	1936-1939
MILTON NOBLES	1892-1895
	1899-1924
FREDERICK O'NEAL	1970-
JAMES O'NEILL	1910-1912
	1941-1945
ALBERT M. PALMER	
First Vice-President	1882-1883
Board of Trustees	1882-1885
President	1885-1897
Board of Trustees	1897-1905
First Vice-President	1904-1905
ANTONIO PASTOR	1885-1899
Second Vice-President	1899-1907
GEORGE PAUNCEFORT	1924-1934
RAYMOND W. PECK	1939-1950
ANTOINETTE PERRY	1941-1944
AUGUSTUS PITOU	1891-1901
JOHN F. POOLE	1882-1887
Second Vice-President	1885-1887
EDWIN H. PRICE	1889-1893
HAROLD PRINCE	1969-
ROLAND REED	1898-1901
MAJOR BERNARD A. REINOLD	1916-1933
Second Vice-President	1930-1940
H. A. ROCKWOOD	1892-1896
RICHARD RODGERS	1950-
J. WESLEY ROSENQUEST	1890-1891
	1894-1896
J. ROBERT RUBIN	1955-1959

FRANK W. SANGER
    Treasurer   1889-1895
    Board of Trustees   1889-1897
    First Vice-President   1897-1899
    Board of Trustees   1902-1904
HENRY W. SAVAGE   1901-1905
                                     1910-1920
SAMUEL H. SCHWARTZ   1967-1969
    Treasurer   1969-
SAM A. SCRIBNER   1912-1917
    Treasurer   1916-1942
WILLIAM SEYMOUR   1916-1921
                                     1922-1930
JOSEPH W. SHANNON   1889-1898
JOHN SHUBERT   1950-1962
LEE SHUBERT   1926-1929
                                     1941-1954
MILTON I. SHUBERT   1963-1967
WILLIAM E. SINN   1882-1889
    Second Vice-President   1883-1885
    First Vice-President   1885-1887
    Board of Trustees   1894-1899
CORNELIA OTIS SKINNER   1956-
OTIS SKINNER   1937-1942
JOHN P. SMITH   1885-1888
HARRY G. SOMMERS   1929-1941
    First Vice-President   1941-1953
EDMUND C. STANTON   1889-1891
RICHARD STERLING   1937-1943
CHARLES STEVENSON   1919-1927
BEATRICE STRAIGHT   1969-
H. S. TAYLOR   1891-1893
AUGUSTUS THOMAS   1912-1914
CHARLES W. THOMAS   1889-1894
    Secretary   1889-1894
FRED W. THOMPSON   1905-1907
EUGENE TOMPKINS   1883-1889
                                     1893-1897
                                     1898-1902
GEORGE C. TYLER   1902-1904

WALTER VINCENT	1912-1922
Secretary	1921-1924
Second Vice-President	1924-1930
First Vice-President	1930-1941
President	1941-1959
CHARLES D. WALDRON	1933-1936
ARTHUR WALLACK	1885-1886
LESTER WALLACK	
President	1882-1883
Board of Trustees	1882-1885
DAVID WARFIELD	1912-1917
HARRY WATKINS	1886-1889
CHARLES B. WELLS	1917-1923
Second Vice-President	1923-1924
JOSEPH F. WHEELOCK	1889-1895
FRITZ WILLIAMS	1896-1898
PERCY G. WILLIAMS	1907-1914
SIDNEY WILMER	1931-1936
FRANCIS WILSON	1898-1902
	1912-1917
THOMAS A. WISE	1909-1910
J. FRED ZIMMERMAN	1888-1889
	1901-1902

Counsels

HON. A. J. DITTENHOEFER	
First Counsel	1882-1902
A. H. HUMMEL	
Second Counsel	1902-1907
MAX STEUER	
Third Counsel	1907-1911
DAVID GERBER	
Fourth Counsel	1911-1923
MESSRS. DITTENHOEFER & FISHEL	
Fifth Counsel	1923-1929
JACOB I. GOODSTEIN	
Sixth Counsel	1929-
Board of Trustees	1942-

*Abbey, Henry E.
Abbot, Anita Whittaker
Abbott, George
Abbott, Loretta
*Abeles, Edward
*Abeles, Mrs. Edward S.
Abeles, Julian T.
Able, Will B.
*Aborn, Milton
*Aborn, Sargent
*Abraham, Carl
Abraham, Lt. Col. Robert
*Abraham, Saul
Abrams, Ben Ford
*Abrams, Hiram
Abrams, Patricia
Abrams, Virginia Payne
*Ackabaz, Mohamed
    (Michael La Mott)
*Ackerman, Charles L.
*Ackerman, Edward
Ackerman, Sigmund L.
Ackerman, Walter
Ackley, Mary
Adams, Edith
Adams, Hattie
*Adams, Milward
Adams, Peter
Adams, William P.
Addiss, Justus
Addy, Wesley
*Adler, Adeline
Adler, Luther
*Adolfi, John G.
Aherne, Brian
*Albee, Edward F.
*Albee, Reed A.
Albert, Dorothy
Albre, Mrs. Laurence Jr.
Alda, Robert
Alder, Else
Aldrich, Richard S.
Alexander, Guido
Alexander, Mrs. Guido
    (Frances Tantillo)
Alexander, John
Allemann, Louis J. II
Allemann, Teresa Butler
Allen, Beatrice
*Allen, Fred

*Allen, Harry R.
Allen, Portland
Allen, Rita
Allen, Steve
*Allen, Viola
Allentuck, Max
Allentuck, Mrs. Max
Allison, Wana E.
*Allister, Claud
Almirall, Lloyd V.
Alter, Paul
*Amada, Louise Finch
*Amann, Andrew F.
Ames, Teal
*Ames, Winthrop
Anderson, Clinton
Anderson, Eddie (Rochester)
Anderson, Judith
Anderson, Warner
Andes, Keith
*Andrews, Albert G.
Andrews, Dana
*Andrews, Floria Vestoff
Anthony, Joseph
Anton-Smith, Gretchen
Aparicio, Manuel
Aplin, Alma
Appel, Louis
Appelbaum, Gertrude H.
Arands, Leo S.
*Arbuckle, Maclyn
Arden, Eve
Arganbright, Charles W.
*Arliss, George
Armes, Sarah B.
*Armstrong, James J.
Arnold, Jeanne
Arrow, Jerry
*Arthur, Joseph
Arvedon, Ruth M.
Ashe, Martin
*Ashebrooke, Florence
*Ashford, Harry
*Ashley, Arthur H.
Ashley, Mrs. Arthur H.
Astaire, Fred
Atkinson, Brooks
Atkinson, Oriana
*Atwill, Lionel
Atwood, Whitney Bourne

Autry, Gene
Ayres, Lew
Babkirk, Alice
Bacall, Lauren
*Backus, E. Y.
*Backus, Lillian Thurgate
Bacon, Catherine
Bacon, Mrs. Chas. Edward
*Bacon, Frank
Badia, Leopold
Baer, Howard F.
*Bainter, Fay
*Baker, George D.
Baker, Ruth
   (Mrs. Edward J. Crowley)
*Balaban, Barney
Ballantyne, Paul
Ballard, Lucinda
Balsam, Martin
Balshofer, Fred J.
*Bame, Joseph
Banas, Robert J.
Bancroft, Anne
Banda, Arthur J. W.
*Banks, Leslie
Banks, Monty Jr.
Banner, John
*Bannon, John T.
*Bara, Theda
Baranoff, Abe M.
Baranoff, Mrs. Abe M.
Barasch, Norman
Barber, Walter "Red"
Barber, Mrs. Walter
*Barbier, George W.
*Barbier, Mrs. Geo. W.
*Barbour, Ada Lytton
Barbour, Thomas
Barker, Margaret T.
*Barker, Mary E.
Barling, Kitty
Barlow, Louise
*Barnablee, H. C.
Barnes, Mrs. Clarence A.
Barnett, Arthur E.
*Baron, Milton
*Baron, Saul J.
*Barrat, Ethel M.
*Barrat, Robert H.
Barrett, Edith
*Barrett, Lawrence
*Barrett, Rabbi Maurice
*Barrett, May

*Barrett, Thomas
*Barrow, Tracy
Barrows, Richard
*Barrymore, Ethel
*Barrymore, Mrs. Irene Fenwick
*Barton, Charles
*Barton, James E.
Barton, Mrs. James E.
Barton, R. G.
Baskerville, Jessie
*Bates, Blanche
*Bates, Marie
Bauersmith, Paula
Baxter, Anne
Baxter, Charles
*Baxter, Warner
Baxter, Mrs. Warner
*Bayes, Nora
Bayh, Mary Alice
Bayne, Beverly
Beal, John
*Beal, Royal
Bean, Orson
*Beane, George A.
Beattie, Dorothy
Beatty, George
Beaumont, Grace
Beban, George, 2nd
Beck, Jackson
*Beck, John
Beck, Mrs. Louise
*Becker, Irving N.
Beckwith, Geraldine
Bedford, Ruth
Begin, Richard
Begley, Dollie Woodward
*Begley, Ed
Begley, Martin J.
*Behman, Louis C.
Behrman, Sam N.
*Beisman, Paul
Bejan, Edward
Belafonte, Harry
*Belasco, David
*Belasco, Fred
Belkin, Jeanna
*Bell, Digby
Bell, Mary
Bell, Ralph S.
Bellamy, Ralph
Bellaver, Harry
*Bellew, Kyrle
Bellini, Muriel Boxton

Belmont, Mrs. August
Ben-Ami, Jacob
*Benedict, Philip P.
Benham, Earl
Benner, Larry
*Bennett, Constance
Bennett, Joan
Bennett, Josephine M.
*Bennett, Richard
*Bennington, Bessie T.
Benny, Jack
*Bentham, M. S.
Bentley, Beverly
Beresford, Frank
*Beresford, Harry
*Berg, Dorothy Bruce
*Berg, Gertrude
Berge, Louis A.
Bergen, Edgar
Bergen, Jerry
Berghof, Herbert
Bergman, Ingrid
*Bergman, Leonard
Berkowsky, Paul B.
Berman, A. L.
Berman, Shelley
*Bernard, Dorothy
*Bernstein, David
*Bernstein, Henri L.
*Bernstein, Herman
Bernstein, Ira
Bernstein, Joseph
Bernstein, Mrs. Joseph
Bernstein, Karl N.
Bernstein, Leonard
Bernstein, Mildred A.
*Bernstein, Ruben
Bethune, Zina
Bettis, Valerie
*Beuermann, Gus
*Bevans, Clem
*Beverly, Mildred
Beyer, Ben
*Bickford, Charles
*Bidwell, David
*Bigelow, Charles A.
Bilodeau, Hervé A.
Bing, Anna Kostant
*Bingham, Leslie
*Birch, Wyrley
Bird, Mrs. Charles Sumner
Bird, Mrs. Francis W.
Bishop, Mrs. Paul

Bisland, Rivington M.
Bisland, Mrs. Rivington M.
*Bispham, David S.
Bissell, Richard
Bissinger, Peggy
Bittner, Jack
Bixby, Mildred E.
*Black, Louise
Blackburn, Clarice
Blackburn, Dorothy
Blackmer, Sidney
*Blackton, J. Stuart
Blaine, Vivian
Blair, Betsy
Blair, Janet
Blanchard, Jean L.
Bland, Lawrence E.
*Blandick, Clara
*Bledsoe, Jules
Bliss, Eileen
Blondell, Joan
*Bloom, Sol
Bloomgarden, Kermit
Blum, Edward A.
*Blumenthal, Ben
Blyth, Ann
Bodkin, Thomas V.
Bohn, Chris
*Boland, Mary
Bolger, Ray
Bolin, Shannon
Bonis, Henry
*Boone, John A. L. H.
Boone, Pat
*Booth, Edwin
Booth, Nellie
Booth, Shirley
Booth, Wade
Boothe, Clare
Borden, Gloria Jones
Borden, Joyce
Bosley, Tom
*Bottomley, Mrs. John T.
*Boudinot, Jessie Burnett
*Bovay, Jane
Bowan, Sibyl
Bowden, Charles
*Bowes, Major Edward
Bowler, Richard
*Bowman, Charles R.
*Bowman, John
*Boyar, Ben
Boyar, Burton A.

Boyar, Jerome I.
Boyar, Robert A.
*Boyd, Andrew
*Brabyn, James
*Bradford, Etheyle Parry
*Brady, William A.
Braham, Gladys Feldman
*Bramley, Edith Speare
Bramley, Raymond
*Brandt, Charles C.
Brandt, Charles D.
*Brandt, George W.
Braxton, Stephanie
*Bray, Charles Edward
Breaux, Marc
*Breese, Edmund
*Brennan, James J.
Brennan, Mary Middleton
Brennan, Thomas L.
Brent, George
Brent, Romney
Breslauer, B. F. Jack
*Brewster, Margaret O.
*Brian, Donald
Brickley, Evelyne
*Briscoe, Johnson
*Briscoe, Lottie
Britton, Barbara
Britton, George W.
*Broadhurst, George
Broder, Jane
*Broderick, Helen
Broeder, Raymond L.
*Bromley, Theodore
Brooks, Geraldine
*Brooks, Joseph
Brooks, Virginia Fox
*Broun, Heywood
*Brown, Albert O.
*Brown, James A.
Brown, Jimmie
Brown, Joe E.
Brown, Mrs. Joshua W.
Brown, Robert Andrew
*Brown, Russ
*Brown, William
Brownstein, Rebecca
Bruce, Carol
*Bruce, Hilda
*Bruce, Nigel
Bruguiere, Ronald
*Brulatour, J. E.
*Bruno, Christopher

Bryant, Mrs. Dorothy N.
Bryant, Mary
Bryce, Edward S.
Brynner, Yul
*Buck, George
Buck, Herb
Buckley, William T.
Buckridge, Kenneth W.
Budd, Norman
Bullock, H. Ridgely Jr.
*Bunce, Alan C.
*Bunny, John
*Burby, Jane
Burch, Charles
*Burke, Billie
*Burke, Edwin H.
Burke, Richard Robert
Burke, Robert M.
Burnett, Elizabeth
Burns, "Hi-Brown" Bobby
*Burns, Nat
*Burnside, R. H.
Burr, Fritzi
Burr, Raymond
Burrows, Abe
*Burt, Ida
*Burt, Laura
Burton, Richard
Butera, Mrs. Joseph C.
Butler, James J.
*Butterfield, W. S.
Buttitta, Anthony
Button-Reynolds, Editha L.
Buttons, "Red"
Byers, Alfa Perry
*Byington, Spring
*Byrne, Mrs. Harry Joseph
*Byrne, William J.
*Byron, Kate
Cabot, Virginia A.
Cady, Anson W.
*Cady, Fred M.
Caesar, Sid
Cagney, James
Cagney, Jeanne
*Cahill, William
*Cahn, Julius
*Caine, Mrs. George R.
Caine, Howard
Caine, Joan-Ellen
Caldwell, Nathan E. Jr.
*Calhern, Louis
Calhern, Marianne Stewart

Callahan, Daniel J.
*Callahan, Emmett R.
Calleia, Joseph Spurin
*Cameron, Hugh
Campanella, Joseph
*Campbell, H. H.
Campbell, Jim
*Campbell, Robert
*Campbell, William S.
*Canby, A. H.
Canetti, Jacques
Cannon, J. D.
Canova, Judy
*Cantor, Eddie
*Cardinal, Arthur
*Cardinal, Florence Nelson
Carey, Betty
*Carey, Joseph A.
*Carhart, James L.
*Carle, Richard
Carmel, Roger C.
Carney, Art
Carney, Grace
Caro, Warren
Carpenter, Frank E.
*Carr, Cornelia P.
Carr, Robert A.
Carroll, Dee
Carroll, Jane H.
Carroll, Leo G.
Carroll, Pat
Carroll, Vincent
Carson, Wayne
Carter, Jewell
Cartledge, Jim
*Caruso, Enrico
Caruso, John
*Casad, Campbell B.
Casad, Mrs. Campbell B.
*Case, Edythe True
*Casey, Pat
Caspare, Leo F.
Cass, Peggy
Cassano, Dorothea
Casson, Bernardette
*Castle, James W.
*Cavanaugh, Florence Heston
*Cawthorn, Joseph
Cella, John G.
Chamberlain, Dora
Chamberlain, Mrs. Henry G.
Chambers, Augusta
*Chambers, Ralph W.

Champion, Gower
Chaney, Lon
Chaplin, Charlie
Chappell, Edna
Chase, Stephen Alden
Chenowith, Walter
*Cherryman, Rex
*Chesterfield, Henry
Childers, Dolores
*Childs, Monroe
*Chisnell, Susan
Choate, Edward
Choate, Mrs. Edward
Chodorov, Jerome
Claire, Ina
Claire, Ludi
*Claire, Willis
Clark, Alexander Jr.
Clark, Al W.
*Clark, Bobby
Clark, Mrs. Bobby
*Clark, Charles Dow
Clark, Mrs. Charles Dow
*Clark, Frances
*Clark, Fred
Clark, Hazel Vernon
*Clark, Marguerite
Clark, Marilyn
Clark, Phillip W.
Clark, Tony
*Clarke, Andrew J.
Clarke, Francis
Clarke, Harry
Clarke, Harry E.
Clarke, Mary A.
*Clarke, Thomas A.
*Clarke, Thomas B.
Clary, Robert
Class, Maurice M., 2nd
*Claxton, Kate
*Clayton, Estelle
Clayton, Jan
*Clement, Clay
Clements, Alice
*Clements, Dudley
*Clements, Mary Frey
Cleveland, Georgine
*Cliffe, Alice Belmore
*Clifford, Mrs. Anna May
Cline, Edward J.
Cline, Louis
Clive, Madeline
Coate, Margie

*Coates, Mildred G.
Cobb, Richard
*Coburn, Charles D.
Coburn, William H.
*Coburn, Mrs. William H.
Coca, Imogene
Code, Grant
Cody, Lou
Cody, Marie
Coe, Fred
*Coghlan, Charles F.
*Cohan, George M.
*Cohan, Helen F.
*Cohan, Jerry J.
*Cohan, Josephine
Cohen, Abe
Cohen, Alexander H.
Cohen, Hildy Parks
*Cohen, Max A.
Cohen, Sydney S.
Cohen, Ted
*Cohn, Harry
Colbert, Claudette
Cole, Albert H.
Cole, Mrs. Albert H.
Coley, Thomas L.
Collamore, Jerome
*Collier, William, Sr.
Collinge, Patricia
*Collins, J. Palmer
Collins, Louise L.
*Collyer, Clayton
Colton, Edward E.
Columbus, Charles
*Colville, Samuel
*Colville, Mrs. Samuel
Comegys, Kathleen
*Comstock, Fannie
Cone, Irving
Cone, Theresa Loeb
Conforti, Gino
Conklin, Charles
Conn, Chester
Connard, Phyllis
Connell, Gerard J.
Connell, Gordon
Connell, Jane
*Connelly, Eugene L.
Connelly, Marc
*Connelly, Sadie
Connolly, Ann
*Connor, Frank A.
*Conried, Heinrich

Conroy, Ora May Ann
Conte, John Charles
*Cook, Donald
*Cook, Joe
Cook, Morton L.
*Cooke, Edward G.
*Cooke, Harry M.
Cooke, Mrs. Harry M.
*Cooksey, Curtis
Cookson, Beatrice Straight
*Cooley, Hollis E.
Cooley, Leland Frederick
*Coolidge, Phil
Cooper, Herman E.
Cooper, Irving
Cooper, Jimmie
Cooper, Melville
Coote, Robert
Coots, Clayton
Cope, Elisabeth
*Coquelin, Benoit
*Corbett, James J.
*Corbett, Leonora
Core, Natalie H. H.
Corey, Edward B.
*Corey, Madison
*Corey, Wendell R.
*Corinne
Cornell, Duchess Dutton
*Cornell, John
Cornell, Katharine
*Corrigan, Emmett
Cort, Mrs. Harry L.
*Corthell, Herbert
*Cortland, Mary Hilforde
*Cossart, Ernest
Cossart, Valerie
*Costello, Maurice G.
Cotey, Ben
Cotsworth, Staats
Coughlan, Mrs. Burton
*Coulter, Frazer
*Courtenay, Mrs. Virginia Harned
Courter, Madeleine Janis
*Courtleigh, William
*Courtney, William H.
*Cowan, Jerome
Coward, Noel
*Cowell, Sydney
*Cowl, Jane
*Cowles, Eugene
Cox, Ray
*Crabtree, Lotta M.

Craig, Helen
Cramer, Gordon
Crandall, Brad
*Crane, William H.
*Craven, Frank
Craven, Robin
Craver, William
*Crawford, Clifton
*Crawford, Edward Hart
Crawley, Robert
Crecca, William D.
*Cressy, William H.
Crocker, Aleen Bronson
Crocker, Mrs. George Glover
*Crompton, W. H.
Cromwell, John
Cronyn, Hume
Crosby, Bing
Crosman, Mrs. Forrest
*Crothers, Rachel
*Crouse, Russel
Crowley, Edward J.
*Crumit, Frank
*Cummings, Robert
Cuneo, Fred
Curley, George F.
Curry, Mason
*Curtin, James H.
Curtis, Julius
Curtiss, Charles C.
*Cushman, Mrs. Abe Lincoln
Cushman, Nancy
Da Costa, Morton
Dahdah, Raymond
Dahlberg, Gilda
Dahlberg, Gunnar
*Dailey, Joseph
*Daily, Peter F.
*Dale, Charles
*Dale, Margaret
Dalrymple, Jean
*Dalton, Charles
Daly, James F.
Dana, Kenneth
*Danforth, William
Daniel, Leslie
*Daniels, Bebe
*Dantes, Marie
*D'Arcy, H. A.
*Darcy, Maurice Sullivan
*Darling, Edward V.
*Darnell, Linda
Darnay, Toni

da Silva, Howard
*Davenport, Eva
*Davenport, Harry
*David, William
Davidson, A. F.
Davidson, Gordon
Davies, Harry
*Davies, Phoebe
*Davis, Alice
Davis, Bette
Davis, Edward H.
Davis, Glenmore
*Davis, Harry
*Davis, Owen
*Davis, Owen Jr.
Davis, Mrs. R. C.
Davis, Sammy, Sr.
Davis, Stephen
*Davis, Will J.
Dawson, Dolores
Daykarhanova, Tamara
*Dazian, Henry
Deak, Lewis J.
*Dean, Dora (Georgia Empey)
Dean, Shannon
Dean, William
*De Angelis, Jefferson
*De Armond, Caprice Lewis
*De Belleville, Frederic
*DeBondy, Fred
Debuskey, Merle
*DeCordoba, Pedro
de Fieore, Mrs. Claire Gamble
de La Viez, Hirsh
de Liagre, Alfred Jr.
Delmar, Harry
*Delmore, Ralph
*Delson, John
DeLugg, Milton
*Demarest, Barney H.
*Dempsey, Clifford
*Denton, Harvey R.
De Ross, Frank
*Derwent, Clarence
*DeSilva, Frank
*DeSylva, B. G. (George Gard)
*Devereaux, Jack
Devine, Berdine Allemann
Devlin, Nancy
Dewhurst, Colleen
Diamand, Ralph R.
Diaz, Louis
Dick, Joe

Dickinson, Mrs. William R.
Dickson, Matilda
Diener, Joan
Dietrich, Marlene
*Digges, Dudley
*Dillingham, C. B.
Dillon, Tom
Dilworth, Hubert
*Dingwall, A. W.
*Ditrichstein, Leo
*Dittenhoefer, I. M.
*Dixey, Henry E.
*Dixon, Harland
Dixon, Jean
*Dobson, Frank Wallace
Doll, William
Dolley, Sara
*Donahue, Jack
*Dondiego, Bernardino
*Donehue, Vincent J.
Donn, Berta
*Donnan, La Rue
Donnan, La Verne
*Donnelly, Dorothy
*Donnelly, John J.
Donovan, King
Doran, Daniel A.
Dorfman, Bertha
*Doro, Marie
Douglas, Helen Gahagan
Douglas, Kirk
Douglas, Melvyn
*Douglas, Paul
Douglass, Amy C.
Douglass, Stephen
Dow, Belle
Dow, Mrs. William Griggs
Dow, Wolford K.
*Dowling, Edward Duryea
Dowling, Robert W.
Dowling, Mrs. Robert W.
Downey, Morton
Downing, Robert
Downing, Virginia
*Doyle, Len
Drake, Alfred
*Drake, Josephine
*Draper, Ruth
*Drew, John
*Drew, Sydney
Drill, Frances A.
Driscoll, George F.
Drury, James E.

Duff, William B.
Du-For, Dennis
*Duggan, Henry
Duggan, Pat
Duing, William Edward
Duke, Patty
*Dullzell, Paul
*Dullzell, Mrs. Paul
Duncan, Angus
*Duncan, Margherita Sargent
Dunetz, Lou
Dunn, Bob
*Dunn, Emma
*Dunn, J. Malcolm
*Dunn, Violette Kimball
Dunnock, Mildred
*Dunstan, Clifford
*Dupree, Minnie
Durant, Jack
Durkin, Gus
*Durrand, Juliet
*Duryea, Dan
Dustin, Robert E.
*Eagels, Jeanne
*Eagle, Oscar W.
Eagle, Mrs. Oscar W.
Earnfred, Thomas S.
*Eberle, Robert M.
Eckert, George A. Jr.
Eckles, Robert M.
Edelstein, Joseph
Eden, Sara
*Edeson, Robert
*Edney, Florence
Edwards, Leo
*Edwards, Samuel
Effrat, Andrew George
Effrat, Anne
*Effrat, John
Egbers, Peggy
Ehrlich, Mrs. Richard A.
Eisen, Max
Elder, Judith
*Eldot, Jesse J.
Eldridge, Florence
Elic, Josip
*Ellinghouse, Alf.
Elliott, David
*Elliott, Gertrude
*Elliott, Maxine
*Ellis, Mrs. Lee
*Elmer, Harry
*Eltinge, Julian

*Elverson, Mrs. James Jr.
*Emerson, Ed.
Emerson, Joe
*Emerson, John
Emerson, Vesta Gilbert
*Emery, John
*Emmet, Katherine
*Emmett, Florence (Fostell)
*Emmett, J. K., Sr.
Emmons, J. Gordon
*Endicott, Samuel C.
Engel, Lehman
Engel, Tala
Erickson, Mitchell
*Erlanger, A. L.
Erlanger, Charlotte
Erskine, Howard W.
*Erwin, Stuart
*Esmonde, Edward
Essex, Harry
*Ethel, Agnes
*Evans, Frank W.
Evans, Madge
Evans, Maurice
*Evans, Millie A.
*Evelyn, Judith
Everett, Mabel Wilber
Everts, Louise
*Evesson, Isabelle
Ewell, Tom
*Fabian, Simon H.
*Factorow, Max
*Fairbanks, Douglas
Fairchild, Charlotte Mae
*Fairchild, Josephine M.
Falkenhainer, Beryl Halley
Farley, Morgan
Farnworth, Betty Brooks
*Farnworth, Dudley
Farrell, Dorothy Butler
Farrell, Edwin A.
*Farrell, Lawrence
Farrell, Walter W. Jr.
*Fassett, Mrs. Julia Morton
*Faversham, William Sr.
*Fay, Frank
Fearnley, John
Feder, Abe H.
*Feeney, John
*Feinberg, George
Feinberg, Ione
Feine, Arthur
Feinstein, Martin

*Fellowes, Rockliffe
*Felton, "Happy"
Fennelly, Parker
*Ferber, Bernie
*Ferber, Edna
Ferguson, Mrs. Albert G.
*Ferguson, Elsie
*Fernandez, Bijou
Ferrer, Jose V.
Ferriday, Carolyn W.
Feuer, Cy
Fickett, Mary
*Field, Al G.
Field, Leonard S.
Field, Louis
*Field, R. M.
*Fields, Joseph
Fields, Totie
*Fillmore, Nellie
*Finberg, Abe
*Findlay, Cora M.
Fischer, Mrs. Herbert A.
*Fish, Margaret
Fisher, Carl
Fisher, Grace
Fisher, Kathleen
*Fiske, Harrison Grey
*Fiske, Minnie Maddern
*FitzGerald, Lillian (West)
Fitzpatrick, Mrs. Edward M.
Flamm, Donald
*Fleischman, Israel
Fletcher, Bramwell
Fletcher, Jack
*Fletcher, Larry
*Flinn, John C.
*Flood, John
Florance, Marian
*Florence, William J.
*Flynn, James Patrick
*Flynn, Joe
*Flynn, Zitella
Foch, Nina
Fonda, Henry
Fonda, Jane
Fontanne, Lynn
*Foot, Mrs. Jessie S.
*Forbes, James
*Ford, Charles E.
Ford, David
Ford, Frank A.
Ford, George D.
Ford, Helen

Ford, Paul
*Ford, "Senator" Edward H.
Forde, Mrs. Benjamin F.
*Foreman, Elliot S.
*Foreman, Jules L.
*Forepaugh, John A.
*Formes, Carl
Fornadel, Jeanne
Forrest, Anne K.
Forrest, Iris
*Forrest, Samuel M.
Forsyth, Robert Hyde
Forsythe, Charles
Forsythe, John
*Forwood, Harry M.
Forwood, Margaret R.
Foster, Alan
Foster, Claiborne
Fowlkes, Julian
Fox, Gertrude
Fox, Janet
*Fox, William
*Foy, Eddie
Foy, Magda
*Fraiz, Mrs. Birtine Farnworth
Francine, Anne
Franciosa, Anthony
Francis, Allan
Francis, Mrs. Allan
*Francis, Kay
Francis, Robyn Denise
Frank, Judy
Frankel, Dorothy M.
Franken, Rose
Franklin, Hugh
*Frayer, Frank
*Frazee, Harry H.
Frazee, Mrs. Walter E.
Frazer, Daniel
*Frazer, Jack
*Frazer, Thomas K.
Freed, Robert E.
*Freedley, Vinton
Freedman, Ben
Freedman, Leo
*Freelyater, W. Rodney
Freeman, Valdo Lee
*Freeman, Y. F.
French, Kate R.
*French, Malcolm Bradley
French, Richard E. ("Dixie")
*French, T. Henry
*Frey, Nathaniel

Fried, Walter
Fried, Mrs. Walter
Friedlander, Emil
Friedlander, Harold
Friedman, Leopold
*Friend, Arthur S.
*Friganza, Trixie
Frisbie, Mabel
Frizzell, Genevieve
Frohman, Bert
*Frohman, Charles
*Frohman, Daniel
Froman, Jane
*Fromkes, Harry
*Fulford, Robert
Fuller, Frances
Fursman, Georgia
*Gaige, Crosby
Gaige, Truman
*Gale, Lillian
*Gallagher, George W.
*Gallagher, "Skeets" Richard
Gambarelli, Maria
*Gannon, Marjorie Mason
Gardiner, James W.
*Garfield, John
Garrison, Duane
*Garrison, Isabel
Garson, Greer
Garwood, Beatrice
Gates, Larry
*Gates, Ruth
Gateson, Marjorie
Gaus, Robert
Gautier, Donat
*Gaxton, William A.
Gelb, Claire Lila
Geller, Daniel
Geller, Iris
Gendel, Max
Geoly, Andrew
*George, Charles
*George, Grace
Geraghty, Tom
Gerber, Ella
*Gerlach, Maxine
German, William J.
*Gest, Morris
Gibberson, William
*Gibbs, Cora
*Gilbert, Billy
*Gilbert, Mrs. G. H.
Gilbert, J. Charles

Gilbert, Louis
Gilbert, Loyd
Gilbert, Margot R.
Gilbert, Paul
Gilbert, Dr. Ruth
Gilbert, Mrs. W. G.
*Gildea, Agnes
*Gildea, Mary
Gillen, Girard
*Gillespie, Joseph
Gillet, Langdon
Gillette, Ruth
*Gillette, William
Gillmore, Margalo
*Gilman, Ada
*Gilmore, Charles P.
Gilmore, Dorothy Quinette
*Gilmore, William J.
Gingold, Hermione
Ginsberg, Jack M.
*Girardot, Etienne
Giroux, John A.
Girvin, Virginia
*Gish, Dorothy
Gish, Lillian D.
Gladstone, Henry
Glaser, Vaughan
Gleason, Jackie
*Glendinning, Ernest J.
Glenkey, Col. Paul G.
Glenn, Daisy
Glick, Harold
Gobel, George
*Goldberg, Harold
Golde, Mrs. Sydney R.
*Golden, John
*Golden, Samuel
*Goldin, Elias
Goldreyer, Michael
Goldreyer, Mildred
*Goldsmith, Rae S.
Goldstein, Marvin
Goldstein, Nathan W.
*Goldthwaite, Dora
Goldwyn, Samuel
Gombell, Minna
*Gomez, S. Thomas
*Good, Rose Gelb
*Goodall, Grace
*Goodfriend, Simon
Goodkin, Viola Clarens
Goodlake, Richard H.
Goodman, Arlene Wolf

Goodman, Frank
Goodstein, Jacob I.
*Goodwin, Nat C.
Goodyear, Elizabeth
*Gordon, Julia Swayne
Gordon, Max
Gordon, Mrs. Max
Gordon, Ruth
Gordon, S. Stanley
Gorman, Robert L.
Gottlieb, Morton
*Gottlob, J. J.
*Gottlob, Joseph
*Gould, Harold W.
*Gould, Harry E.
Goulet, Robert
*Goulston, Mrs. Ernest J.
Grady, Cecilia
*Grady, Hugh
*Grady, Jere
Graham, June F.
Grandin, Edna
Grant, Bernard
Grant, Cary
Grant, Leopoldine
*Grau, Maurice
Gray, David Jr.
Grayson, Kathryn
Grayson, Richard
*Greaza, Mary N.
Greaza, Walter
Green, Charlie
Green, Martyn
*Green, Philip A.
Green, Ruth
Green, Tom
Greene, Bernard Ben
Greenhouse, Martha
*Greenwall, Henry
Greenwood, Charlotte
Greeran, John
Gregg, Katherine
Griffin, Arthur L.
*Griffin, Gerald
Griffin, Gerald, Jr.
Griffin, Mrs. Gerald
*Griffin, Gerald 2nd
Griffith, Andy
*Griffith, Robert E.
Grimes, Gene
Grimes, Ray
*Grismer, Joseph R.
Grismer, Mrs. Joseph R.

Grizzard, George
Grody, Cyril H.
*Groesbeck, Amy Bradish
*Grosner, Lewis
Gross, Sherman
Grossman, Bernard A.
Guettel, Henry
Guilford, Carol
Gutterson, Lyman P.
Gutterson, Mrs. Lyman P.
*Gwenn, Edmund
*Haagsma, Alvira P.
Hackett, Buddy
*Hackett, James K.
Hadley, Arthur G.
Hagen, Uta
Hahlo, Jet
Hahlo, Sylvia
Haines, Larry
Hale, Allan
*Hale, Creighton
Hale, Frank J.
*Hale, Louis Closser
*Hall, Charles P.
Hall, Patricia
*Hall, Thurston
Hamer, Gerald
*Hamilton, Henry H. Jr.
Hamilton, Jane
Hamilton, Laura
Hamilton, Margaret
Hammerstein, James
*Hammerstein, Oscar 2nd
*Hammerstein, William
*Hammond, Virginia
*Hampden, Walter
Hampden, Mrs. Walter
*Hamper, Genevieve
Hampton, Hope
*Handy, George
*Handy, Mabel Thorndyke
Haney, Mrs. Earl P.
*Hanley, Martin W.
Hanna, Ruth R.
*Hans, David J.
Hanson, Gladys
*Harbach, Otto A.
Harding, Ann
Hardy, Joe
*Hardy, Sam B.
*Hardy, Mrs. Sam B.
Harmon, Charlotte
Harmon, Lewis

Harms, Carl
*Harrigan, Edward
Harrigan, Nedda
*Harrigan, William
*Harrington, Henry John
*Harrington, Joseph
*Harris, Charles
*Harris, Henry B.
*Harris, Mrs. Henry B.
Harris, Jeremiah
Harris, Jonathan
Harris, Joseph
Harris, Mrs. Joseph (Geraldine)
Harris, Joseph P.
Harris, Julie
Harris, Lewis H.
Harris, Lillian
Harris, Robert
*Harris, Sam H.
Harris, Victor
*Harris, William
*Harris, William Jr.
Harrison, Edward
*Harrison, James Dunbar
*Harrison, Robert S.
Harron, Donald
*Hart, Annie
*Hart, Bernard
Hart, Charles
*Hart, Max
*Hart, Moss
*Hart, Teddy
*Hartley, Frances
Hartley, Neil
Hartman, Paul
*Hartz, Al F.
Harvey, Kenneth
Harwood, Gwen
*Harwood, Harry
*Hassan, Edward J.
Hasso, Signe
*Hastings, Ernest
*Hastings, Harry
*Haswin, Carl A.
Haswin, Frances
Hatch, Ruth
*Haven, Jane
*Hawkins, R. C.
*Haworth, Joseph
*Hawthorne, Charles W.
Hayden, Mrs. Paul C.
Hayes, Helen
Hayes, Irene

Hayes, Vernon H. Jr.
*Hayman, Al
*Hayman, Alf.
*Heath, Thomas K.
Hecht, Albert
Heckart, Eileen
Heckscher, Ernest M.
Hedden, E. G.
*Hedges, Harry H.
*Hegeman, Alice
*Heiman, Marcus
*Hein, Silvio
Heineman, Bernard
*Heineman, Hermine Shone
*Helburn, Theresa
Hellender, Elsa S.
Heller, Betty Dair
Hellman, Lillian
Helm, Geneva
Helmers, June
*Helwitz, Aaron
Heming, Violet
*Henderson, Ettie
Henderson, Florence
*Henderson, Frank E.
*Henderson, William
Hendricks, Beatrice
*Hendricks, Ben
*Hendrickson, Rod
Henninger, Adolph T. Jr.
Henry, Bill
Hepburn, Katharine
*Hepner, William
Herd, Richard
*Herendeen, Fred
*Herk, I. H.
Herlick, Jety
Herlie, Eileen
*Hermann, Alexander
Herndon, Dixie Dunbar
*Herne, Chrystal
*Herne, James A.
*Herne, Mrs. John
*Herrmann, U. J.
Hershfield, Harry
*Hersholt, Jean
Herz, William Jr.
Hewitt, Alan
*Heyward, Mrs. Dubose
*Hickey, Sylvester M.
Hickox, Harry
Highland, Geo. Arthur
*Highley, Richard

Hildegarde
*Hildreth, Albert W.
Hildreth, Margaret E.
Hill, Arthur
*Hill, Gus
*Hill, Mrs. Gus
*Hill, Harry H. (Metz)
Hill, James N. B.
*Hill, Kenneth
*Hilliard, Hazel E.
*Hilliard, Mack
Hilt, Ferdinand
*Hines, Earle Remington
Hirsh, Anna
*Hirsh, Louis A.
Hirshhorn, Naomi Caryl
Hirst, Frank S.
*Hitchcock, Mrs. Raymond
*Hobart, George V.
Hobbs, Rebekah
*Hodge, William
*Hoerle, Helen
*Hoey, William F.
Hoffman, Bern
*Hoffmann, Gertrude
*Hoffmann, Max
Hofford, Mrs. H. Ray
Hogsett, Marie
*Hohl, Arthur
*Holbrook, Carrie
*Holbrook, Joshua
Holden, Fay
*Holland, E. M.
*Holland, Joseph J.
*Holliday, Judy
Holly, Margaret M.
Holm, Celeste
Holm, Jan
*Holmes, Coney
*Holmes, Rapley
Homan, Edward A.
*Hooley, R. M.
*Hope, Francis X.
*Hopkins, Arthur
Hopkins, Miriam
Hoppenfeld, Elsa
*Hopper, De Wolf
*Hopper, Edna Wallace
*Hopper, George F.
Horkheimer, Ellwood D.
*Horkheimer, H. M.
*Horlick, William
Horner, Richard

*Jessel, Patricia
*Jewell, Helen
Jewell, Izetta
*Johnson, Ben
*Johnson, "Chic"
*Johnson, J. Moffat
*Johnson, Orrin
*Johnson, Tefft
Johnson, Mrs. Tefft
Johnston, Justine A.
*Jolson, Al
Jones, Al
Jones, Barry
Jones, Charlotte
Jones, Hazel
*Jones, Henry Arthur
Jones, Jennifer
Jones, Philip Cary
Jones, Viola Paulson
*Jordan, Walter C.
Jory, Victor
Jostyn, Jay
Joyce, James J.
Judd, Carl C.
*Juliska, Gyori
*Jungen, Grace
Kadison, Harry
*Kalmine, Harry M.
Kaminskas, Charles
Kane, Mikel
Kanin, Garson
Kaplan, M. C.
*Karloff, Boris
Karolyi, Elizabeth
Kasha, Lawrence N.
Kaufman, Albert A.
*Kaufman, George S.
*Kaufman, S. Jay
*Kaye, Benjamin
Kaye, Danny
Keach, Stacy
Kean, Norman
*Keane, Davis
Keegan, Robert
Keel, Howard
*Keenan, Frank
Keenan, Harry G.
*Keene, Thomas W.
*Keit, John J.
*Keith, B. F.
Keith, Dorothy Tierney
*Keith, Paul
*Keith, Robert L.

*Kelcey, Herbert
*Keller, A. M.
*Kelley, Barney
Kelley, Francis Beverly
Kellogg, Gertrude
Kelly, Charles P.
Kelly, Emmett L.
*Kelly, Patrick J.
*Kelly, Paul
*Kelly, Walter C.
*Kelly, William J.
*Kemper, Collin
*Kendall, Messmore
*Kendall, Ruby Marion
Kennedy, Bob
*Kennedy, E. G.
Kennedy, Madge
Kennedy, Mary
Kennedy, Mildred Mickey
Kennedy, Hon. Stephen P.
Kenney, Wm. E. (Billy)
Keogh, Agnes Carlton
*Keogh, William T.
*Kernan, James L.
Kerr, Geoffrey
Kerr, John
Kerr, Philip
*Kershaw, Willette
Keyes, Donald
*Keyser, Irving A.
Keyser, Pearl
*Kidder, Kathryn
Kiefer, John A.
*Kilbride, Percy
*Kilbride, Richard
*Kimball, Jennie
King, Edith
*King, Josephine Cameron
*King, Leslie
King, Lila Rhodes
King, Madeleine
*Kingsford, Walter
Kingsley ,Sidney
*Kingston, Winifred
*Kiplinger, Mrs. M. L.
Kippe, Sonny
*Kirby, William E.
Kirkpatrick, Scott
*Kirkwood, James
Kitchen, David
Kitchen, Frances Cameron
*Klaw, Marc
*Klawans, Bernard

*Klein, Charles
*Kleist, A. J. Jr.
 Klenk, W. Clifford Jr.
 Klipstein, Abner D.
 Klipstein, Randy Brett
*Knight, Frederick
*Knight, John
 Knight, June
*Knight, Mary Eleanor
 Knill, C. Edwin
*Knowles, Edwin F.
*Koerfer, Henry J.
*Koerper, Mrs. Henry J.
 Koestler, Isabel
 Kohn, Marvin
 Kolen, Anita B.
 Kornblatt, Samuel F.
*Kornzweig, Ben
 Kornzweig, Mrs. Benjamin
 Korvin, Charles
 Kosta, Tessa
 Kramer, Fred D.
 Kramer, Leslie A.
 Kranz, Benjamin D.
 Kreling, Mrs. Ernestine
*Krembs, Felix
 Kressen, Sam
 Kron, Arthur A.
 Krones, Fred H.
 Kruger, Otto
 Kurlan, David
*Kurtz, Harry L.
 Kusell, Harold
 Kutlow, Thomas
*Kyle, Howard
*Kyle, Mrs. Howard
*Lackaye, Helen
*Lackaye, James
*Lahr, Bert
 Laire, Judson
 Lambert, Sherry
*Lamont, Jennie
 Lamour, Dorothy
 Landau, Lucy
*Landis, Jessie Royce
 Landry, Alma R.
 Lang, Murray
 Langford, Frederic
*Langner, Lawrence
*Langtry, Lillian
 Lansbury, Angela
 La Pidus, Edward M.
 La Pidus, Mrs. Edward M.

 Larsen, Rosemary
*Larson, Robert G.
*Lasky, Jesse L.
 Lastfogel, Abe
 Latham, Cynthia B.
*Latham, Fred G.
*Lauder, Edwin G. Jr.
*Laurie, Joe Jr.
 La Verne, Eddie
 La Verne, Grace
*La Verne, Lucille
*Lawford, Ernest
 Lawlor, David
*Lawrence, Arthur R.
*Lawrence, Gertrude
 Lawrence, Lawrence Shubert Jr.
*Lawrence, Pam
*Lawrence, Robert Webb
*Lawrence, Walter
*Lawrence, Walter N.
 Layton, Joe
*Leahy, W. H.
*Lean, Cecil
*Learock, Henri (Tony Williams)
*Leblang, Joseph
*Le Clair, Maggie
*Le Conte, Fred E.
*Lee, Jane Elisabeth Banahan
*Lee, Katherine Elisabeth Banahan
 Lee, Lorraine Sobel
 Lee, Valerie
 Lee, Will
 Lefkowitz, Nat
 LeGallienne, Eva
 Lehman, Martin
 Leigh, Gilbert
*Leigh, Mabel
*Leigh, Vivien
 Leins, Herman S.
 Lek, Nico
*Leland, Rosa M.
 Le Massena, William
 Lemmon, Jack
 Le Noire, Rosetta
 Leon, Joseph
 Leonard, David A.
 Leonard, Jack E.
 Leonard, Margaret
 Leonard, Marion
 Leoree, Joanne
 Lerner, Alan Jay
 Le Roy, Adele
*Leslie, Bert

*Le Soir, Jane Schenck
Lesser, Sol
Lester, Edwin
Levene, Sam
Levenson, Sam
*Leventhal, Jules J.
Lever, Charles
Levere, Rose
Levin, Herman
Levine, Dave
*Levitt, M. B.
Levkova, Sonja
Levy, Asher
*Lewers, William H.
*Lewin, Herman
Lewis, Abby
*Lewis, Ada
Lewis, Brayton
*Lewis, Dave
Lewis, David
*Lewis, Fred Irving
*Lewis, Jack X.
*Lewis, Joe E.
*Lewis, Kathryn Howard
Lewis, Michael
*Lewis, Ted
*Liddy, Pat F.
Lieberman, Judge A.
*Liebling, William
Liebman, Mrs. Max
Lieff, Irving
Liff, Samuel
*Light, Norman
Light, Mrs. Norman
Lilley, Edward Clarke
Lilley, Pauline G. MacLean
Lillie, Beatrice
*Lincoln, E. K.
Lindblom, Maria de Gerlando
Linden, Hal
*Lindroth, Helen
*Lindsay, Howard
*Ling, Richie
Linn, Bambi
Lipsky, David
Lipson, Paul R.
*Litel, John B.
*Litt, Jacob
*Little, Anna
Little, Guy S. Jr.
*Liveright, Horace B.
Llewellyn, Barbara C.
Llewellyn, Col. John G.

Lloyd, Prince
Lochner, Don
*Locke, Mabel Dunham
*Lockhart, Gene
Lockhart, Jeanne B.
Lockhart, June K.
Lodge, Marguerite
*Loeb, Philip
Loew, Mildred Z.
Loewe, Frederick
*Loftus, Cecilia
Logan, Joshua
Loiacono, Carmine
Lonergan, Lenore
Long, Sumner A.
*Longfellow, Mrs. Henry W.
*Lo Porto, Camille J.
Lord, Walter
Loring, August T.
Loring, Mrs. Royden
Lo Russo, Joseph P.
Lotito, Louis A.
Lotito, Mrs. Louis A.
*Lotto, Fred
*Lovejoy, Frank
*Lovely, John
*Lovenberg, Charles
*Loverich, Samuel
Lowe, Eugene K.
Lowe, Ralph
*Lowell, Helen
*Lowry, Rudd
Loy, Myrna
Lucas, J. Frank
Luce, Claire
Ludlam, Helen
Lukas, Karl
Luke, Keye
Luley, Frank
Lummis, Dayton
Lunt, Alfred
Luria, Joan
*Lurie, Louis R.
*Lytell, Bert
*Lytton, Louis
McAllister, Paul
*McAree, John
McCaffrey, William
*McCallen, Agnes Carroll
*McCann, W. R.
McCarthy, Frances
McCarthy, James
*McCarthy, Joe

McCarthy, Viola
McCauley, Amy Revere
McCauley, John B.
*McClanahan, Barbara
*McCleery, Albert K.
*McClelland, Charles F.
*McComas, Carroll
*McCormack, Frank
*McCormick, Myron
*McCourt, Peter
*McCowan, John J.
*McCoy, Frank
*McDermott, Aline
McDevitt, Ruth
McDonald, Leo
McDonald, William
McGauley, Hugh J.
McGeehan, John R.
McGrath, Mrs. Michael F.
*McGrath, Thomas
McGuire, Dorothy
*McGuirk, John
McHenry, Don
*McHenry, Nellie
McHugh, Frank C.
*McIntyre, Frank
*McIntrye, James
*McKean, Ethel
*McKee, Frank
McKnight, Vince
McLain, George W.
*McLaughlin, Leonard B.
McLauthlin, Muriel L.
McMahon, Clarissa
*McMahon, Rod
McMartin, John
McNab, Horace Greeley
McNally, Horace V.
McNeil, Claudia
*McNeill, Lillian
McNulty, M. E.
*McPartland, Edwin
McPartland, John F.
McPeake, Edith H.
McQueen, Butterfly
McQueen, Steve
*McRae, Bruce
*McVicker, J. H.
*McWade, Robert
MacArthur, James
Macbeth, Edna
MacDonald, Eva
*MacDonald, Jeanette

*MacDonald, Nan
Macfarlane, Mrs. John
MacIntyre, Elizabeth
*Mack, Andrew
*Mack, Mrs. Andrew
*Mack, Bobby
*Mack, J. Herbert
Mack, Jess
*Mackay, F. F.
*MacKellar, Helen
*MacKenna, Kenneth
*MacLarnie, Thomas
MacLaughlin, Don
*MacLean, Douglas
Mac Mahon, Aline
MacNichol, Mrs. Gordon E.
Macollum, Barry
*Macomber, Sherwood G.
*MacQuarrie, George
*MacSweeney, John P.
Macy, William
Madann, Michael
Madden, William
Maharis, George
Maibaum, Norman
Maidman, Irving
Maison, Edith
Malcolm, Edith Fisk
*Malcolm, John
Malden, Karl
Mallicoat, Basil B.
*Mallory, Marshall H.
*Malone, Pat
*Maloney, John J.
Maltby, Myrna Dean
*Manchester, Robert
*Mandel, Frank
*Mandelstam, Abraham
*Maney, Richard
*Mann, Harry
*Mann, Louis
*Mannering, Mary
Manners, Jayne
Mannix, Julie
*Mansfield, Richard
*Mansfield, Mrs. Richard
*Mantell, Robert B.
Mantia, Charles
*Mantle, Burns
Manulis, John Bard
Marcato, Robert E.
Marcato, Russelle
March, Fredric

Mardo, Fred
*Marian, Annie
*Marian, Frank (Patrick)
*Marinoff, Fania
*Marion, George F.
*Markham, Frances
Markson, Greta
Marlow, William J.
Marno, Marc
Marone, Terry
*Marron, Louis
Marshall, Armina
*Marshall, Edna
*Marshall, Herbert
Marshall, Jay
Marshall, Pat
*Marston, John
*Martell, Oliver
Martin, Ernest H.
Martin, Helen D.
*Martin, Mrs. Jacques
Martin, Mary
Martin, Nan
*Martinot, Sadie
Martyniuk, Helen
Marvin, Earl C.
Marx, Albert L.
*Marx, Melville
*Mascolo, Emma
*Mason, Reginald
Massey, Raymond
Masters, Polly Jo McCulloch
Masterson, Harris
*Mather, Charles P.
Mathews, Carmen
*Matthews, Bert
Matthews, Hale
*Matthison, Edith Wynne
*Maude, Cyrill
Maude, Margery
Maxwell, Marguerite
May, Jean
*Mayfield, Cleo
*Mayo, Alfred
*Mayo, Edwin F.
Meadows, Audrey
Meadows, Jayne
Mearian, Mike
Meeker, Dainty Marie
Meeker, Earl Franklin
Meeker, James Matthew
Meeker, Ralph
Meeks, Louise Furlong

Meighan, James E. Sr.
*Meighan, Thomas
Meiser, Edith
Melfo, Frank
Melfo, Therese
*Melford, George H.
Melnick, Jack
*Melville, Rose
Menard, Paul H. A.
Mendelson, Bert L.
Mendelson, Ruth
*Mendum, Georgie Drew
*Menjou, Adolphe J.
*Menken, Helen
Menken, Kenneth C.
*Menzeli, Elizabeth
Meredith, Burgess
*Merivale, Philip
Merkel, Una
Merle, Janet
Merman, Ethel
Merrell, Jan Miner
Merrell, Richard
Merrill, Beth
Merriman, Randy
Meskill, Katherine
Messer, Mrs. Theodore P.
*Metcalfe, Earl
Metz, Raymond G.
Meyer, Charles
Meyer, Edgar
Meyer, M. E.
*Meyerfeld, Morris
*Meyers, Beatrice
*Meyers, Max Lang
*Meyers, Paul Henry
Meyers, Peter
*Meyers, Sam
*Miaco, Thomas E.
Michel, Mrs. Leon
Mielziner, Jo
*Miller, Bertha Lovejoy
Miller, Charles W.
*Miller, Eddie
*Miller, Gilbert
Miller, Mrs. Gilbert
*Miller, Henry
*Miller, James E.
*Miller, James S.
Miller, Leatta
*Miller, Marilyn
*Miller, Marshall
Miller, Marvin

Miller, Oscar
*Mills, Frank
*Miltern, J. E.
*Miner, Edwin D.
*Miner, H. Clay
*Miner, Henry C.
Miner, Henry C. Jr.
*Miner, Thomas W.
Minot, Anna
*Mitchell, Grant
*Mitchell, Irving
*Mitchell, Maggie
Mitchell, Ruth
*Mitchell, Thomas
*Modjeska, Helena
*Moller, John
Molter, Mrs. Walter H.
Mong, Mrs. Chas. Leroy
*Monroe, Geo. W.
Monroe, Helen
Monroe, Lucy
Montague, John
*Montague, Mrs. John I.
Montand, Yves
*Montfort, Stanley
*Montgomery, Elizabeth
Moore, Carroll Jr.
Moore, Dennie
Moran, Betty Joan
*Mordaunt, Frank
*Moreno, Antonio M.
Moreno, Rita
Morgan, Claudia
Morgan, Cosmo
*Morgan, Helen
Morgan, Henry
*Morgan, Kate
Morgan, Kathleen P.
*Morosco, Oliver
*Morris, Chester
*Morris, Felice T.
*Morris, Felix
Morris, Katie
Morris, Mary Margaret
*Morris, Mildred H.
Morris, Ruth H. E.
*Morris, William
*Morris, Mrs. William
Morris, William Jr.
*Morrisey, John
Morrison, Bret
*Morrison, Helen Stewart
Morrison, Irving

Morrison, Martin M.
*Morrison, Mary Horne
*Morrow, Doretta
Morse, Robert
*Morton, William H.
Mosconi, Charles S.
*Moss, B. S.
*Moss, Paul
*Moss, Theodore
Mostel, Zero
Mott, Hamilton
*Moulton, Harold M.
*Mountford, Harry
Mower, Margaret
*Moxley, George Baine
Muchnick, Ronald
*Mudge, Mrs. Augusta V.
*Mudie, Leonard
Mulhern, Leonard A.
Mulkeen, Mrs. James P.
*Muni, Paul
Munsel, Patrice
Munsell, Warren P.
Munsell, Mrs. Warren P.
*Munsell, Warren P. Jr.
Munsell, Mrs. Warren P. Jr.
*Murdock, Ann
*Murdock, J. J.
Murphy, Mrs. Harry J.
Murphy, James J.
Murphy, John F.
Murphy, Kathryn Walsh
Murray, Betty
Murray, Jan
Murray, Lola
*Murray, Martin M.
Myerson, Bess
Myrtil, Odette
*Nagel, Conrad
Nalchajian, Mrs. Willard D.
*Nash, Florence
*Nash, George
Nash, Mary
Nasker, William H.
Natwick, Mildred
*Nazimova, Alla
Nazzo, Angelo
Nederlander, James
*Neher, John W.
Neill, Louise W.
*Neilson, Caroline
Nekola, Louis William
Nell, Maralyn

*Nelmes, Harry B.
Nelson, Barry
Nelson, Gene
*Nelson, Ruth
*Neslo, Henry Craig
Nettleton, Lois
*Newburger, Mrs. I. Edward
Newhall, Patricia
*Newman, Charles
*Newman, John K.
*Newman, Ray
*Newton, Theodore
*Niblo, Fred
*Nichols, Anne
*Nichols, Eldon
Nichols, Elsie J.
Nichols, Josephine
Nichtern, Claire
Nicol, Alexander L. Jr.
*Nicolai, George H.
Nielsen, Karl
Niesen, Gertrude
Nigro, Harry
Nigro, Joyce P.
*Niven, Philip
*Nixon, S. F.
Noa, Jane Salisbury
*Noa, Julian
Nobile, Mrs. Anthony P.
Noble, Ruth
*Nobles, Dollie
*Nobles, Milton
Nolan, Jeanette
Nolan, Lloyd B.
*Noonan, Frank J.
North, Clyde
North, Elizabeth
Norton, Coe
Norton, Lola Andre
Nugent, Elliott
Nuyen, France
*Oakland, Mrs. Will
*Ober, Robert H.
Oberon, Merle
*Oberworth, Louis Jacques
O'Brien, Josephine
O'Brien, Pat
O'Brien, Rt. Rev. Thomas J.
*O'Connell, Hugh
O'Connor, Edward J.
*O'Connor, Una
O'Connor, Walter G.
O'Connor, Mrs. Walter G.

O'Dell, Larry
O'Donnell, Eve
O'Donnell, John E.
Ogden, Angela
*Ogden, Vivia
*O'Hara, Charles
*O'Hara, Fiske
O'Hara, Mrs. Fiske
O'Hara, Warren
*O'Hay, Cap't. Irving
*O'Keefe, Dennis
*Olcott, Chauncey
*Olcott, Mrs. Chauncey
*Olcott, Sidney
Olesen, Oscar E.
Oliver, Burns
Oliver, Clarence (Larry)
*Oliver, Edna May
Olivier, Sir Laurence
Olsen, Carl
Olsen, Janice
*Olsen, John S. "Ole"
*Olver, Hal
O'Malley, William J.
O'Malley, Wini Shaw
O'Neal, Frederick
O'Neil, Betty
*O'Neil, James
*O'Neill, Frank F.
*O'Neill, James C.
O'Neill, James L.
*Onorato, James Michael
*Onri, Adele Purvis
Oppenheim, Justin S.
*Oppenheimer, S. C.
Oram, Harold
*O'Ramey, Georgia
*O'Rourke, Tex
Orr, Mary C.
Ortega, Santos
Osborn, Paul
*Osgood, Charles
*Oshier, Irene
*Oshrin, George
Ostertag, Barna
*Ostrander, Leslie Ira
O'Sullivan, Maureen
*Packard, Mrs. Beaumont
Paget, Ffolliet
Pagliaro, Sam
*Painter, Eleanor
*Palmer, Albert M.
Palmer, Betsy

*Proctor, David Gould
*Proctor, F. F.
*Proctor, Mrs. F. F.
Proctor, James D.
*Purcell, Charles
Purcell, Mrs. Charles
*Pyper, George D.
Qualen, John M.
Quick, George
Quinn, Anthony
*Quirk, William
*Quitman, Max D.
*Rains, Claude
Rains, Jessica
Raitt, John
*Ralph, Jessie
*Ramey, Margaret P.
Randall, Anthony L.
*Randall, William W.
Randell, Ron
Randolph, Donald
Randolph, John
Randolph, Joyce
Randolph, Mimi
*Rankin, Phyllis
*Ranney, Frank
*Rapley, W. H.
*Rathbun, William J.
*Ratoff, Gregory
*Ravold, John D.
Rawley, Ernest M.
*Ray, Helen
Raymond, Gene
*Reano, Bob
*Rechelle, Lizzie
*Reed, Florence
Reed, Philip
*Reed, Roland
*Reeves, Al H.
*Reicher, Frank
Reid, Carl Benton
Reid, Elliott
*Reid, John H.
Reiley, Helen Baysinger
*Reilly, George
Reilly, Hugh
Reilly, John J.
Reiner, Carl
Reiner, Elaine Ellis
*Reinold, Bernard Adolph
Reiter, Hazel McLaughlin
*Rennie, James
*Rennie, Mrs. James

Repetto, Mrs. F. Edward
Reynolds, Charles H.
Reynolds, W. J.
*Rhea, Mlle. Hortense
Ribner, Clayre
*Rich, Charles J.
Rich, Irene
*Rich, Isaac B.
*Richard, George N.
*Richards, Augustus
*Richardson, Thomas H.
Richman, Harry
Richmond, Ruth
Rickles, Don
Riemer, Walter
*Riggs, Benjamin
Rimmer, Mrs. Frank H.
Rinaldo, William J.
*Ring, Blanche
*Ring, Frances
*Risdon, Elizabeth
Ritchard, Cyril
*Ritter, Thelma
Robards, Jason
Robbins, Barbara
Roberti, René
Roberts, George
Roberts, Mrs. George
Roberts, Maurice J.
*Roberts, Theodore
Robertson, William
*Robins, Edward H.
*Robinson, Bill
*Robinson, Charles A.
Robinson, Edward G.
*Robson, May
Rocco, Jean
Rock, Ella
Rodgers, Richard
Rodgers, Mrs. Richard
*Rodner, Harold
Roerick, William
*Rogers, David
*Rogers, Emmett
*Rogers, John R.
*Rogers, Lucille
Rogers, Saul E.
*Roig, Julio
Roland, Ed
Roman, Ruth
*Romberg, Sigmund
*Ronchetti, Gladys D.
Ronson, Adele

Rorke, Hayden
*Rose, Billy
Rose, Irene
Roseman, Yvonne
Rosen, Albert H.
*Rosen, Samuel
Rosenberg, Ben
Rosenberg, Mrs. Ben
*Rosenfeld, Sydney
*Rosenquest, J. Wesley
Roski, Margaret
*Ross, Harriet
*Ross, Hope
Ross, Lanny
*Ross, Lee
Ross, Paul L.
*Ross, Thomas W.
*Ross, Mrs. Thomas W.
Ross, William
Rossi, Frank P.
*Rosskam, Charles H.
Roth, Helen
*Roth, Joseph
Roth, Lillian B.
Rotondo, Peter Joseph
Routledge, Patricia
*Royle, Edwin Milton
*Row, Arthur William
Rowan, Frank M.
Rubber, Violla
Rubin, Arthur
Rubin, Mrs. Arthur
Rubin, Jack
*Rubin, J. Robert
Rucinski, June Blane
Rueff, Annette Herbert
*Ruggles, Charles
*Ruman, Sig
*Runkle, Edgar
*Rush, Isadore
Russell, Evelyn
*Russell, Harold
*Russell, Jay
*Russell, R. Fulton
*Russell, R. Fulton Jr.
Rutter, Lillian H.
*Ruyle, Ben
*Ryan, Alice G.
*Ryan, Elsa
*Ryan, James J.
*Ryan, Mae Burgess
*Ryan, Mary
Ryan, Robert B.

Ryan, Thomas J.
Ryback, Dr. Julius
*Ryley, J. H.
Ryschkewich, Tanya
Sabinson, Eric
Sabinson, Harvey
Sabinson, Mrs. Harvey
*Sablosky, Abraham
*Sack, Nathaniel
*Sackett, "Mollie Revel"
Sager, Max
*St. James, Rhea Bacon
*St. James, William H.
St. John, Howard
Saitta, Peter
Sallee, Hilmar
*Sammis, George W.
Samples, M. David
*Sampson, William
*Sampter, Martin
Samrock, Victor
*Sanders, Albert
Sanders, Honey
Sanderson, Julia
Sands, Dorothy
Sanford, Cordelia R.
*Sanford, Walter
*Sanford, Mrs. Walter
*Sanger, Frank W.
Sardi, Vincent Jr.
Sarnoff, Daniel Jay
Saul, Hyman
*Saunders, John E.
*Sauter, James
*Savage, Henry W.
*Savo, Jimmy
Sawyer, Mrs. Frank
*Schack, Harry
Schaefer, George J.
Schafer, Natalie
Schaff, George
*Schaff, Germaine
Schallen, William W.
*Schanberger, Fred C.
*Schanberger, Fred C. Jr.
Schanberger, J. L.
Schapiro, Seth
Schary, Dore
Schattner, Lenore Tobin
Schattner, Meyer
Scheer, Jules
*Scheff, Fritzi
*Schildkraut, Joseph

*Schiller, Samuel
*Schira, Adam
 Schlesinger, Leon
 Schlissel, Jack
*Schnebbe, Allan J.
 Schneider, Bert
 Schneider, Irving
 Schneider, John J.
 Schnitzer, Robert C.
 Schnur, Jerome
*Schoeffel, Agnes Booth
 Schoen, Jules
 Schoenfeld, Gerald
 Schreiber, Virginia
 Schwartz, Betty
 Schwartz, David S.
 Schwartz, Jean A.
 Schwartz, Samuel H.
 Schwartzman, Ethyl Van Riper
 Schwartzman, Sam
 Schwenk, Herman C. Jr.
*Schwenk, Dr. J. A.
 Scott, Alan R.
*Scott, Cyril
 Scott, Donald
*Scott, L. N.
 Scott, Lizabeth
 Scott, Martha
 Scott, Ray
 Scourby, Alexander
*Scribner, Sam A.
*Seamans, Nina A.
 Seamon, Morrie R.
*Seddon, Margaret
 Seelig, Arthur
 Seida, Kuraji
 Seidman, David E.
*Seigman, Edward
 Selden, Albert
 Seldes, Marian
*Selwyn, Edgar
*Selznick, David O.
 Selznick, Irene Mayer
 Senate, Muriel
*Senfeld, Dr. Matthew M.
*Serlin, Oscar
 Serlin, Mrs. Oscar
 Seymour, Anne
 Seymour, John Davenport
*Seymour, May Davenport
*Seymour, William
*Shafer, George
 Shaff, Monty

*Shannon, Effie
*Shannon, Frank L.
 Shannon, Margie Dalton
 Shatner, William
*Shauer, Emil E.
 Shaw, Reta
 Shaw, Robert
 Shayne, Al
*Shea, Michael
*Shedd, Mrs. Frederick
 Sheehan, Jerome J.
 Sheehan, Tess
*Sheldon, Arthur
*Sheldon, H. S.
 Shelley, Rev. William
*Shelton, George C.
*Sheridan, Frank
 Sheridan, Mrs. Frank
*Sheridan, John Carroll
*Sheridan, Phil H.
 Sherman, Hiram
 Sherman, Paula
*Sherman, Robert
*Sherry, William L.
 Sherwood, Lorraine
 Shevett, Irene
*Shields, Helen
 Shipley, Charles W.
 Shoemaker, Ann
*Shoninger, Frederick E.
 Shoninger, Katherine Murray
*Short, Florence
*Short, Harry
*Short, Hassard
*Shriner, Herb
*Shubert, J. J.
*Shubert, John
*Shubert, Lee
*Shubert, Commander Milton
 Shumlin, Herman
*Shurr, Lester
 Shwartz, Martin
*Sidman, Sam
 Signoret, Simone
*Sills, Milton
 Silver, Sam
 Silvers, Phil
*Simmons, Vi Bowers
 Simon, Louis M.
*Simpson, Ivan
 Simpson, Pamela
*Sinclair, George H.
*Sinn, William E.

*Sinn-Hecht, Isabel
Sirola, Joseph A.
Skala, Lilia
Skelley, Hugh
Skelly, Madge
Skinner, Cornelia Otis
*Skinner, Otis
*Slavin, John
Slezak, Walter
*Smart, J. Scott
*Smirl, Harry
Smith, Albert C.
Smith, Albert E.
Smith, Alexis
*Smith, C. Aubrey
Smith, Edward L.
Smith, Ethel Ursuline
Smith, Mrs. Henry E.
Smith, Joe
Smith, Kent
*Smith, Lee Thompson
Smith, Loring B.
Smith, Philip John
Smith, Sammy
Smith, Truman C.
Smith, Will C.
*Smith, Winchell
*Snader, Edward L.
*Snelling, Winthrop
*Solomon, Lep
*Solomon, Tessie
Solotar, Jacqueline
Soloway, Leonard
Solters, Lee
Somers, Donald Benton
Somlyo, Roy A.
Sommers, Ben
*Sommers, Harry G.
*Sosso, Pietro
Soteras, Dorothea
*Sothern, Edward H.
*Sousa, John Philip
Southern, Hugh
*Spachner, Leon
*Specter, Julius
Spencer, Clinton
Spiegelberg, Barbara J.
*Spitz, Eugene
Spratt, Charles E.
*Stack, Josephine Evans
Stafford, Mrs. George F.
*Stahl, Rose
*Stair, E. D.

*Standing, Sir Guy
*Standing, Herbert
*Stanford, Henry
*Stanton, Edmund C.
Stanwyck, Barbara
Starr, Frances
*Steel, Oscar B.
Steele, Virginia Spottswood
Stehli, Edgar
Steinberg, Harry
*Steinert, Mrs. Alexander
Steinhauer, Edward W.
*Stept, Sam H.
Stevens, K. T.
Stevens, Lee
*Stevens, Sydney G.
*Stevenson, Charles A.
*Stevenson, Earle W.
Stevenson, Isabelle
*Stewart, A. A.
*Stewart, Charles G.
Stewart, Genevieve
Stewart, James
Stewart, J. Ross
Stewart, Robert Wood
Stickney, Dorothy
Stillman, Louise Huff
Stinnette, Dorothy
Stoddard, Margaret
*Stoker, Floyd W.
Stone, Carol
Stone, Dorothy
Stone, Ezra
*Stone, Fred
Stone, Harold J.
*Stone, Julius
Stone, Norman J.
Stone, Theodore
Stoneburn, Tilda
Stonzek, Morris
*Storrs, Frank Vance
Story, Bill
*Strakosch, Claire
Strasberg, Susan
*Stratton, Samuel R.
Straub, Mrs. Mary W.
*Straus, Lionel F. Jr.
Straus, Sylvie
*Stroock, James E.
Struble, Helen Gates
*Stryker, Gustave A.
*Stryker, Rex
Stuart, Doris Rich

*Stuart, Ralph
Stuckmann, Eugene
Sturtevant, Collin
Styne, Jule
Sullivan, Ed
Sullivan, Liam
*Sullivan, Neil
Sullivan, Pauline E.
Sullivan, Thomas D.
Sulzberger, Mrs. Arthur Hays
*Summerville, Amelia
*Sumner, Engel
*Sun, Gus
Sun, Gus Jr.
*Sun, John
Surace, Francis Anthony
*Sutherland, Albert
Sutherland, Albert Ed.
Sutton, Dolores
Sutton, Henry R.
*Sutton, Kitty
*Swan, Ethel F.
*Sweeney, Joseph
*Sweet, Mrs. Alfred J.
*Sweet, Chandos
Swete, E. Lyall
Sweyd, Lester
Swire, Willard
Swope, Herbert Jr.
Swope, John
Sylva, Daphinee
*Taber, Richard
Taishoff, Sol
*Talbot, Lewis
*Taliaferro, Edith
Taliaferro, Mabel
*Tamminga, Ethel
Tandy, Jessica
Tannehill, Frances
*Tannen, Julius
Tannenbaum, Samuel W.
Tanner, Annette Simonet
*Tanner, Wilson P.
Taviner, Edgar N.
Taykee, Princess To'Naya
*Taylor, Dr. M. Sayle
Taylor, Philip P.
*Taylor, Stanner E. V.
Taylor, Mrs. Stanner E. V.
*Teal, Ben
*Tearle, Godfrey
*Tellegen, Lou
Templeton, Olive

Tender, George
*Terriss, Tom
Terry, Helen
Tesoriere, S. A.
*Thall, Mark
*Thall, Sam
*Tharp, Norman
Thatcher, Leora
*Thayer, Mrs. Ezra R.
*Thayer, Royale
*Thayer, Mrs. Royale
Thibault, Conrad
*Thomas, Augustus
*Thomas, Charles H.
*Thomas, Charles W.
Thomas, Christine
*Thomas, John Charles
*Thomas, Ruth
*Thomas, Walter
*Thomaschefsky, Boris
*Thompson, Charles H.
Thompson, Charles P.
*Thompson, Denman
*Thompson, Fred
*Thompson, Marion B.
Thompson, Mrs. Richard L.
Thomson, Archie
*Thorne, Harry
*Thorne, Millie
*Thurston, Adelaide
*Tiller, Leo
Tobin, Genevieve
Tobin, Vivian
*Todd, James
*Todd, Michael
Tombes, Andrew
*Tompkins, Eugene
Tonken, Philip
*Totten, Edyth
Townes, Harry
Tozere, Frederic
*Tracey, Thomas P.
Tracy, Arthur
*Tracy, Lee
Traubee, Jacques
*Travers, Henry
Treacher, Arthur
Treacher, Mrs. Arthur
Tremayne, Les
Trevor, Claire
*Trovato, Tony Arcaro
Truskauskas, Juozas
Tucker, Forrest

*Tucker, Sophie
*Tupper, Sheridan
*Turner, George
Tustin, Florence
*Tyler, George C.
*Tynan, Brandon
*Vail, William J.
Valdemar, Odette Carey
Valle, Luis
*Van, Billy B.
*Van Beuren, Ameede J.
*Van Buren, A. H.
*Vanderbilt, Gertrude
Vanderbilt, Gloria
VanderKloot, Robert
*Van Horn, Rollin Weber
Van Runkle, Al
*Van Vechten, Carl
*Varden, Evelyn
*Vekroff, Perry
Velie, Jay A.
*Velsey, Graham
*Vermilyea, Harold
*Vincent, Eva L.
*Vincent, Frank W.
*Vincent, Walter
*Vinton, Arthur R.
Vitelli, Vincent B.
*Vogel, Joseph R.
Vola, Vicki
Vollono, Mrs. Vincent J.
von Zerneck, Frank
Vroom, Paul
Waddington, Patrick
*Wagenhals, Lincoln A.
Wagner, David
Wagoner, Maria Ascarra
*Walburn, Raymond
*Waldron, Charles H.
Waldron, Harriett Fowler
*Waldron, Jack
Waldron, Martin
Walker, Cora
Walker, D. S.
Walker, Johnny
Walker, Nancy
*Walker, Stuart
Walker, Sydney
Wallace, Regina
Wallace, Vesta Ethel
Wallach, Eli
Wallach, Florence
*Walsh, Blanche

Walsh, Blanche Slattery
Walters, Casey
*Walters, Charles L.
Walters, Henry A.
Walters, J. Henry
Walters, Mimi
Walterstein, Al
*Walton, Charles
*Walton, Eugene W.
Ward, Charles
*Ward, Fannie
*Ward, Hugh J.
*Ward, Mary
*Ware, Helen
*Warfield, David
Warlock, Robert
*Warner, Major Albert
*Warner, Harry M.
Warren, Fran
Warriner, Frederic
*Warrington, Ann
*Watson, Frederick
*Watson, Joseph K.
*Watson, Justice
Watson, Kathleen E.
*Watson, Lucile
*Watson, Minor
Watson, Mrs. Ralph G.
Watson, Vera
*Watson, William B.
Wayne, David
Wayne, Ken (F. Wayne Klaiss)
*Weber, John
*Weber, Joseph M.
*Webster, Harold McCloud
Wedge, Maura K.
Weidhaas, Arthur E.
*Weinburg, Gustave C.
*Weiner, Celia J.
*Weiner, Lawrence
Weiner, Norman Lewis
Weinstock, Helene B.
*Weintraub, Milton
Weisberg, Daniel
Weitzner, Lillian
Welch, Charles C.
*Welch, Jack
*Welch, Thomas
Wellesley, Arthur
*Wells, Charles B.
*Wells, Otto
*Wendelschaefer, Felix R.
Werner, Gerson H.

Wessel, Isaac
*West, Buster
*West, Edna Rhys
West, Madge
*West, Olive
*West, Will
Weston, Edward
Weston, Mrs. Joseph F.
Whiffen, Peggy
*Whiffen, Mrs. Thomas
*Whippler, Truevilla
Whitcomb, Mrs. Stanwood E.
White, Charles
*White, Clayton E.
*White, George R.
White, Joan
White, Onna
White, Thomas H. Jr.
Whitelaw, Arthur
Whiteman, Charles
*Whiteman, Paul
Whitley, Albert
Whitman, Frank
Whitmore, James
*Whytal, Mrs. Russ
Whyte, Jerome
Whyte, Mrs. Jerome
Wiegand, William E.
*Wilder, Marshall P.
Wilder, Thornton
Wilkins, Polly R.
*Willard, E. S.
*Willat, Dr. C. A.
Willi, Arthur
Willi, Mrs. Arthur
*Williams, Arthur
Williams, Eleanor W.
Williams, Eva
Williams, George Francis
Williams, Gwilym
*Williams, H. Y.
*Williams, Harold
*Williams, Hattie
Williams, John
Williams, Mrs. John Burr
*Williams, Joseph R.
Williams, Lottie
*Williams, Malcolm
Williams, Malvina Roth
*Williams, Percy G.
*Williams, Tony
Willis, Austin
*Willis, Richard

Willmann, Mrs. Alfred W.
Willys, Mrs. John North
*Wilmer, Sidney
Wilmot, George
Wilson, Eleanor D.
*Wilson, Francis
*Wilson, George W.
Wilson, Hansford B.
Wilson, Henry W.
*Wilson, Jeanette
Wilson, Jessie L.
*Wilson, John C.
Wilson, Lois
Wilson, Lou
*Wilson, William
*Wiman, Anna Deere
*Wiman, Dwight Deere
*Winchell, Walter
Windom, William
*Winlocke, Isabelle
*Winninger, Charles J.
Winters, Marian
Winters, Maurice H.
Winters, Shelley
Wise, Berva G.
*Wise, Thomas A.
Wolf, Edward
Wolf, Jay
Wolff, Richard
Wolfington, Iggie
Wollett, Sidney
*Wood, George
Wood, Mrs. John C.
*Wood, Nicholas Schaberger
Wood, Peggy
*Woodall, Walter
*Woodruff, Henry
*Woods, A. H.
*Woods, Mrs. A. H.
Woods, Richard J.
*Woodward, George
Woolford, Guy
*Woolley, "Monty" Edgar
Worlock, Frederic G.
*Worthing, Frank
Wray, Fay
*Wright, Arthur W.
Wright, Bob
Wright, Ethel
Wright, Horace H.
Wright, Teresa
*Wyatt, H. C.
Wyatt, Jane

*Wynn, Ed
*Yale, Charles H.
*York, Chick
 Yorke, John
 Young, Aston S.
 Young, Gig
*Young, Loduski
*Young, Roland
 Yurdin, Anna

---

*Deceased

 Yurka, Blanche
*Zell, Gladys
*Zell, Violet J.
*Zoar, Millie
 Zorn, George
 Zukor, Adolph
 Zulkie, Lambert
 Zwissig, W. J.

ASSOCIATE LIFE MEMBERS

Adamec, Joseph
Adamson, Robert
Adler, Chas. Jr.
Ahrens, Theodore
*Amend, Ottilie
*Amory, John J.
Anable, Courtlandt V.
Anspach, Andrew A.
*Anspacher, Mrs. Louis K.
Apple, Mrs. Jerome
Armour, B. R.
*Asnas, Max
*Astor, Vincent
Atkins, Charles M.
Babin, Elmer J.
Babione, Sandra J.
*Bache, Jules S.
Baer, Julius B.
Baldinger, Milton I.
*Bamberger, Louis
Bangs, F. S.
Barnet, John S.
Baron, Irwin
*Baruch, Bernard M.
*Bascom, George
Bass, Robert
Bass, Mrs. Robert
Baumgarten, Paul J.
Beauregard, Vivian W.
Beck, Walter S.
Belth, Herman
*Benson, Bernard
*Berezniak, Leon A.
*Bernard, Betty
Bernard, Robert W.
Bernheim, Mrs. Lucile M.
*Billingsley, Sherman
*Bing, Leo S.
Blacher, Lillian
Blackwell, Jerry E.
*Bliss, William H.
Bloch, Harry
*Block, Jean
Bloom, Vera
Blum, Herman
*Blume, Joseph S.
Boardman, Mrs. Queen W.
Bogusch, Mrs. Ernst W.
*Boldt, George C.

Booth, Mrs. Benjamin H.
*Bourne, Fredk. G.
*Bowman, John McE.
Boynton, H. W.
*Brady, James Buchanan
Brandenstein, George
Breiner, Dr. John
*Briggs, C. A.
*Bristol, John I. D.
*Brokaw, George T.
Brown, Mrs. J. Thompson
Brown, Margaret L.
Bruckner, Martha P.
*Brundage, Mrs. J. Robert
*Bruns, Edwin G.
Buck, James P.
*Buhler, Joseph S.
*Burkan, Nathan
Burke, Joanna Arrington
Burns, Edward N.
Cabaniss, George H. Jr.
Calder, Mrs. Alexander Sr.
*Campbell, Frank E.
Carl, John W.
Cassel, Hugh
*Castle, W. A.
Chadwick, Mrs. E. Jerry
Chapin, Cornelia Van A.
Chapman, Rose Marie
Cheever, Mrs. H. Durant
Chopnick, Max
Christenberry, Robert K.
Churchill, James
Coakley, Mrs. Henry B.
Cohen, Louis J.
*Cohen, William W.
*Cole, Edward Franklyn
*Cole, Mrs. Edward Franklyn
Collins, Cecelia
Condit, Mrs. Hedwig S.
Cone, Frederic W.
Conried, Richard G.
*Cooke, Walter B.
Cooper, Mary
Cooper, S. Robert
Cousins, Sarah Louise
Crafts, Elisabeth S.
*Crandall, Edward H.
Cravath, Paul D.

Crehore, Mrs. Sara B.
Crocker, Hon. Edward S.
Crocker, Mrs. Edward S.
Croghan, John T.
Curtis, Wm. Edmund
D'Agostino, Maria
*Dane, William H. 3rd
Danzig, Aaron L.
Danziger, Daisy C.
Davidson, David
*Davidson, James E.
Davies, Julien T.
*Davis, Anna D.
Davis, Leslie
*Davis, Robert H.
*Davison, Daniel Frohman
Davison, Mrs. Daniel Frohman
Daw, Mrs. Harold J.
*Day, Joseph P.
Deane, Dr. W. C.
de Fieore, Michael
De Lamar, Alice A.
De Laura, Rt. Rev. Anthony F.
*Demoulin, Mrs. Edward A.
Deutsch, Joseph
Dexter, Mrs. Elliott
Doblin, Leo C.
*Donaldson, William H.
*Donaldson, Mrs. William H.
*Downey, James J.
*Downing, Euphemia
*Dreyfus, Mrs. Carolyn S.
Dronsick, Michael
Duffy, Bernard C.
Dumler, Egon
Dunn, Mrs. Harvey
*Earle, Dorothy Kirchner
Eckstein, M. Maurice
Eisenbach, Richard
*Elkan, Leo H.
Ellenbogen, Franklyn
Elliott, Alice
Engstrom, Mrs. C. William
*Fahy, Rev. Martin E.
Farrell, John R.
Fasse, Marie
Feathers, Henrietta
Feathers, Joan
Feathers, Mrs. Leonard C.
Feinman, Alfred
Feinson, Helene
*Feist, Leo
Ferber, David M.

*Ferriday, Elsie
Field, Mrs. Meyer
Fischer, Dr. N. Arthur
*Fleischmann, Paul W.
*Ford, Dorothy Jane
*Foster, Edwina
Fox, William Jr.
Fraunhar, Gilbert
*Freeman, Mrs. Hadley F.
Freeman, Dr. Sumner L.
Freen, Alfred
Freen, Mrs. Alfred
*Freiday, William
*Frick, Henry Clay
*Frieder, Dr. William
Friederich, Babette
*Friedsam, M.
Friend, Arthur S.
*Frohman, Emma
Frost, Betsy
Gaisman, Henry J.
Gardner, Rev. Gerald
Geist, Irving
Geppert, Otto Emil
Gertner, Herman
Gertner, Maurice
*Giannini, Dr. A. H.
*Goelet, Robert Walton
Goldiner, Nate
*Goldstein, Jonah J.
Goldstein, William A.
Goode, Mrs. Richard Wallace
Goodstein, Aaron
Gordan, John D.
Gordan, Mrs. John D.
Gould, Mrs. C. Smith
Graham, Mary Stoner
*Greenfield, Mrs. Geo. J.
*Greenhut, B. J.
Grierson, Robert C.
Griffis, Stanton
*Grossman, William
Gruberg, George
Guggenheim, Isaac
*Guggenheim, Murray
*Guggenheim, Simon
Gutman, Albert K.
*Hader, George
Haggerty, H.
Haggin, L. T.
Hamburger, Evelyn
*Hamburger, Samuel B.
*Hanna, Leonard C. Jr.

*Harbach, Mrs. Otto A.
Harding, Eugene C.
*Hardy, Lamar
Harkness, Marcia
Hartigan, Stephen P.
*Hauge, Robert L.
Hauser, Margaret
Hay, Robert
Hayes, Adeline Z.
Hayes, Timothy J.
*Hearst, William Randolph
Heckscher, Mrs. Florence
Heidingsfeld, Ben.
Heins, Mrs. Elmore D.
Hemley, Margaret M.
Hendricks, John J. H.
Herendeen, John
*Hering, Henry
Hibbs, Mrs. Russell A.
Hildreth, Frank E.
Hildreth, Robert E.
*Hilprech, Prof. H. V.
*Hilprech, Mrs. H. V.
Hirsch, Laurence J.
Hirsch, Marx
Hitchcock, Frank H.
Hobson, Dr. Sam
*Hockstader, Leonard A.
Hoffman, Robert L.
Holden, Anne M.
Hollerith, Charles
Holt, Roland
Hoye, James B.
*Huber, Richard M.
Huber, Solomon
*Hughes, Hon. Charles E.
Hughes, Franklin
Hunker, Robert L.
*Huyler, Frank Dek.
Impellitteri, Hon. Vincent R.
Indzonka, John J.
*Jacobs, Abraham L.
*Jacobs, S. M. Jackson
Jacobson, M. J.
Jacobson, Mrs. M. J.
*Jennings, Walter
*Johnson, Eldridge R.
Johnson, Genevieve Joyce
Jones, Aaron J.
Jones, Roy N.
Joyce, William B.
Jungmann, Anne-Marie
*Kahn, Otto H.

Kaltenbacher, Joseph C.
Kanzer, Beth K.
Kaplan, Emily R.
Kaplan, Kivie
Kaplan, Mrs. L. J.
Katz, Louis F.
Keelan, Dr. Edward M.
*Keller, Albert
Kelley, Walter E.
Kennedy, William Sr.
Kennedy, William Jr.
Kersten, Anne H.
King, Margaret Carmichael
*Kirchner, Mrs. Julia E.
Kirsch, Luther H.
Klar, Arthur
Knapp, Robert P. Jr.
Komoroff, Samuel
Kudin, Dr. Alfred
Kuehn, Dr. Conrad
*Langley, William H.
Langworthy, Marjorie C.
Lanz, John
Larsen, Carol Dempster
Latz, Mack
*Layton, Marie
Leff, Lillian
Leisure, Lucille Pelouze
Leland, James J.
Lenke, Mrs. Mark A.
*Lennen, Philip W.
Leo, Jack G.
Leslie, Frank H.
*Levy, Myron
Lewis, Arthur
*Lewis, Mrs. William
*Lewisohn, Sam A.
*Liebman, Walter H.
Linden, Sidney
Lindermann, Jan
*Lippincott, Arthur H.
*Lippincott, Henrietta Porter
Livingston, Charles Lauriston, Jr.
Livingston, Florence S.
*Livingston, Julian M.
Lloyd, Eric
*Lotto, Mrs. Fred
*Lowe, Emily
*Lowe, Joe
Lunder, Beatrice
Lyle, Mrs. William Gordon
*McAlpin, Charles W.
*McBride, T. J.

*McEldowney, H. C.
McGuirk, Katherine M.
*McHenry, I. M.
McIntyre, W. H.
McKenna, J. P.
*Malone, Dudley Field
Marks, David
Marks, Dr. David N.
Marran, C. Charles
Maschas, Carolina A.
Massoletti, H. E.
Massoletti, J. D.
*Metz, Herman
Meyer, Maurice Jr.
*Michel, Dr. Leo L.
Miller, C. L.
Miller, Mrs. Danforth
*Miller, Peter A.
Morison, William S.
Morley-Fletcher, John
*Morrison, Dr. W. W.
Morrow, Naomi
Mosbacher, Emil
Mount, George A.
*Muller, J. P.
Mungovan, Michael J.
*Munsey, Frank A.
*Murdock, David V.
Mytinger, Lee S.
Nathan, Emily S.
*Naylor, Edwin J.
*Nelson, Carl E.
Nichols, Humphrey Turner
Niden, Zivel B.
Noyes, Katherine
Ohrbach, Nathan
Olmsted, L. N.
O'Neil, Daniel J.
*Orth, Louise M.
*Osborne, Helen Wadsworth
*Osborne, Hull
Patrick, Mary B.
Patrick, Patrick Rodger
Paul, Erich F. A.
Perlman, Jess
Perrin, George R.
Pfeiffer, Curt G.
Pforzheimer, Carl H. Jr.
Phillips, T. T. Jr.
Pier, Garrett Chatfield
Platt, Abraham S.
Plumb, Margaret Grant
Pollock, Helen Channing

*Powers, A. J.
*Powers, Wallace M.
*Putnam, Henry
Quinlan, Mrs. John H.
Randel, Murray
*Rawll, Rita
Reichenbach, Marie H.
Reid, Lillian M.
Renthal, Charles H.
Reynolds, William H.
Rich, Samuel
Ring, Edward A.   ·
Robins, Mrs. James W.
Robinson, Joyce
Rocker, Louis P.
Rodrique, George (Sgt.)
Rogers, Bertha F.
Rose, Alfred L.
*Rose, Mrs. Caroline B. W.
Rose, Charles
Rose, Irving
Rosenthal, Dr. Randolph
Rothberg, Sidney
Runyon, Carmen R.
*Ruppert, Col. Jacob
Ryan, Mrs. Byford
*Ryan, J .L.
Ryan, John D.
Sadowsky, Jack P.
Salisbury, Philip
Samson, Charles F.
*Samuel, Edith
Savidge, Mrs. Eugene Coleman
Sawahata, Alfred
*Sax, Carol M.
Saxe, Sigmond
Sayle, Florence M.
Schaefer, Rudolph J.
*Schindler, Raymond C.
Schlenoff, Michael R.
Schlesinger, Charles J.
Schneider, Irving
Schoenhof, Edward W.
Schrettner, Jerome H.
Schuman, Henry
Schuman, Mrs. Henry
*Schumer, Harry
*Scott, Col. Walter
*Sells, E. W.
Senft, Jean Hildreth
Shapiro, Dr. Mortimer F.
Shea, Mary E.
Shea, Mrs. Michael

Shero, Caroline
Sherry, Lilian
Shone, Al E.
Silberstein, Meyer
Silbert, Theodore H.
Silver, Bertram S.
Simon, Harry M.
Sloan, William
*Smith, Dr. Harry
Smith, James Nichols
*Sokolow, Benjamin D.
Solinsky, Sam S.
Somach, Mrs. Irving
*Spalding, J. W.
*Speyer, James
*Spitz, Mrs. Eugene
Squires, Dorothy Nagel
Starr, J. Joseph
*Stearn, Allene A.
Stearn, Alva E.
Stearn, Mrs. Alva E.
Stein, Herbert M.
Steiner, S. S.
Stern, Mrs. Leopold
Stetson, G. Henry
Steuer, Bertha
Stone, I. F.
Storm, Jules P.
Stragnell, Dr. Gregory
Straus, Charles B.
*Strauss, Charles
Stupel, Abner B.
Summerfield, Solon E.
Suydam, Horace
Swadley, Mrs. Frank L.
*Synnott, Jane
Taub, Mrs. Ronald B.
*Terry, Mrs. Lillian E.
Thayer, Lyman E.
The Sidney S. Loeb Memorial
    Foundation Inc.
Thomas, Louise V.
*Tilford, Frank
Tobias, Sidney
Todd, Webster B.
*Toensfeldt, Ralf
Traum, Dr. Arthur A.
*Tucker, Mrs. Preble

Tuerk, John R.
Tumpeer, Joseph J.
Tyrone, Anthony R.
*Underwood, John T.
Vance, E. D.
Van Cleef, Felix
*Vanderbilt, Major Cornelius
*Vanderbilt, William K.
Van Dyke, Mary Douglas
Vogel, Jerry
Wacker, J. Samuel
Walker, Fay H.
*Walker, William B.
Wall, Daniel C.
*Walsh, Clara Bell
*Wanamaker, Rodman
*Warren, Edward K.
Warren, Mrs. Edward K.
Washington, Dr. I. E.
*Waterman, Frank D.
Watson, Roy Garrett
Webster, Nell
Weeks, Antoinette
*Weikel, Jacob
Weinberg, Julia
*Weinberger, William Degan
Weininger, Richard
Wentworth, Margaret
Wilcox, William G.
Wilder, Charles P.
Wilderman, Louis H.
Willens, J. R.
Willets, Howard
Willets, Mrs. Howard
*Williams, Arthur
Williams, Barbara
Williams, Sydney A.
*Willmsen, Phebe Bates
Wilson, R. Thornton
Wood, Thomas J.
Woolfolk, A. Wheeler
Wright, Mrs. John B.
Wright, Loyd
Wyner, I. A.
Yegen, Mrs. Christian
*Zabriskie, Mrs. Cornelius A.
Zinner, Jay
Zuckerman, Mrs. Henry

*Deceased

INDEX